In Your Times

In Your Times

A 20TH CENTURY GRANDFATHER WRITES TO HIS 21ST CENTURY GRANDCHILDREN

Farrell F Neeley PhD

Copyright © 2016 Farrell F Neeley PhD
All rights reserved.

ISBN: 0990625605
ISBN 13: 9780990625605

Table of Contents

Author's Preface · **xxi**

Chapter 1 ·**1**

If You Ain't Fallin', You Ain't Climbin' · · · · · · · · · · · · · · · 1

Living Under The Bridge · 2

Fewer Regrets · 4

We're Holding Gold For You · 5

Misdirection… Fooled Again · 6

Inflation Is All In Your Imagination · · · · · · · · · · · · · · · · · 6

Stay Skeptical, Children · 7

Taking A Break From Other People's Voices · · · · · · · · · · · 9

The Passage of Time · 11

Voyage Of Discovery · 12

Rabid Consumerism · 14

How To Create A Social Misfit · · · · · · · · · · · · · · · · 16

The Dumbing Down Of America · · · · · · · · · · · · · · · · 18

They've Fired Ron Johnson · · · · · · · · · · · · · · · · · · · 20

Good Cop, Bad Cop · 22

Econ 101 For Politicians · 24

Chapter 2 ·27

Nothing To Fear But Fear Itself · · · · · · · · · · · · · · · · 27

Pursuing Your Own Star · 28

Stop And Smell The Hummingbirds · · · · · · · · · · · · · · 29

No Sunglasses · 30

Extended Self-Sufficiency · 30

Whose Dream Is It Anyway · · · · · · · · · · · · · · · · · · · 32

A Leader Who Didn't Know It All · · · · · · · · · · · · · · · 34

Not If But When · 36

Young Taxpayers Are The Victims· · · · · · · · · · · · · · · · · 36

On The Playing Fields Of Life · · · · · · · · · · · · · · · · · · 38

The Power Of Voices · 40

Clearing The Decks · 41

Clearing The Decks Of The Extraneous · · · · · · · · · · · · · 42

Clearing The Decks Of Poisonous Friends And Family · · 44

Clearing The Decks For Your Life Work · · · · · · · · · · · · 46

Clearing The Decks Of Windmill Slaying · · · · · · · · · · · 48

Chapter 3 ·51

A Million Gadgets, And They're Still Lost · · · · · · · · · · · 51

Some Days Are Diamonds · 53

Fool's Gold · 53

Yourself In Your Children · 55

Bankers, Gangsters, And Banksters· · · · · · · · · · · · · · · · 57

Aesop's Ancient Wisdom · 59

Financial Caution · 59

What's Your Solution? · 59

Now That The End Has Not Come · · · · · · · · · · · · · · · · · 61

While You Still Have It · 62

Reality Checks · 64

Your Small Decisions Matter · 66

Saving Your Savings · 67

Wisdom's Children · 68

Mercantile Fatalities · 70

We Know What's Best For You · · · · · · · · · · · · · · · · · · · 72

Chapter 4 ·75

What's It Worth To Me · 75

You're Never Too Young To Die · · · · · · · · · · · · · · · · · · 76

Red-Shouldered Hawks: Enjoy Their Show · · · · · · · · · · · 77

Experiment In Social Engineering · · · · · · · · · · · · · · · · · 79

Everybody Doesn't Need A Doctorate · · · · · · · · · · · · · · 81

The Final Needle · 82

Political Terminal Illness · 84

A Panel Of Experts · 85

Grounded In Reality · 86

Class Reunions · 87

We All Lose · 89

Risk And Reality · 90

Appearances Drive The Frenzy · · · · · · · · · · · · · · · · · · 91

A Perfect Plan · 93

Build No Nation Before Its Time · · · · · · · · · · · · · · · · · 93

Chapter 5 ·96

Rest In Peace John Maynard Keynes · · · · · · · · · · · · · · · 96

Those Who Can't… Criticize · · · · · · · · · · · · · · · · · · · 98

Religious Relics · 98

Be Good To Your Body · 100

Rolling In Manure · 101

Great Dividends · 102

Lessons In Business Ownership · · · · · · · · · · · · · · · · · · 103

The Uncivil Wars · 105

Tax The Daylights Out Of them · · · · · · · · · · · · · · · · · 106

Black Swan Events I · 107

Black Swan Events II · 108

Black Swan Events III · 110

Black Swan Events IV · 112

Black Swan Events V · 113

Avoiding Other's Negative Emotions · · · · · · · · · · · · · 115

These Days Pass Quickly · 117

Spending Time Wisely · 117

Chapter 6 · 119

What Lifestyle Can You Sustain · · · · · · · · · · · · · · · · · 119

A Fish Rots From The Head Down · · · · · · · · · · · · · · 120

Lords Of The Manor · 121

Tactical Trolls · 122

Your Own Worst Enemy · 128

Responsible Adult · 128

You Raised Them · 129

Of Diet And Research · 132

Good Or Bad, Eventually Word Gets Around · · · · · · · · 133

Of Presidents And Emperors · 135

Unconsumed By An Earlier Catastrophe · · · · · · · · · · · · 135

Get The Facts Before You Make Judgments · · · · · · · · · · 137

Take A Deep Breath · 138

Eulogies · 139

No Place Like Home · 140

Pushing Back · 141

Chapter 7 · **144**

Careless, Poorly Educated, Or Illiterate · · · · · · · · · · · · 144

The Human Touch · 145

Dealing With Mad Men · 146

Altruism Or Competitive Advantage · · · · · · · · · · · · · · 148

Life Is A Moving Target · 149

Of Course We Were Young Once · · · · · · · · · · · · · · · · · 150

What Makes Your Day · 151

My Best Laid Plans · 152

One Percent Error · 152

Lessons Of The Vietnam War · 157

Casualties Of War · 159

Always Arguing · 160

Good Intentions · 161

You're The Parent · 162

Your Work Or Your Life · 164

A Thief At Your Side · 165

Relearning The Lessons of War · · · · · · · · · · · · · · · · · · 166

The Road To Ruin · 167

Chapter 8 · **·169**

Define Your Own Success · 169

Is Anyone Following You · 169

Bitterness And Bitter People · 170

There Are No Winners Here · 172

Other Career Paths · 173

Handle The Family Business with Care · · · · · · · · · · · · · 173

Your War On Poverty · 174

Twilight Of Civility · 175

Blessed To Live In America · 176

Slower To Judgment · 177

Your Holiday Traditions · 178

Wisdom Is Justified Of All Her Children · · · · · · · · · · · 178

Values Can't Be Legislated · 180

The Stupidity Pit · 182

Healing Your Own Anger · 182

You Might Want To Catch Up First · · · · · · · · · · · · · · · 183

He's An Original · 184

Circumspection · 185

I Was Misquoted · 185

Let Sleeping Dogs Lie · 186

Announced Faith Or No Faith · · · · · · · · · · · · · · · · · · 188

Chapter 9 ·189

May Your Future Be Bright · 189

Your Ancestors Are Watching · · · · · · · · · · · · · · · · · · · 190

Enemies Of Excellence · 191

Great Swelling Words · 192

Managing Dilemmas · 193

Difficult People · 195

Anything But Golden · 196

Protected To Death · 196

The Distant Future Belongs To Graduates · · · · · · · · · · 198

Beware The Politician Who Would Save You · · · · · · · · · 199

On The Lookout For Stupid · 201

Help Or Sympathy · 203

Affliction · 204

Giving Less And More · 205

Self-reliance · 206

Evil And Evil Men · 208

Awakening The Sleeper · 208

A Tipping Point· 209

When Happiness Arrives · 211

Older & Wiser · 211

Chapter 10 ·213

Raising Trees And Children · 213

Be Careful Out There · 214

Our Debt To Future Generations · · · · · · · · · · · · · · · · · 217

No Special Training Required · · · · · · · · · · · · · · · · · · · 218

Competition Of Religious Ideas · · · · · · · · · · · · · · · · · · 221

Lifetime Implications· 224

Ethical Slippery Slopes· 228

Living With Yourself· 230

Where Will You Live · 232

Child Of The Universe · 234

Chapter 11 ·236

Pleasure Versus Happiness · 236

Friends And Friendships · 239

Mayberry Is Gone Forever · 241

Making Allowances For Imperfection · · · · · · · · · · · · · · 242

Anger Will Be Your Only Companion · · · · · · · · · · · · · · 244

There Are Words · 247

Give The Jealous A Wide Berth · · · · · · · · · · · · · · · · · · 247

A Shared Resource · 248

Burning Bridges · 250

Speaking Truth To Power · 251

Not Conducive · 252

Brain Injured · 253

Taken With A Giant Grain Of Salt · · · · · · · · · · · · · · · · 254

Technological Trojan Horses · · · · · · · · · · · · · · · · · · · 255

Assuming The Worst · 256

What Goes Around Comes Around · · · · · · · · · · · · · · 257

Chapter 12 · 259

These Are The Times · 259

Your Electronic Tethers · 259

Real Problems... Faux Problems · · · · · · · · · · · · · · · · 261

Evil With No Consequences · 261

The Proof's In The Pudding · · · · · · · · · · · · · · · · · · · 262

The Slough Of Despond · 263

Dangerous Deceivers · 264

Are You Qualified · 265

Intellectual Dissemblers · 267

Talking The Talk · 267

On The Lookout For True Need · · · · · · · · · · · · · · · · 268

No More To Take · 270

Are You Buying This · 271

Nature Isn't Perfect · 272

Commercial Affection · 274

The True Face Of Evil · 277

That Final "I Love You" · 280

Author's Afterward · **283**

Dedication

This is the second written work I've published; the first was my doctoral dissertation and I dedicated it to my Momma and Daddy. By then, neither my Momma or Daddy were alive to read it, and honestly I'm not certain my doctoral committee was able to wade through it either. As I set out to write this my intended audience is my grandkids. If you chance upon a copy of it, know 'going in' it's personal.

I want to dedicate these writings to my daughters: Christina, Melody, and Rachel. I love them more than I can ever adequately express. I make this dedication in recognition of their continuing love, faith, and support of me through the hardest years of my life, following the death of their brother Ryan and the breakup of my marriage to their mother Sheree.

Thank you ladies; you've become fine, strong, Christian women in the proudest traditions of all your Neeley and McCormick family lines.

Author's Preface

When I began work on this book a little over two years ago, I set out to talk about 'Wisdom'. I did this because in the back of my mind, I wanted to leave my experience on many topics to my daughters and my grandchildren. What has emerged is more of a retrospective of my own school of hard knocks experiences; the things I've done right, the things I've done wrong, and the expensive lessons learned along the way.

For you grandchildren, your mother was raised on my views, as my grandchildren you spend far less time with me and know me mostly by the grandfather myths your mother and others have passed along to you. I'm addressing these issues for you because I believe there can still be great days ahead for civilization in general and for you, daughters and grandchildren, in particular.

I share my views on politics, religion, relationships, economics, marriage, family, education, wealth, healthcare, birth and death, war and peace, business, governments, nature, international development, and some odds and ends I couldn't properly categorize. Every one of these pages was written in response to some experience or encounter I've had during the course of my life. This approach allows me to range far afield, unlike the way I was taught to write as an academic. As your father or grandfather, I'd ask only that you read these pages with an open mind.

You've been told by others all your life there were topics which were taboo for discussion because of the rancor or discomfort they create. I suspect you could take many of the issues I raise here and create a tempest at your next family gathering, church supper, cocktail party, or faculty reception. This causes me to wonder if the reason so many of these topics eventually spill over into the streets is because we conceal them until they fester like an untreated wound. Then when the wound finally bursts open from the pressure of its own putrefaction, polite society behaves as if it has no idea how this could've happened.

Many times during my early adult years, while serving as a pastor in Christian ministry, I liked to remind audiences I'd come to this place to "…comfort the troubled and trouble the comfortable." This is a cute little saying which hides a very serious matter. This is so because we all move back and forth across the troubled/comfortable continuum on a host of issues during our lifetimes. When we find ourselves troubled, we're much more likely to look for answers and change. When we find ourselves comfortable, we're much more likely to feel we already have the answers, and we don't want any change.

My task as a lifelong contrarian was much easier with those who were troubled than with those who were comfortable. The physical, mental, emotional, financial, or spiritual underpinnings have been torn away from the man or woman who's troubled, while the comfortable man or woman feels entirely secure within their safe harbor of personal certainties. To some degree both parties are deluded, since life is rarely as good or as bad as it seems to the person caught up in the current moment's tempest. Keep this in mind as you live out your lives.

My chief concern for you who'll one day read this, is a day might come where life so abuses you that you cease considering other people's points of view, other people's lives, and other people's feelings. If this occurs, it'll be the day your intellect, your humanity, and your soul begin to shrivel and die. Fight with all you have to make sure this never happens.

Farrell F. Neeley, PhD
October 28, 2014

CHAPTER 1

If You Ain't Fallin', You Ain't Climbin'

Life is a lot like being the lead climber on a rock-climbing expedition. The challenge for the lead climber is to find the route up the rock so the climb can go forward. Most of the time, there is a period of calm and deliberate observation and consideration the lead climber and his partner(s) go through on the ground while looking up at the rock. But once you get on the rock face itself, it's not nearly as easy to spot the way up as it was from the relative peace and safety on the ground.

A climber is constantly fighting gravity, his or her own physical limits, and of course the structural elements of the climb. When I was young and still climbing regularly, there were periods of immense calm followed by moments of sheer terror at the effort required to execute a certain move and the fear I didn't have it in me. Despite being on the rock and rope with others, you are in essence totally alone. The joy or climber's high in all this comes from having challenged the rock and safely traversed it.

Just as I've had people comment about how calm and deliberate my climbing leads once looked, I've had them make the same sort of comments about my life. I have to laugh at this line of thought in both instances. My life is just like everyone else's—periods of intense calm followed by moments of sheer terror. Each of us is laboring to execute the next move we know we have to make and simultaneously fighting back the fear we don't have it in us. Just like a lead climber, eventually each of you must call out to the world the word 'climbing' to indicate climbing is beginning, and move on.

The joy or the high in your life comes from having challenged it and safely traversed it. Climbers know those who choose to remain spectators on the ground will never know how this feels. There's no end to the climb, only another pitch on another rock face. Similarly, there's no end to the challenges you'll face in life. Only another day to be encountered and passed over in the best fashion you can manage. I fell often while climbing and I learned by heart the old climber's adage, "If you ain't fallin', you ain't climbin'."

Living Under The Bridge

My ex-wife—your mother or your maternal grandmother—used to say I was a "dream-killer." For years, I took this as a bad thing and didn't want clients to catch on to that aspect of my advising business. But for more than twenty years now, one of the things I do routinely to earn a living is to look at business plans and search for flaws; more specifically I look for fatal flaws. You see, in the case of a simple flaw you may work around it, but a fatal flaw will inevitably kill your effort. What I've found is instead of being embraced for this talent; I've been rejected and even vilified. Through the ensuing years, I've learned to take this in stride. As time has gone by, many of those who rejected my earlier counsel have come back to say I was correct, and they're sorry. The sorrow is mine! Some of them dumped their life savings into plans I assured them would fail. Many lost their marriages and friendships. For the lucky ones, they were only broke for a few years.

There is a verse in the scripture of Christianity. I think it's among the wisdom attributed to Solomon, but it could have been the words of his father, David. In either case: "Faithful are the wounds of a friend." I've always taken this to mean a true friend will tell you the truth, even if it hurts you, makes you mad, or leads to the dissolution of the friendship. I lost a friendship a couple of months back over speaking the truth to a friend regarding a legal matter. She didn't take it well. She saw me pointing up the law to her as taking her adversary's side. In fact, what I was trying to do was steer her away from a lawsuit where I felt she was completely in the wrong and could not prevail. In another recent instance, where I pointed out to one of my friends she was being abused by an elderly parent, she rejected my counsel and verbally attacked me. I haven't heard from her since, but I have no doubt if there's no intervention this parent will be abusive to her until the day one of them dies.

So where does this lead us? For you kids, I hope it points up the need to be truthful in your relationships if they're to be anything more than smoke and mirrors. I believe each of you should do as I do and take any ability to guide friends, clients, or family as a sacred trust. If you've been so educated, qualified, and/or gifted, it's preponderant upon you to take this charge seriously and not as though it was trivial. I've no difficulty accepting each of you is uniquely gifted. Whether this gift is at times is interpreted negatively is not the issue. The issue is whether or not you'll be true to those things which you know to be correct, even if it offends others, antagonizes friends or family, or breaks up relationships. Life is short and resources are finite. If it's more important for you to be a friend than a good source of wise counsel, will you still visit them when they are living under a bridge?

Fewer Regrets

I'm at an age where I frequently find myself in conversations with similarly aged individuals who are expressing regrets about the way they've lived their lives. Many have made up bucket lists (wish lists) they want to complete, but in some cases, the train they wanted to ride left the station years ago and there's not much they can do to ever get on-board now. As your mother has probably told you by now, I returned to college full-time at age forty-three to complete my education. Even then some people I knew questioned the wisdom of such an effort at such an advanced age; I knew I would regret not doing so for the rest of my life and ignored the naysayers.

None of you can turn back the hands of time; I certainly haven't been able to. I hope some of you children read this, and if you're still young enough to either engage or re-engage your dreams, you'll seriously consider doing so now. Regardless of what change it is you need to make in order to finally realize your dream, you'll have to put enough energy (e.g., time, money, mental effort, physical effort, etc.) into the attempt to make it a reality. Nothing will ever take the place of your dreams, and you'll always know a substitute is just a substitute. Do yourself a favor while there's still time and pursue your dreams so you can live with fewer regrets.

We're Holding Gold For You

In the current year, 2015, we have a program known as Individual Retirement Accounts (IRAs) where regular folks can set aside money with the taxes deferred until they begin to use it in their old age. My guess is these accounts or something similar will still be around when you grow older and begin to think about saving for your retirement years. Make no mistake about it, you'll grow up, you'll grow old, and you'll someday either fully retire or take on a lesser role in life than you now enjoy. I said this would never happen to me and yet, like so many other things I was certain about in life, I was wrong.

Right now it's time for me to roll over my IRA. This means it's time to renew its term of investment for another year or more. I'm appalled at the paltry rates of interest my bank is willing to pay versus the rate of interest they are asking of people for a loan. There seems to be a serious disconnect there. But I'd have to say the offers which strike me with a mixed sense of concern and amusement are the ones offering me a way to buy gold or some other precious metal and place it in my IRA. Many of us like the idea of owning "tangible wealth" which holds its value as inflation creeps up. I suspect this will remain true even in your time. My generation also has fears we might get taken in by a clever con artist intent on stealing our retirement savings.

I'm in the group which isn't opposed to holding precious metals as part of an overall wealth strategy. What I'm opposed to is the idea I'm going to send currency (e.g., cash, check, money order, bank draft, etc.) and in return some unknown 'they' will send me back a paper certificate, assuring me of how much precious metal they have in custody for me. Call me suspicious, but when I get an offer from some company I've never heard of, operating from a post office box in Dog Trot, Nebraska, how can I possibly confirm they actually have gold which belongs to me? Why should I or you trust faceless entities which appear in our email, on television, or pop-ups on some website?

I'm not any crazier about the current spate of retirement account investment opportunities out there than anyone else my age, but I'm going to hold off on jumping into these paper certificates until other people I know and trust let me know how they're working out for them. I've never been what is termed a 'fast-follower' in these matters. I tend to wait and see if it's a vat of water people are diving into or a vat of hydrofluoric acid. I've attended the economic funerals of a lot of industry leaders and I've encountered more than one formerly wealthy man or woman who was too enthusiastic, too trusting, or too willing to take a flyer on the next "better mousetrap." Caution may in fact cost you money. However, cautious people rarely starve to death from lack of funds.

Hedge your bets, never buy a Rolex from a guy in a parking lot, and be sure to hold your own precious metals.

Misdirection... Fooled Again

I hope you kids realize regardless of what political party you're affiliated with now, all anyone has to do to get elected to office in this country is to do a better job of misdirecting you than their opponent or opponents. Once elected, politicians have somewhere between two, four, or six years to figure out a whole new strategy to fool you all over again.

Inflation Is All In Your Imagination

If your times are anything like those I'm living in, you'll keep hearing all the money they're printing at the United States

Treasury isn't having any inflationary impact on the nation's currency. I'm not certain how they define inflationary impact, and there's no telling how they'll explain it to your generation in the future, but it occurs to me if Pinto beans used to be about a $0.69 a pound, and now I'm paying $1.69 a pound, something is causing the price to go up.

The same thing goes for beer, beef, gasoline, macaroni, and just about any other thing you need to survive. It seems both the Democrats and the Republicans figure if they tell us anything they deem true long enough, soon we'll all believe it. I'll try to keep things simple here as I write these pages to you, so your old papa will believe there's no inflationary impact from all the stimulus money which was printed in these times, just as soon as I can buy Pinto beans for $0.69 a pound again.

You'll need to become a student of economics in your time, just as a matter of self-defense and not as an academic pursuit. You're going to learn, if you look at governments all over the world throughout history, the governments' and associated politicians' chief complaint has always been there's not enough revenue being raised from taxes. Then the people paying the taxes will routinely be pressed to pay more, either directly or indirectly. Inflation is a veiled tax and your politicians know this; so should you!

Stay Skeptical, Children
Remain skeptical when all about you have given themselves over to gullibility. Case in point, I was listening to a panel discussion recently on the effect of current political policies on the economy while driving home and one of the panelists started an argument with, "Most economists agree that..." He went on to make a claim in an area of economics I've always found to be

fraught with controversy and not one which appears to me to be nearly as settled as his sweeping statement implied. Now despite the fact his pronouncement supports one of my pet opinions, I knew he'd at the very least exaggerated the facts greatly, and at the very worst he had outright lied. I don't want to win a critical political or philosophical point through lies; that's the first step onto the slippery slope of self-deception and rejection of truth.

When I got home, I checked the radio channel's website to see if I could determine the panelist's academic credentials and discovered he had them, but not in economics. He was actually an ex-athlete, a communications major who'd tried standup comedy for a while and somehow ended up on cable news. Let me say he certainly could've developed 'credentials' after his other careers ended, but if he did I couldn't find a record of it. The tragedy here is more and more people form their opinions on all sorts of life and death issues based on the blather they routinely hear coming from their radios, televisions, computers, or smartphones. This is particularly troubling when you realize people believe these instant facts, incorporate them into their mindsets, and then order their lives based on faulty logic, exaggeration, or outright lies.

It occurs to me we have folks like this panelist on the news because in my time, we've come to the place where we have to be entertained every moment of every day. I understand there have to be people who can make witty quips so listeners don't turn the dial and cost their corporate masters advertising revenue. Tragically, we seem to have no time to actually read, think, discuss, and evolve a position on any issue for ourselves. Instead, we appear to be basing our lives and our opinions on one-liners and late-night monologues. On the one hand we hold up the ideas and Socratic methods of the ancients as our preferred path to knowledge, while on the other when someone who actually has a background in the area of discussion speaks we turn the dial because they lack Hollywood looks, fail to wear designer clothes, or have a dry, pedantic style of delivery.

Demand more of yourself! Stop being satisfied with the baby food versions of the issues and begin to read, think, and discuss matters with your friends again or for the first time. There'll be those, who upon hearing your plan for how you propose to spend the next hour with them, will simply beg off and avoid your future invites. This is okay. Not all your friends have to be deep thinkers, but a few of them should be. You can use this book as a starting point. Read it to them! Tear it apart! Criticize the style! Criticize the subject! But at least begin to remake the connections between thinking, speaking, and debating an issue. Some of your companions will be as off-base as the panelist I mentioned earlier. That's okay too; error is sometimes desirable to season the debate. Conversely, devolution to nothing but the entertainment value of the discussion is never beneficial. Stay skeptical, children!

Taking A Break From Other People's Voices

I've found if I'll allow myself to become inundated in any of the various media streams which bombard me daily, I become poisoned by it. It doesn't matter if it's liberal or conservative, Democrat or Republican, capitalist or communist; the end result is the same. I begin to lose overall perspective and sink into disillusionment or outright depression. In talking with friends, family, and business associates, I find I'm not alone in this reaction.

Three years ago I made the conscious decision to detox from large daily doses of social media, and media in general.

It wasn't long before I remembered reading, reflecting, conversing, looking, listening, and living once again. Before you launch in about me being an old-fashioned grandpa, I'm not opposed to social media or media in general. However, I'm opposed to being drowned in so many other peoples' voices I can no longer hear or recognize my own voice. It's my guess this will only become more of a problem in the years in which you'll live out your life.

There are very few things in life unique to us. Our view of the world and the way we interact with it is one of them. In my opinion it's one of the most precious things about life. It's easy to be so overwhelmed by the voices of the experts or our friends. At these times we begin to doubt our own voice and damp it down in response to the daily tidal wave of other voices. One of life's constant challenges is to hold firm to ourselves and avoid becoming a nameless member of the homogenized universal mind. Your mother has told you this already: "Just because everybody else does something is no reason you have to do it."

You can best accomplish this deliberate break with other voices by holding yourself responsible to know who *you* are. To this end it would do you well to spend time figuring out who and what your ancestors were all about. In knowing more about them, you might well want to come to know more about you and the times you live in. You can then strengthen this knowing who you are by nourishing the positive aspects within yourselves which are worth nourishing and starving those negative aspects which need to die. If you listen to experts all day long on every topic, and are willing to give your life over to them completely, what's the purpose in even trying to have your own life?

Carefully consider what I'm saying here and ask yourself if it might be time to take a break from all the other voices and rediscover your own.

The Passage of Time

My reflexes are not nearly as quick as memory assures me they once were. So I find it stunning at times when put to the test to realize the years take a toll on each of us, even me. The toll is taken with such subtlety one never realizes reflexes you were sure were there have been gone for God only knows how long. I try to accept these new realities with grace, but some days it's harder than others.

Except for my daughters and the oldest grandchild reading this, I've always been a gray-haired old man to you. I know it's hard for you to feature me any other way except when some picture of me in my younger years is placed before you. Let this be a cautionary tale to each of you. Now you're young, but just as surely as I grew old, you will too. It's not a terrible thing so don't view it this way, but it does take some getting used to.

In fact, my advice on aging would be you learn to accept and make the best of whatever age you're at. Youth is a wonderful time, but far too many young people have an absolute fear of old age. Old age isn't the problem; it's the deterioration which sometimes accompanies it which is the real devil in life's details. One hopeful thing we've learned in my lifetime is you can definitely improve your quality of life by making better lifestyle choices when you're young. So make better choices now!

As I write this I'm sixty years of age and come from a line of fairly long-lived parents and grandparents. However, it would be good to mention here my Daddy and my brother both cut their lives short with the daily long-term use of tobacco. Your great-grandfather chewed tobacco from the time he was seven years old. They were poor, tobacco was easy and cheap to grow, and it kills appetite. Instead of living to be ninety-four or older, as many of his ancestors and siblings had done, he died in his early eighties from cancer of the jaw, tongue, and esophagus.

I'd also suggest you plan a life which can accommodate aging. Far too many members of my generation worked and played as though they were going to be twenty-five years old forever. Not only did they find their bodies couldn't handle this pace in their later years, they also discovered they'd made lifestyle and retirement plans which hadn't taken into account their bodies would be thirty to forty years older when retirement finally arrived.

Let me close this passage by saying once again you shouldn't be trepidatious in growing old; don't fear it. For every negative I've encountered in aging there've been an equal or greater number of positives. This doesn't mean all those positives line up in the same column with all those negatives to balance them out. It just means you begin to be grateful to be alive, even in an aging body, when you live long enough to see your dreams come true and you get to your hold your latest grandchild in your arms.

Voyage Of Discovery

The headline read, "Puzzling Find Ruins Scientific Theory." I ran across it a few days back on the Internet with regard to physicists apparently determining protons are smaller than previous theories have suggested. I was staggered by the headline, not because protons might be smaller than previously believed and

I had money riding on the old theory. I was staggered because the author obviously didn't have a clue how science is supposed to work. You see scientists posit theories about how data they have at the present leads them to believe this data represents fact. In truth, one of the things you're hounded about in writing up scientific research is you must use words which indicate you're not certain (e.g., posit, perhaps, seems, appears, suggests, apparently, etc.), because we can never be certain of anything in science. We're even taught to be suspicious of the natural laws we all take for granted every moment of every day.

I fear we're living in a dumbed-down age which is growing more so with each passing school year. I also fear it will only grow worse in your time. Finding new information doesn't ruin anything. In fact, finding new information is at the very heart of knowing what is. This isn't the middle ages where we cheer for our favorite scientists because our city-state has hired them to come and do their research in our town. Having said this I feel immediately compelled to admit institutions of higher learning do appear at times to have exactly this mindset. Yet be this as it may, for the average man or woman there is no advantage in continuing to embrace popular science, bad science, or junk science because it's more convenient than inculcating the newest information into our outlook and adjusting our textbooks. Just accept it too will be challenged with new data at some future point.

As parents you'll need to talk with your children about this dangerous aspect of modern science and those who'd thwart its efforts to sort fact from fiction in order to fit their pet theory or drive their political agenda. This planet and its people are still on a great voyage of discovery. Lies, half-truths, hidden agendas, and competition for research dollars all have the ability to warp science or set it back. When all science, for all which is around us is settled once and for all, discovery will be a dead issue and the voyage will have come to an end. Man's insatiable curiosity is at the very core of what it is to be human. I would even go so far as to say those who wish to obscure, hide altogether, or downright destroy new facts are the enemies of mankind and certainly not the saviors they often portray themselves as being. Be wary of geniuses, politicians, and mad men; they each have tremendous destructive potential.

Rabid Consumerism

As I grow older I notice I have to work harder to stay on top of the latest changes in technology. It's not I feel overwhelmed by new technology, it's more I feel bombarded with gadgets I'm not sure I need nearly as badly as some of the world's most profitable corporations try to convince me I do. A couple of weeks back, as a favor to a client, I agreed to check out a piece of electrical equipment they had which was functioning in a questionable manner. When I arrived and pulled out an analog device to check the equipment, the young man assigned to assist me wondered aloud why I didn't have a digital version. He appeared surprised when I told him I did have the digital version but felt the older analog model was just as reliable and had proven itself to be physically more robust than the digital device. The digital version has been in for repairs twice in two years and the analog has never been back for repairs in thirty years. I've had similar experience with other items, so allow this to provide you a sense of where my trepidation lies.

It seems we need to regain a sense of the utility of gadgets rather than owning the latest toys for the cachet they carry. My phone model is the old flip-type (an archaic clamshell even now) and all I use it for are calls, though I know it can also be used for texting if the urge to text were ever to strike me. As my child or grandchild, you've openly wondered why I don't own an iPhone® or a Droid® or some other model of smartphone so I could take advantage of all the hundreds of apps you've either downloaded for free or purchased by the dozen. Each of you children have looked at my desktop and laptop computers and wondered aloud why I don't have an iPad® or some similar tablet device. Here I need to admit I was once 'an early adopter' of new computer technology. But over the last three decades I've seen how Microsoft®, Apple®, and Intel® have worked us into a near-frenzy of fear of being left behind so we'd rush out to buy their very latest version of their very newest profit-maker. In the early days of personal computers, I was taken in by the newest bells and whistles but received little actual improvement from the new and improved versions.

I live in a capitalistic society, and I'm an unabashed capitalist. However, that doesn't mean in order to be a faithful capitalist I have to take my hard-earned capital and plunk it down on the latest and greatest offering from some of the cleverest and most profitable companies in history. In fact, it might be a better indication of my capitalistic views if I refrain from spending $500 to $1,000 on an item which will be passé in two months and obsolete in six. You see, what we have here is actually a form of rabid consumerism I'm not sure is at all healthy in the long run. If you were to forego the immediate gratification of purchasing the latest smartphone or other similar technology and invest the same money in an item with long-term value, might it not be a wiser choice than lining up at the Apple® store five days before the next release so you can be one of the first to own (or be owned by) the latest gadget? Be wise out there, and be sure you're getting value for the dollars you spend.

How To Create A Social Misfit

I recall how driven his parents were to see 'Rex' become a great athlete. His father attended every sports practice we had. His mother and siblings were at every game, cheering him on and telling him how great he was. All of his friends, I among them, truly admired Rex and figured he'd go to the pros someday. As the years went by he honed his athletic skills, apparently ignoring to large degree his education and people skills on his way to a professional athletic career. He was eventually recruited by a professional team and all of us who had known him figured he was on his way. I lost track of him. The next time I saw him was nearly fifteen years later.

Rex's giftedness never quite panned out. The professional athletic career fizzled out, along with an early marriage and early parenthood. I was happy to see him after fifteen years and to get the chance to catch up on life. Rex was clearly not happy to be encountered working at what he quickly told me he felt was a job which was beneath his skills. After this encounter I lost track of him again and didn't hear anything out of him until another twenty years had passed. By then he'd worked long enough to retire from the job he hated and was looking to launch a second career, one more closely associated with his athletic glory days.

Apparently, that second career never locked in for him; perhaps he'd been away from the sport too long. Other people reported increasingly angry encounters with Rex. He took to lambasting acquaintances who'd lacked his athletic skills but went on to become successful in their 'lesser' fields of endeavor. When old friends were unable to help him find a new career, he accused them of being jealous of his athletic gifts and taking it out on him thirty-five years later by not trying hard enough to help him in his hour of need. Eventually Rex burned his local bridges and moved on. I'm unsure of his whereabouts or status today.

What's the point to you in all this? This saga began back in the 1960s. Athletics were important then but not nearly as important as people seem to think they are today. I see parents doing the same things Rex's parents did; perhaps even more so. I see parents honing children for a professional sports career which may or may not ever be possible for their son or daughter. Maybe the most tragic thing I see is these children too are allowed to neglect getting an education and developing the people skills they'll need to survive. These parents never hold out the possibility to their child there needs to be a fallback plan in place if the giftedness falters or the pros never call.

In all honesty I don't see any athletic giftedness in any of you at this point, but since the majority of you are less than eight years old, this could all change in a moment. The other place it could crop up is if you are musically or artistically gifted. Both of those life courses can hold pitfalls similar to those I've mentioned regarding athletics. You could also easily become consumed by video games and suffer an identical ne'er-do-well fate. The bigger question here is how so many well-meaning families end up creating social misfits instead of the world-changer they were sure they were fostering? I believe it happens because parents lose sight of the fact a parent's first goal should be to raise children to be responsible adults and responsible citizens. If the responsible child should grow to be celebrated or famous, it would be icing on the cake. If a responsible child doesn't grow to be celebrated or famous, they'd still have a child they and society could interact with and enjoy.

So, if you or your future children have a gift, I encourage you to nurture it. But at the same time I hope you'll be nurturing abilities and traits like conversation, compassion, humor, kindness, and learning. I took some time recently to do a little research on child prodigies from several fields. Apart from their early novelty and the inevitable appearances on television, many of them are unable to ever parlay their childhood *wunderkind* status into an adult career. The brilliant musician, or mathematician, or athlete may in fact turn out to be the unhappy, angry adult, who strikes out at all those about him. By the time you're grown you'll have met many of these people, often in roles as teachers, columnists, coaches, commentators, and the like. Whenever you find a sour, failed child prodigy (athletic or otherwise), please recall this essay.

I frequently see the parents' poison in the grown child before me. By ignoring school work in lieu of more practice of one sort or another, the education suffers. By ignoring basic social skills in lieu of developing intense concentration on one area of life, the humanity suffers. By telling the child all her fellows are jealous of her gift, the potential for close relationships suffers. In other words, future mommies and daddies, if you encourage your child to pursue one track to the exclusion of all others, there's a very slim chance of success. But there's an enormous likelihood you'll create a social misfit.

The Dumbing Down Of America

There are now those who routinely muse the average American is not quite as well educated or knowledgeable as those in prior generations. My Momma, your great-grandmother, was born in 1918, and her formal education ended with the eighth grade. Other than algebra, I'd guess my Momma was at least as well educated as the high school class I graduated from in 1972. This begs the question as to whether there's been a decline going on for a long time. I still encounter the occasional young man or woman who's in love with learning and has benefited from all the love of learning entails. But more often than not I encounter young people who seem to be completely unaware of their personal history (i.e., who were your ancestors and where did they come from), much less knowing anything about their state or nation.

I saw a YouTube® video recently where someone was claiming the government has put fluoride into much of the drinking water in an effort to dumb down the populace to make us easier to control. I have a hard time swallowing this one (no pun intended), since it implies the ability to create an enormous conspiracy and carry it off over multiple generations without anybody ever finding the smoking gun it would take to blow the lid off such a conspiracy. I have my doubts because those in government can't even seem to run the postal service efficiently or use the IRS to secretly attack their political enemies without falling on their face and having the whole world find out about it. So, if we're dumbing down, it may be as simple as weakened curriculum, poorer study habits, larger classroom numbers, or mom and dad not caring enough to get involved in assuring the kids receive a proper education.

To the best of my knowledge, you grandchildren's parents have done a workman-like job of pushing education with you. Whether the life lesson in education 'takes' or not will be as much on your shoulders as it is on theirs. What I hope you've seen from our lives, especially mine, is education is not the cure all and be all of existence. On the other hand, I can assure you a poor education, or a lack of one, can definitely impact how high your horizons can be. There'll come a time when you'll understand every family has responsibility for the education of its own children. I don't mean everybody should homeschool their kids. What I mean is the education of your children is far too important to be left solely to public hirelings. If your child grows up to be a dunce because of bad schools or bad teachers, neither the schools nor the teachers will be hurt by it nearly as much as you and your child.

They've Fired Ron Johnson

I'm not sure the department store chain JC Penney® will still be around when you finally get your hands on this book, but I shopped there most of my life. Then about a year and a half ago the board of Penney's hired a man named Ron Johnson to be their Chief Executive Officer. Johnson, fresh off a successful stint over at Apple® (I think they'll still be around in your time), set out to remake Penney's into a newer, hipper kind of store. Gone were the sales and the coupons; in were the fair pricing schemes and portable checkout systems. The end result was sales fell nearly twenty-five percent and profits followed. His effort to create 'stores within a store' fell flat and former customers stayed away in droves. I haven't been back to Penney's since I got my first look at the changes Johnson made almost a year ago. They did away with a brand of underwear I'd worn for forty-five years. In short, the board brought Johnson in for a face-lift and a physical check-up and Johnson did a full facial reconstruction and a heart transplant.

Apparently the Penney's board decided the experiment was over. In the past few days they gave Johnson his walking papers and a large severance package. I'm sure he'll pop up again and he may well have other successes. In the meantime it'll take an enormous effort (read tons of cash invested) to pull buyers back from Target® and Internet vendors after the drubbing they took from Johnson and his new world order vision of this old American institution. Here's what you need to take away from this if you ever own a business and you have a downturn which requires some fresh counter-cyclic thinking. If the basic mechanics of your operation are good, figure out which areas are problematic and deal with those specific areas. For God's sake, don't decide just because the front door is damaged the whole house should be torn down. Furthermore, you might want to ask your present customers what it is they like about your company before you decide to scrap your moneymakers.

I've seen this re-imaging happen far too much in recent years, and as often as not, the effort was disastrous. Old people like me who received clothes from Penney's when they were a child learned some of their favorite and most successful lines were dropped entirely. Other lines were modified so much customers didn't recognize them. At the end of the day many Penny's customers did what I did and went elsewhere. If you're going to try and look like Walmart®, then most folks would just as soon go over to Walmart® and get better pricing. I'm glad to hear they came to their senses and fired Ron Johnson. Here's the worst of it though, this doesn't mean I or the other customers who fled are heading back to Penney's immediately. I've developed new preferences and new loyalties while I've been away and like most consumers, I take my time leaving and I'm slow to return once I've been burned.

In my time a man named Alvin Toffler wrote at length about the accelerated speed of change which was coming to my twentieth-century world. This calls to mind the old axiom about turning a great ship. You may or may not know this, but it can take miles to bring a big ship around. If it's done too quickly the result can be a disaster. If it's done too slowly, it can also end in disaster. So while I'm fully conversant in the idea of creative destruction, I'm always quick to remind folks who want to implement such a process that the word 'creative' has to be given equal weight with the word 'destruction' or the paradigm fails. You must be able to turn the ship without turning it over or running into the pier. It's a delicate balance you'd do well to remember in seamanship and your future business life.

Good Cop, Bad Cop

You may at some point get the feeling, depending on who is in power in the state or nation's capital at the time, our two political parties play good cop bad cop with the people. In my estimation, you'd be correct. It appears to me they alternate roles as the situation requires, but once regular folks go back to the holding cell of their daily lives the politicians slap one another on the back and have a friendly drink together after work. I urge you to consider this deception and be wary of buying in too much to the positions espoused by any political party.

Instead, you owe it to yourself and your progeny to know the critical issues of your day and be conversant in them. Lazy and uninvolved citizens, as much as self-interested politicians, are what got us to the place we're in now and are at least as much to blame. There's always the tendency to want to go home at the end of your day and vegetate. There's always too much willingness on the part of the citizenry to abdicate personal responsibility for the state of their nation's social and political affairs. This comes about so we might be about our rest and enjoy our leisure. This absence of the citizenry in the political arena has created a vacuum which the vote seeker has all too willingly filled.

Certainly politicians throughout recorded history have understood this truth and capitalized on it. They've made it exceedingly easy for us to place government in their hands so we might fill our own hands with the implements of a pseudo-leisure class. I make this fine point about a pseudo-leisure class because the true leisure class has enough money to live a life of leisure AND remain vitally connected to their personal and business interests, whereas a pseudo-leisure class *does not.* On Monday you go back to your eight-to-five job; on Monday they go back to counting their assets.

Don't be fooled by appearances! Just because you go skiing in Vale and see some of the Kennedys, Duponts, Musks, or Gates on the same slopes, it doesn't mean you live in the same world they do or you and they are paying the same price for leisure time. Families of this financial stature can afford to hire experts to look after their business and personal interests, including their political and social interests. Unless you personally manage to amass this kind of wealth, you'll likely have had to set aside or ignore your similar political and social interests in order to indulge in such an amazing ski trip.

Finally, I've rarely, if ever, outright hated a politician. There've been many I disliked intensely, but wasting time outright hating someone you've almost no control over is an exercise in ulcer production, and the ulcers will be yours. The troubling part is every once in a while you're going to see a truly selfless man or woman enter the political fray and perhaps even rise to some lofty height. Unfortunately, most of the time all this really does in the long-term is ruin a good man or woman and get the electorates' hopes up politics have turned a corner and a better class of politician is on the way. History doesn't support this cheery view!

Econ 101 For Politicians

I had a very troubling thought recently which for some unknown reason I've never had before in my sixty years. It was a troubling political thought related to economics. You see, the present state of the world's economics provides me with pause for great concern. Consequently, I worry about your future, daughter or grandchild. The troubling thought I'm having is so simple it's easily overlooked, and I've overlooked it all my life. Apparently, I've done this along with millions of other people around the world. I'll try to frame it in a way which makes sense, so you can ruminate over it as I have now it's found its way into my thought stream.

Here's some background. Most colleges and universities require a course in political science or some similar class designed to give the well rounded man or woman some inkling of how their country's political system works. As I recall, I was told it also created a "...better informed citizen." This being the case, why don't we also require some kind of basic course in applied economics related to the political system our country espouses? In a communist country, it would be the economics of communism. In a socialist country, it would be the economics of socialism. In a capitalistic country, it would be the economics of capitalism.

In this manner all the citizens of a country with higher education would then have some common basis for understanding how their economic system was supposed to work. They'd understand the political system and the economic system. I've always felt that people claiming higher education should at least be conversant in their nation's economic system; sadly it's my experience most are not. The term 'economic illiteracy' comes to mind. Okay, taking an econ class doesn't seem like such a big deal, does it? But here's the *very* troubling thought! How is it (as far as I've been able to determine) *no country* has any requirement whatsoever people seeking political office have even a basic understanding of economics?

Throughout the world we place people in charge of the economic health and welfare of our nations while giving little if any thought to whether or not these people even know how to balance their own checkbook. We elect former soldiers, actors, singers, lawyers, organizers, comedians, bankers, and activists of every stripe. I concede once in a while an accountant does get elected to public office, but by temperament they're quickly consumed by the facts in front of them, never to be heard from again. We elect these folks without any apparent regard for the fact we're about to place the economic lifeblood of our city, county, state, or nation into the hands of (for the most part) economic neophytes. Look around the planet! In the light of this economic knowledge deficit, is the economic shambles you see at all unexpected?

What all nations need going forward isn't more glib men and women who present themselves well and are expert at glad-handing potential constituents and donors. What all nations need, and perhaps should ask for, are candidates who've at least taken Econ 101, or something similar. Furthermore, it should be a favorable characteristic if candidates have actually gone beyond the basics and taken advanced work in microeconomics, macroeconomics, accounting, or some equivalent classes. It wouldn't even have had to be at a college or university, most of us would be happy if they'd even read a book (e.g., Economics for Dummies, etc.) on the subject.

You can't immediately fix the state of your political world in your time any more than we could here in mine. Yet moving on into this century you might want to add 'economic education' as one of the filters you engage when measuring the next great leader. I find it troubling we eagerly place a seventeen trillion dollar annual economy in the hands of elected officials who may have never been responsible for as much as a single million-dollar budget in their lives. Look at your local elected officials. How many of them demonstrated any degree of business acumen before they were sent to manage the business of the people? Now ask yourself, would you—should you—hand over your checkbook and budget and let them handle it for your family?

CHAPTER 2

Nothing To Fear But Fear Itself

There are many motivators in the human experience. Fear is one of them and it's very powerful! Fear's greatest drawback is once people enter into a fearful state, they're no longer behaving as rational individuals. Frequently, this fact is why some politicians, preachers, and prophets like to trot out fear at every opportunity. Rationality rarely serves a fearmonger. As a consequence fearmongering behavior seems to have reached the state of an art form in my time, especially in the media. There's money to be made from fear, and there's power to be gained from purveying it.

Here's an idea for you to hold onto. Begin to listen to the messages you're being inundated with and make a conscious effort to determine what form of motivation the message bearer intends. Anytime you recognize someone is using fear as a motivation, try to quickly determine if it's a caring approach (i.e., don't put your hand in the fire) or a selfish approach (i.e., "Call now! We only have three of these watches left at this price, and if you don't call now, they'll be gone!"). If you don't take charge of the filters available to you and aggressively use them to tune out unnecessary fear, fear-driven behavior will be your way of life from now until your grave.

Pursuing Your Own Star

I'm not one of those folks living in 2015 that has to know the latest information from *TMZ* or *Entertainment Tonight* (popular television in this time). Celebrity doings and goings-on have never intrigued me to any large degree. As I enter my seventh decade on this planet, I'm less and less able to identify the stars and am often completely at a loss as to who folks are when I see news clips of people walking the red carpets of the innumerable awards shows out there these days. I'm not angry with any of these people, nor do I begrudge them their fame. What does concern me though, is the number of people I meet who seem to be living out their lives vicariously through celebrities.

I suspect a good many people are thwarted in pursuing their dreams and recognizing their potentials because they get caught up in the lives of others they've judged to be better people than themselves. They then give up on their own lives to imitate their idols. I've been working with, leading, and advising people for decades. One of the sadder things people in my position see is wasted human potential, where people have given up on themselves because they don't match up with some kind of an imaginary ideal created by overbearing parents or the marketing minds of Madison Avenue. Very few of us could ever hope to be as attractive, intelligent, fashionable, or witty as Hollywood can make folks appear to be.

Remind yourself, your sibling(s), your offspring, and their offspring of the things about each of you which are unique and altogether wonderful. Many studies I've seen indicate most of us are very uncomfortable giving or receiving praise. Consequently, there's a societal-wide hurdle in place which has to be overcome before each person may hear and receive a true assessment of who they are. You're not perfect, your mother's not perfect, and neither am I. Each of us has strengths and weaknesses. Each of us has positive and negative attributes. The reason so many of the famous and near-famous are able to appear so together is because they have a dozen other talented people working frantically to help them hide their weaknesses and negative attributes while helping them always put their best foot forward.

Don't give up on yourself! Don't give up on your children! Don't give up on your grandchildren! Never give up on your dreams! In fact, this may be the dividing line between those who eventually achieve their dream lives and those who watch the dream lives of others. Are you following your dream? Are you pursuing it passionately? Or, have you settled because you aren't quite sure you're good enough to pull it off? Why not turn off the television, shut down the computer, put away the smart phone, and invest some of your imagination in capturing or re-capturing your dreams? Then let those dreams ignite your passion for the greatness which lies within you. It's a greatness which has the power to make *you* THE star in whatever world you choose to walk in.

Stop And Smell The Hummingbirds

Your great-grandmother, Opal McCormick Neeley, loved flowers and hummingbirds about as much as anything I'm aware of. She always did her best to have a yard full of flowers, and these in turn gave her a steady stream of hummingbirds. She often reminded me to take time in life to stop and smell the roses. She clearly worried I was too much about work and not enough about any of life's other important business, such as relaxing. Momma was a hard worker, but she also knew to sit down and enjoy your company and a glass of sweet tea.

One malady I suffer with my which Momma did not have to endure is allergies. So, I've been somewhat limited in my ability to enjoy the flowers as much as Momma did. I too love birds, especially hummingbirds, and do my best to keep plenty of feeders out for them around the otherwise barren landscapes I've kept as an adult. In either case, I'd like to offer this advice to you, if for one reason or another you cannot enjoy one or more of the delights in life which others can; you truly need to stop and smell the hummingbirds.

No Sunglasses

When you're grown, you'll discover you can make three or four trips to the store to buy a pair of sunglasses, and each time you'll come home with a carload of items... and no sunglasses.

Extended Self-Sufficiency

Over the past few years I've noticed our government has shifted the timeline of its ability to care for people in times of local, regional, or national crises. Years ago we were led to believe if the worst happened, the National Guard, Red Cross, or one or more federal agencies would respond almost immediately to get the situation in hand. Then we saw a series of disasters which exposed the fact the National Guard, Red Cross, and all the consolidated federal agencies, currently known as the Federal Emergency Management Agency (FEMA), were often unable to respond in less than seventy-two hours. Sometimes they haven't been able to respond properly for two or more weeks!

Now I'm noticing government-sponsored billboards around the country encouraging people to be prepared for disasters by having adequate supplies to survive for up to seven days without outside assistance. The upward trajectory of how many days we'll have to be self-sufficient seems to be steadily increasing. So here's what I've taken away from all this; yes, it may be crazy to try to have five years' worth of food, water, and other supplies on hand for times Without Rule of Law (WROL) or when we reach The End Of The World As We Know It (TEOTWAWKI). But it may be good sense to have enough supplies on hand to survive a couple of weeks if you experience an earthquake, hurricane, wildfire, terrorist attack, or visiting relatives.

I don't have a crystal ball and can't say what kinds of natural or man-made disasters you may have to deal with in the years and decades ahead. In my time I've seen volcanoes virtually shut down the planet, or at least large sections of it. There have been some horrific earthquakes which laid waste to entire regions of the world. As if those weren't bad enough, we've experienced tsunamis around the earth's oceans' shorelines which have killed hundreds of thousands and left hundreds of thousands of others homeless. My suspicion is, since these calamitous things always have been, they always will be. You can either pretend they won't happen to you, and if you're lucky they won't, or you can prepare to encounter and survive life's dangerous inevitabilities.

This will require you take the long view of your life and the necessities of daily existence. When I was a boy, your grandmother or great-grandmother prepared in whatever fashion we could afford to have food on hand to survive a workless winter period when income was either slim or none. We learned to raise gardens and to preserve and store food. The irony was not lost on me when, during my master's degree study in International

Development, we were being taught how to pass these ideas along to impoverished families in developing countries as a way to stabilize and improve their quality of life. I was often puzzled we didn't make the same efforts with American families in general and poor American families in particular.

My advice to you is to learn whatever you can about taking care of yourself and/or your family. Society has a very thin veneer of manufactured civility; it's one which easily disintegrates under duress. Personal safety, food security, extended pantries, and even learning to live, not off the grid but in the absence of the grid, are valid pursuits in this old man's opinion. I'm not suggesting you become some gun-toting, conspiracy-theory-laden madman hiding in a bunker somewhere, planning to kill your neighbors rather than offer them food. I'm suggesting you utilize common sense and recognize if a rainy day does come along, the guy who owns an umbrella is in better shape than the poor fool who always laughed at the people who owned an umbrella.

Whose Dream Is It Anyway

I cautioned a young grad student today to think hard before she decided to press on and earn a PhD; she was shocked! Don't get me wrong, I'm happy to have earned one and am always glad to see someone pursuing one in earnest. In this case she was certainly young enough at twenty-four to get plenty of mileage out of the degree and pay off any resultant debt incurred while earning it.

However, I didn't hear any fire in her voice about how this had been her lifelong dream/obsession. What I heard was she had just about wrapped up her master's degree, her husband wanted her to press ahead for the PhD, and it had been a lifelong dream of her parents she would someday earn a PhD, teach at a university, and be called doctor.

I assured her if she was ambivalent now about pursing this goal, it wouldn't necessarily get better over the next four to seven years in a doctoral program. For any of you kids trying to inspire your child, your sibling, or your spouse to pursue a dream, you might want to make sure it's their dream and not yours. I worry far too many people are pursuing dreams which are not their own.

Dreams are incredibly powerful stuff and can take little people and turn them into giants. Dreams can cause a child who stutters constantly to one day speak or sing clearly before thousands. Dreams can convince a child born an impoverished farm worker he can one day be a teacher and writer. Dreams will carry you when everything and everyone around you says your effort is futile. So nurture you're your dreams and other people's dreams, and when those dreams comes true, enjoy them.

Everybody doesn't need a terminal degree. Everybody doesn't want to be a surgeon, lawyer, accountant, stockbroker, banker, professor, or rocket scientist. For all the lip service parents pay to encouraging their child to pursue their passions, you can often hear the letdown in their voices when they say, "Yes, our Jayne has decided to give up medical school to become a yoga instructor." In those instances it sounds as if when Jayne found her dream, her parents' dream died.

I encouraged your mother, and you to get a college education. Ignoring my advice for the most part, your mother has managed to have a successful and fulfilling life, and as of this date, neither she nor any of her sisters have earned a college degree. This has convinced me you can be happy and fulfilled and won't starve to death if you don't earn a degree. It has also shown me if people aren't allowed to pursue their dreams, happiness and personal fulfillment may never be theirs.

A Leader Who Didn't Know It All
One of the most liberating things I ever witnessed was when the CEO of a company I worked for was hearing a presentation and he stopped the speaker and asked him to explain a concept the speaker had introduced which he said he'd never heard before. This shocked me because it was something current in our line of business. Truthfully it had been around a couple of years at this point. The liberating part for me came from the fact even though I knew what the speaker was talking about; here was the head of a multi-million dollar, multi-national, publicly-traded company in a room with twelve of his top level executives from all over the world, admitting he didn't know something.

As I looked around, I noticed several people looked relieved. It was then I realized others had had no idea what the speaker was talking about either, yet didn't want to look like an incompetent by asking him to explain. The speaker graciously took about five minutes to lay out the technical aspects of the concept, and then he picked up his presentation and took off from where he'd been interrupted. It was in this moment I saw great leaders (and this man, now deceased, was a great leader) were not afraid to admit they didn't know something. Contrast this with the leaders you may have followed who'd never admit their own knowledge was any less than God-like.

When I was a young man I took great pride in my knowledge. I loved to learn and loved sharing it. I also loved the adulation it created. But as the years have passed, I slowly recognized, even though I knew more than some others, the areas of my knowledge where I know little or nothing are cosmically vast. Pride in all of us, not just our leaders, will make it hard to admit there's something others around us may know which we don't. It's a strange combination of pride and arrogance bordering on hubris in many of today's 'great leaders'. This holds true in all fields; practitioners of religion, politics, medicine, science, art, and all other disciplines are not immune to this malady.

As an aging man working daily to be a wiser man, I find myself upon someone's questioning; admitting more and more often I don't know the answer. Yes, there are some fields where I'm a Knowledge Area Expert. But there are literally thousands where I'm not. The great leaders allow the expertise of others to be recognized, acknowledged, and celebrated. The bad leaders pretend to know it all, to be able to do it all, and to be insulted if anyone so much as hints perhaps they don't know everything. By the way, this seems classically narcissistic. Institutions in America and around the world need more leaders who'll admit they have gaps in their genius and are big enough to ask for others to advise or lead in these areas.

I point this truth up to you because, knowing most of you well already, it's clear to me you're bright, and unfortunately you've inherited some of the Neeley's penchant for vanity, pride, and a temper. If you're fortunate, life will beat some of this out of you without killing you or destroying those qualities altogether. A little vanity, a little pride, and a little temper can be a good thing. People who don't possess any of these three in small portions don't seem to care about or be willing to fight for important things like their appearance, their possessions, the world around them, and their relationships. It's good to know something, just don't behave as if you know everything. Conversely, be cautious of those who behave as if they know everything.

Not If But When

When it was just the United States, Soviet Union, Great Britain, France, and China who had nuclear arsenals, I figured the threat of mutual annihilation was enough to make sure we didn't have to worry about a bomb coming down on our heads. But with the proliferation of nuclear weapons over the past seven decades, I now believe sooner or later another nuclear device will be employed against some population somewhere on this planet. Regretfully, I predict you and your children will live to see it.

This has become a near certainty as the methods by which the bomb was developed became common knowledge and most of the equipment required to manufacture one can be purchased on the Internet. When you couple this ease of availability and common knowledge with the number of petty dictators who are either developing the weapon or already have it, you begin to see the source of my concern. When it happens, it will be horrible beyond imagination, a thousand times worse than it was in 1945. That is, unless you are an initial victim. In which case, it will happen so quickly your senses will likely not even register the flash of the detonation.

Young Taxpayers Are The Victims

I just noticed a piece come across Facebook®, posted by a local conservative politician, regarding the state of California's finances and who's going to pay the bills. If I recall the latest numbers correctly, California has a total outstanding debt of more than $600,000,000,000. That's six hundred billion for those of you who struggle with so many zeros. As far as who's going to pay the debt, I have two thoughts I want to share. The short answers are "The taxpayers of California" and "No one." You're the taxpayer!

My first response is the taxpayers of California have either directly (ballot initiatives) or indirectly (elected officials) placed themselves and their grandkids on the hook for a massive amount of debt. At last count, California was borrowing about $40,000,000 a day to keep all the balls in the air. Acting as though came about without the electorate's consent is naïve. The people of California wanted things, and they or their elected representatives voted themselves things. Only later do we think about what things cost. The bill will definitely be coming due.

My second response is no one is going to pay this debt, and it's because we've already passed the point of critical mass, and it's in runaway mode due to the inability to even pay the interest. The financial system of California and the United States could still be saved if our economy were to lurch into high gear and produce record employment, record earnings, and the accompanying record tax receipts. However, it would then have to continue in this mode for several years without recession. This isn't likely or even probable based on history.

There is a school of thought which says a deliberate collapse of the economy of the state and the nation is what's really going on here. All conspiracy theories aside, I do think an economic collapse is a strong possibility. I have to wonder how long people can see the price of food go up dramatically each time they visit the market and not revolt. If I were a politician, I'd pay close attention to what happened to politicians after they presided over the economic collapse of their nations. A hungry crowd will dine on blood when there's nothing else left to satisfy their hunger.

Unless you want to be slaves all of your lives, meaning the state continues to demand a bigger and bigger share of what you have and what you earn, you'll need to band together with other people who are similarly situated economically to rally against this abuse. Now to be sure, there are other folks in your time who'll be rallying with others of their ilk who really like a system which takes away from the haves and gives to the have-nots. In theory this is not a bad plan, but in reality the have-nots have increased in their percentage across the decades of my life, and all the while their level of wants have grown geometrically as well.

On The Playing Fields Of Life

I was contemplating a game we played in the grammar school classroom at recess one rainy day back in 1962. The teacher was a kindly older woman and one of the best instructors I ever had. You're thinking, "There's not much to report there." But here's where the screw turns. This game involved her performing a task which required rhythmically tapping a yardstick on the floor while reciting, "Little is the man who can't do this." The students were then asked to come to the front of the class one at a time and do *exactly* what she had done. The point of the game was to see how closely we were watching her so we could precisely mimic her behavior. Each time a student failed, she would repeat the instruction. Time after time students failed and went back to their desks. Eventually, some caught on. In the course of using up all the recesses for the day, everybody managed to figure it out. The trick was before she started to speak, she pretended to clear her throat. Kids focused on the words, the tapping, the posture, and just about every other nuance while trying to get the point of the game. Eventually everybody figured out how critical the throat clearing was to satisfying the game's criteria.

In the course of the day kids got upset, whined, became petulant, sulked, and manifested all the emotions which go along with losing. You have to remember, in 1962 we accepted the fact in life there would be winners and losers, and this teacher was willing to take all day for this scenario to play out. Eventually, every classmate was a winner, but for some of the less observant students, it took all day. The teacher never stopped when some classmate burst into tears at their failure or said, "Oh, never mind, I'll tell you what the answer is." She ignored their unhappiness and the game went on. I contrast this with some of what I've seen over the years where parents and society seem to do everything they can so a child never experiences a personally profound sense of failure. I recognize a constant diet of failure is deadly. But I suspect a constant diet of always being a winner may be just as deadly; it just takes longer. We do both children and society a disservice by creating a make-believe world where everybody is a winner every time. Failure and the resultant loss can be one of the most powerful and important teachers in life.

Or we could pretend every response is a winning response, and every performance is a stellar performance, and eventually come to a point where we live in a narcissistic age of teens and young adults who've never been allowed to fail. They would be alternately crushed or furious when they begin to encounter failure in a world where not everybody gets to be honored as student of the week. Having never previously been allowed to fail, they would blame their parents, their schools, their curriculum, the church, their state, their fellows, and their God. Many would go on to feel angry because they were being denied this right to win which they erroneously learned from their parents, teachers, ministers, politicians, friends, and their God. When it's written down in stark contrast like this, it almost seems as if we've already reached this place in many first world countries. Meanwhile, those people in nations where there are still winners and losers learn to overcome failure and fight on. So, is it any wonder the children from these 'winners and losers' societies frequently consume our little first-world children when they meet on the playing fields of life?

The Power Of Voices

I suspect each of you will sooner or later discover whatever it is your mind feeds on; eventually the food begins to have an impact on your day-to-day existence. I know this is true for me from both a practical and a philosophical point of view. With regard to the social media present in my day, I've learned it too, has an impact. If the information pouring into my head throughout the day is on the whole positive, I feel physically better and have a better mental outlook at the end of the day.

If the information pouring into my head is on the whole negative, I feel physically drained and have a poorer mental outlook. Some of you may regard this as too trite an example, coming from an old man, and simply ignore it while others of you will read this book, hear what it's saying, and reexamine your daily intake. You should each be careful what voices you let fill your world and what messages you allow yourselves to be inundated with.

You'll need to work hard to recognize the voice of God speaking to your heart. You need to work equally hard to recognize your own voice speaking from your heart. The latter is not nearly as easy as it sounds when you're inundated with people who want or need you to think as they do and have some ability to compel you to do so (e.g., friends, spouses, family, bosses, teachers, ministers, etc.). The old adage, "To thine own self be true," will be just as valid in 2035 as it is in 2015. You matter, and your voice matters. Don't let it be silenced by other people's inflated egos or overbearing behavior.

Clearing The Decks

The following 'Clearing The Decks' essays are written as a group and are intended to address some issues you'll not likely encounter until you're into or approaching your middle age, still more than twenty years away. Grandchild, you can read them now while you're young, but I suspect they'll be of more benefit to you when the proper stage in your life arrives. They may more quickly benefit your mother, should she look at them before you do. The key message is one of figuring out what your priorities are and pursuing them to the exclusion of all else.

Many years ago a doctoral professor said something to me in a counseling session which had, and continues to have, a profound impact on my thinking and behavior. I want to share some expanded thoughts on the topic with you in hope they may be as beneficial for you as they've been for me. At the time of the counseling session, I'd nearly completed my doctoral studies and was preparing to write my dissertation. In those moments you become painfully aware of how finite time is, about how painful bad choices can be, and the financial consequences of allowing a deadline to pass unmet.

It was in this frame of mind the good professor and I sat down over iced tea one very hot afternoon in Phoenix, Arizona. Shortly after starting our conversation, she put her finger on the problem I was presently wrestling with without me even telling her what it was. She knew because she'd been where I was. In the course of an hour's conversation, she helped me see in each of life's passages, there are parts of the old life we can't take into the new. We must release one or the other. If we try to hang onto both, we'll have neither. Sometimes this also requires releasing people.

In explaining this truth to me, she used the nautical reference 'Clearing the Decks', a term which denotes ridding a ship's deck of loose objects and anything else which doesn't need to be there prior to a battle or a storm. I now think of this term every time I sense I've come to one of life's passages where I must deal with the need to release a part of the old life. I hope these musings on the various applications of the topic are helpful and assist you in making better quality decisions in your life when the proper time arrives.

Clearing The Decks Of The Extraneous

I plan to be specific about exactly what has to be cleared from the decks of your life in later paragraphs. But right this moment, I want to use the broad term 'extraneous' to address the smaller items. As I've aged I've become aware of all the things I own, or more accurately, the things which own me. House, car, furniture, clothes, toys, and my list goes on and on, just as yours does, even at this age. We amass so many items which at some moment were meaningful to us, but as time passes they've lost their meaning or usefulness and have instead become a shackle of one form or another. I'm acutely aware of all the extraneous things I lug along which no longer serve the purpose they once did, but I still can't repurpose them or let them go unless I force myself to look at what they cost me versus what they're actually worth.

I see other people are more or less the same as I am in this department. Most families have a junk drawer or a junk room where they store miscellany they don't know where else to place. We each have physical, psychological, and spiritual junk drawers, or entire junk rooms we need to wade into regularly and clean out. But we don't do this cleaning unless life sends us a storm or a battle. People instinctively understand when it's a matter of life and death; they have to pare down the cross-section of their ship so they have the best chance possible of weathering the storm or winning the battle. However, it doesn't take a life or death situation to rob your life of its joy and purpose. Maybe it's simply you're sick of mowing the lawn and caring for a too-big house and think a condo fits you better than the home you raised the kids in.

We each need to attune ourselves to the small things in our lives which are robbing us of the simple pleasure of living a life without a constant nagging sense of regret, worry, or frustration. Once attuned, we must heed those things which we hear our heart saying to us, about what actually succors us and makes us happy we're alive. Contrast this with living forever with nagging feelings of missing out on a real life and suppressing those feelings until it's too late to do anything about them. You know, in my view it's rarely too late to change! Admittedly, the closer we get to the grave the harder it seems to become, but change is a good thing if it positively affects a year, a month, a week, or even a single day of the time you have remaining. Let go of your anger, anxiety, pride, fear, and jealousy. They're small items, but they're a heavy weight, which like so many others in life can sink a ship once they fill the deck.

You entered this world naked and without possessions, worries, deadlines, or expectations. Clearing the decks of the extraneous seeks to take us back as close to this place as we can be.

Our lives don't consist of all the things we own as much as what we've been able to give away. I encourage you right now to think about what you could give away that would improve the quality of your life. Pick a single item and pass it along to someone for whom it would hold the same meaning or purpose it once held for you. In doing this, you lighten your soul and your closet, while at the same time bringing new meaning to someone else' life. What they do with it in time is not your problem, but unburdening yourself is certainly your reward.

Clearing The Decks Of Poisonous Friends And Family

I want to make this writing not more than four or five paragraphs so it doesn't ramble and you lose interest. When you address an issue this tough, you have to hit it head on. So if this offends you, I'm okay with you being offended. What I have to say to you here isn't for everyone. As time goes by you have to be able to move on to the next phase of your life, and sometimes this means letting go of some close relationships because they've become a continuing source of poison. You know the ones I'm talking about—the friends who stop growing or turn down a side path. They can be the parents, grandparents, siblings, uncles, aunts, or cousins who've taken histrionics, narcissism, or passive aggressive behavior to new heights. They can be the formerly loving spouse who sabotages you for fear you'll outgrow him or her and move on without them. I told you this would be head on and perhaps too painful. Please read on for your own sake.

Some of you will find you have friends you outgrew years ago because they chose to remain the exact same person they were at age fifteen and you're nearing thirty-five. Here's some news for you: every relationship doesn't stand the test of time, and both parties in a relationship have the absolute right to make personal choices. This doesn't mean you can't part on friendly terms and still get together now and then, but if they make a point of ridiculing who you've become, they're saying they don't like *this* you and they're trying to force their desired change on you! This means they don't like what you've become, and the why or why not of the matter isn't your problem, it's theirs. If, as you've grown up, you became some sort of intolerable jerk, I can't blame them. But if you got out of the old 'hood, got a life, made something of yourself, and have even higher dreams for your kids, there isn't anything to apologize about. Shake 'em loose and move along; they'll only drag you down.

My Momma, God rest her soul, did her best to keep peace among her children. But over the years (and the twenty-year span between her youngest and oldest kids), life didn't turn out as Momma wanted. I don't think this is nearly as rare as some families pretend. I see a lot of families who have learned, to get along you have to go along, or you have to get out. Sometimes getting out is the very best choice. During my years as a minister, I counseled people living in all sorts of family situations, and it never failed the victims felt as if they were to blame. If family have abused (e.g., mentally, physically, financially, emotionally, or sexually) you in the past, and you continue to be around them and leave that abuse unchallenged, you're the one who needs the most help! I've come to the place where I've infuriated some people when they told me of ongoing abuse from a family member, and I told them I wouldn't counsel them anymore until they ended the relationship. These weren't youngsters, they were people my age. Sadly I must conclude some people have grown comfortable being abused.

How can you as adults expect to ever find yourselves, find your place in the sun, and actually enjoy the great and small moments of your lives if you're willing to let people who claim to love you perpetrate acts of mental, physical, emotional, financial, or sexual battery upon you at will? Worse yet, do you willingly make the trip on a regular basis to visit with these monsters and pay for the fuel and wear and tear on your vehicle so it can happen again and again? I'm saying clear them off the decks of your life, the sooner the better. Even at your age they're not planning on changing, and you're a fool for continuing to put yourself in a position to be treated this way. Don't tell me, or your psychologist, or your pastor how much you want to be happy if you're not willing to remove the source of your unhappiness, or at least remove yourself from their company.

You have the right to distance yourselves from me! In fact, everyone has the right to distance themselves from me. There's nothing so special about anyone in your life the relationship can't sour. I'm aging in mind and body, and my mindset is pretty steadfast at this point. I've long believed you can love people in the sense you wish the very best for them and at the same time not necessarily like them. At times these phases pass, but in some instances people change and the only way we can enjoy them at all is from a distance. If I should ever become such a person in your life, then by all means distance yourself regardless of how much I may bemoan it at the time. God knows there have been far too many young lives rained on by older relatives, which only left the younger generation wet, cold, and alienated. Feel free to practice some personal and emotional self-defense where needed!

Clearing The Decks For Your Life Work

Are you in the wrong job? Do you already hate your job? Is there another job you want to do and have never gone after it? Then you're in luck because this is what this passage is all about.

The fact is you may need to be clearing the decks of your life of work you hate and replacing it with work you love. I've been fortunate enough to have had the opportunity to have enjoyed several careers. Over the years I've been a welder, a mechanic, an engineering construction contractor, a pastor, a business owner, a manager, a counselor, a social worker, a CTO, COO, and CEO. The truth is I'm not done yet; I keep plugging along in law school when my health permits. In my case I've worked for more than forty companies and I like to think at least thirty-seven of them would want me back. The other three are still recovering from the people who formerly worked there which I helped send to prison or otherwise ended their criminal on-the-job careers.

Your mother joins your aunts in saying I re-invent myself frequently. I did this for a couple of reasons; either the job I was in became unfulfilling, or the time in my life where I wanted to perform that job any longer had passed. While I hope you're not like me in this sense of restlessness, I have friends who've said they envy my courage in this re-invention area. I don't see it as courage. I see it as a matter of survival one not only is able to make a living at what they do, but also have a life! For many folks I know they've sometimes been in a job for decades, a job which pays the bills but has left them a sad zombie. With troubled economies such as the one we're currently in, there are millions who want a job, any job. Rest assured there'll be troubled economies in your time. These precarious economic conditions force millions to go to a job they hate every day in order to provide for themselves and their families. The term I've heard used most in my adult life to describe this phenomenon is wage slave. Ask yourself, are you a wage slave? Are you a happy wage slave? If you're not happy, clear the decks.

Clearing The Decks Of Windmill Slaying

Throughout my working life I've had the opportunity to train a number of foremen, supervisors, managers, executives, and other leaders. One piece of advice I've given to each of them is "Pick your fights." To me, and I hope to them, this means in any great undertaking (and even some less than great undertakings), you'll be faced with many potential fights. Consider here a true fight cannot ensue unless both parties are willing to square off, either literally or figuratively. A lot of leaders and a lot of just regular folks want to take on every potential fight which comes their way, great or small. The 'all-comers' notion is a noble but unworkable one; sheer fatigue will take you out of the fight long before your opponent's blows will.

The Neeleys have historically been great fighters; it could be the Irish in us or any of the three other cantankerous, clannish groups we hail from. The problem with this all-comers approach is eventually you'll find yourself fighting someone somewhere every minute of every day. Nothing else will get done. All other efforts will become secondary, and fighting will become the end-all of your existence. When I ponder this, I think of Don Quixote and his penchant for jousting with windmills. We all look at his example and chuckle, some of us a little more knowingly than others. When I was young, I took an all-comers approach and usually won the battle, but I lost some important wars in the process. You must decide among all the little scraps and potential tussles coming your way, which are worth fighting and which best avoided.

Windmills are an impossible foe. But so are many of the other minor irritants we drag along through life, only to be forced to fight the periodic delaying action, never quite letting go and yet never quite vanquishing the enemy. To be truly happy, I think each of you have to learn to clear the decks of windmills. How, you ask does one accomplish this? To many people's surprise, windmills generally are not mobile and just putting distance between you and the windmill works wonders. Walk away! The windmill cannot follow you. It's true you may hear the windmill squeaking in the distance. Yes, it will still be there in the same place, and perhaps even remain a minor mental irritant, but it won't occupy your attention to the exclusion of all else as it previously has.

Modern lives are filled with an unimaginable amount of worthless possessions, ideas, entertainments, and worries. In your time I suspect this will only grow increasingly more so. If you want to move on to the next phase of your life, you have to pick your battles, and you have to let at least some of the windmills go unchallenged. Otherwise you'll gain the reputation for being a Great Fighter and a Great Windmill Slayer, but you'll not be recalled as a Great Foreperson, Supervisor, Manager, Executive, or Leader. When I offer the advice I opened this text with, I always remind the person I'm giving it to, it's their decision, and no one else can make it for them. If I'm fortunate, years later they tell me they've learned to pick their fights and are better for it. If not, then someday I eventually hear through the grapevine of their figurative or literal death and sadly sigh at the wasted potential.

Since I expect much of what I write here will be read by you youngsters as much as ten or fifteen years hence, I doubt I'll get to see much, if any, of how this impacts your behavior. I write to you as an aging man covered in scars which, for the most part, could've been avoided. If you doubt the wisdom of these words, pull your mother or any of my surviving friends aside and chat with them about the price I paid for routinely fighting windmills in my youth. It's a price I don't want you to bear one minute longer than youthful foolishness can induce you to do so. There are great and important battles which will need to be fought in your life. Figure out which ones are important as quickly as possible and turn your back on windmills.

CHAPTER 3

A Million Gadgets, And They're Still Lost

Following maps or directions is always a problem for some people, but the problem at this time in history seems to be compounded by people's near total lack of the ability to determine north, south, east, or west. In 2013 I needed to find temporary help for a charitable event I was involved in. This required I hire four people to assist with minor food preparation tasks throughout the eight-hour period of the fundraiser. All four of the temps became lost and only two were able to find the event site. This happened despite the fact it was in the middle of a major city and immediately adjacent to a major local landmark. In all four cases, it turned out any reference to points of the compass confused them.

When I initially made contact with these young people through their college culinary arts program, they each assured me two weeks in advance they'd be there. Since the event was located just off a major thoroughfare, and right next to our county's fairgrounds, I figured with MapQuest® or Google® maps, and everyone seemingly having GIS on their phones these days, it would be no problem finding the location. I was dead wrong!

It seems I threw them off when I gave them the street address and mentioned the location was exactly one block north of the County Fairgrounds on P Street; P Street is between O Street and Q Street in most cities, as far as I can determine.

I find this misadventure sad; I find it alarming; and I find it a fact of modern life. No matter how much I'm dismayed by this latest turn of geographic ignorance, it will probably only get worse in your time as people increasingly rely on Magellan®, TomTom®, or the latest phone application to help them find their way. In this case, all four students had applied because they needed to make money. I sought their help because I needed help. The two who did eventually find us got to work (albeit late) and were paid. The two would-be workers who never found the location didn't earn any money and made my day a good bit harder for their ignorance and their absence.

There's a good deal to be said for kids taking the time to learn to navigate the world without an electronic device. I began to learn about maps and compasses as a cub scout and much more later as a boy scout. By the time I was twelve I could find my way around a forest with just a map and compass. I never worried again about being lost as long as I had access to one or both of those items. I tried to teach this to my daughters; I don't think the lessons took perfectly, but they have the necessary outlines in their minds if they need them. The danger for you is what happens if your magical device loses its source of power? A bad battery, a power outage, a solar flare, or an intentional electromagnetic pulse can each leave the active device you need impotent.

There are a lot of ideas and actions from this time which you'll regard as 'old-timey' in your time; please don't ignore learning about them or how to perform them on a being outdated basis. Items such as maps, compasses, tape measures, and abilities like reading a map, performing math without a calculator, learning to spell accurately without a spellchecker, learning how to print words, learning how to write words in cursive, and even interacting with devices which won't recognize a human voice are important survival-level skills. Two of the richest men in my world are talking a lot right now about the danger humanity faces as we give more and more of our abilities and jobs to the burgeoning world of artificial intelligence. As I regularly encounter young people who are eager to work, yet lacking in rudimentary skills, it points up to me a serious and ominous society-wide problem.

Some Days Are Diamonds

Some days are diamonds, some days are stones. Then there are those days when you can't figure out why you got out of bed. The older you grow, the fuller your understanding of the meaning to be found in the passage of your days will become. I can assure you this actually makes those confusing earlier days, the days where you can't figure out what's going on or why you were ever born, much easier to accept as a meaningful part of your life. It's one of the small consolations of growing old!

Fool's Gold

When I was a young boy, there were many outcroppings of iron pyrite in the nearby Tehachapi and Sierra Nevada mountain ranges. Most of the kids in my area saw it, played with it, and eventually threw it away. This compound is more commonly known as 'fool's gold' because of its ability to fool old-time prospectors into believing they'd struck the mother lode when they'd in fact found a lode of iron compound. If you journey into our nearby mountains today, nearly fifty years since my boyhood adventures there, you can still find it easily. I suspect people visiting our locale from out of the area are still often convinced upon running across these veins they've found real gold or flecks of it for their amateur prospecting efforts.

Anchored firmly in the present, I'm learning that fool's gold of another sort is being mined, processed, and sold on both the Internet and traditional precious metal vendors around the world. There've always been people who knew how to cheat others out of their gold. In the gold rush days, assayers and merchants would put prospectors' gold in a leather bag or pouch and shake it out of sight of the owner, in order to knock off flecks which stuck to the inside of the leather bag. Others cut the edges off gold coins to extract unnoticeable amounts of gold, thus cheating the next holder of some of the value. Scams in the precious metals business are as old as time. But we've entered a dangerous new age which outpaces any of the efforts made by past generations to bamboozle people out of their precious metals.

There's currently an alarming rate of counterfeiting going on with gold and silver coins and bullion, and even people claiming to hold gold and silver certificates for investors. It will do you little good to invest your life savings in bars or coins of gold or silver if thieves have cast bars or coins of similarly weighted materials and simply coated the outside with gold or silver. It's common practice for buyers of gold or silver to 'core' the proffered metal to determine its legitimacy. In this manner they can visually inspect the material and physically expose it to chemicals to help determine its authenticity. Remember, in life it's okay to trust, but it's critically important to verify.

The coring and acid testing which takes place now, was not as commonly practiced in the past as it is today. Therefore, it's completely possible someone might have gold or silver they bought a decade or more ago, and upon attempting to sell it, discover they were taken and there's little, if any, recourse. If you go back to the original vendor, he can easily claim what he sold you was real and he has no idea where you got the bar or coins you claim to have purchased from him. This is a serious and growing problem as people try to flee failing paper currencies around the world in their search for true money. It will continue to be so in your time; don't fall victim.

If you have enough money to purchase gold or silver, then you have enough money to spend some time and effort learning how not to become a victim of this scam. Don't ever be in such a rush to own something you let your emotions overrule your common sense! If you have a thousand dollars or less to invest and get a great return on, stay away from this precious metals game and buy non-perishable grocery items that can be consumed in the coming year. Currently you'd make at least nine percent on your investment, perhaps more if they keep the printing presses smoking in Washington, DC. Fool's gold doesn't only come in the form of iron pyrite, and today's swindler is more studied and practiced than ever.

Yourself In Your Children

I was listening to news this morning on the radio as I drove to my office; once again the report about the performance of our public schools is disheartening. About the same time I was listening to the news, I drove past a billboard touting the fact each year the state lottery puts an additional billion dollars into public education which wouldn't show up otherwise. A few minutes later, I passed a growing private high school near my office which is bereft of public funds, is less than twenty years old, and yet has already established itself as both an academic and sports powerhouse. It occurred to me at this point tossing public money at our public schools will only result in more tossed money. In your time you'll hear the arguments over and over again about how spending more money on education will fix all the problems found there.

I know children in both private schools and who are home schooled who are scholastically amazing boys and girls. Each of you has been either privately schooled, homeschooled, or a combination of the two. Yet the key factor I see is not the relative wealth of your family or these other privately-schooled children's families; some of them scrape by, and many of the kids who are in private schools are there on reduced cost or full scholarships. The key factor is a home in which both parents are present and actively involved in making sure little Johnny or Susie is growing up to be a productive human being. This means they're well behaved, respectful of one another and adults, go to school ready to learn, and come home knowing their homework is their priority.

Until all mothers and fathers make their children the primary focus in their life, our nation will continue its educational and moral decline. If it declines long enough, it will do as every other great civilization before it has done; it will fall apart. Money alone cannot solve the problems of our public educational system. Certainly an adequate amount of money is needed to provide for a solid education, public or private. But adding layer upon layer of bureaucratic programs to supposedly support learning how to read, write, and perform arithmetic only seems to have created bloated bureaucracies where academic excellence isn't nearly as important as scoring high on standardized tests so the adults involved can continue to receive better pay, better benefits, and other teaching incentives.

Bankers, Gangsters, And Banksters

One of the concepts you'll learn early in your exposure to capitalism is you can lose your capital; all of it! You can go in a matter of seconds from being in a positive capital position to a negative capital position, and if you're lucky, back again. Consequently, we've all learned in these times you can go broke and there's no one to ask to give you back your capital. Due to our training as good Americans, when this happens we hang our heads and walk away. This minimal societal knowledge of how capitalism functions has worked all too well for a decidedly criminal element. They stole our wages, our pensions, our jobs, and our futures, and for the most part, we hung our heads and walked away. Let this be a cautionary tale to you in your time!

We were told there were banks and other financial institutions which were "Too big to fail," and if government didn't take money from the taxpayers and rapidly loan or outright gift it to these financial behemoths, they'd collapse and our whole world would fall apart overnight. Ignore for a moment the fact our whole world did fall apart anyway and keep your mind fixed on the issue of losing your capital. You see, with many of these giant losers, we pumped in vast amounts of capital, and they tanked anyway. Then other economic behemoths bought up their assets at fire sale prices. When we heard they were broke, we recalled those early lessons in loss of capital, behaved as though it was our fault for not having given enough quickly enough, hung our heads, and obediently walked away.

Wait a minute; this is where this whole scandal breaks down. This money, billions of dollars worth of it, was alleged to have vaporized. Well, did it? No one I know seems to be able to explain where all these billions of dollars went, and yet they were real enough when we loaned them or granted them or whatever it was we did. Some people in the financial sector have played on our ignorance and limited knowledge of capital to bamboozle us out of a lot of money. I heard this term recently and I like it! I share it with you here because it conveys so much in a single word. If you cross bankers with gangsters, what do you get? You get banksters. As the twenty-first century advances and I pass on to my reward, I think banksters will still be with you youngsters.

We keep hearing of all the alleged criminality in regard to the housing bubble, sub-prime mortgages, and loan guarantees coming out of Washington. We hear so much chest-beating by members of the Congress about this, you'd think the attorneys general of every state would be up to their necks in indictments and the attorney general of the United States would be handing us the head of a newly convicted bankster each week. You'd think those things, but you'd be dead wrong. If a thief steals your wallet, and you don't make a fuss, nothing comes of it except the thief is enriched at your expense. If banksters engage in the same kind of behavior, and you don't make a fuss, they'll be enriched at your expense. Oh, and someday they'll come back for more.

This 'coming back for more' scenario will occur in your time. My advice is to never believe real wealth can be created out of thin air; it can't be. All factors being the same, a house which was worth $200K last month can't be worth $250K this month in the absence of tangible changes to the property or economy somewhere to justify this kind of pricing spike. You can figure out the other applications of what I'm suggesting, but the point is the same. When people start to sell you blue sky, know there's a bankster somewhere blowing smoke and waiting for the money to roll in. Don't be fooled. Know this also, there's a politician somewhere smelling future campaign contributions and willing to do the bankster's bidding.

Aesop's Ancient Wisdom

> "We hang the petty thieves and appoint the great ones to public office."
> -Aesop-

Financial Caution

The ability of the financial markets to seemingly rally and then vaporize almost as quickly as they initially rallied is a cautionary tale to those who'll heed it. When stocks, bonds, precious metals, or pork bellies begin to roller coaster in their pricing, it's time for all but those with the strongest stomachs and the largest wallets to wait out the ride. Yes, it's true fortunes are won or lost in times like these. But if they happened in equal number, you'd have heard a lot more stories in your young life of "How I made my fortune" rather than stories of "Did I ever tell you I used to be wealthy?"

What's Your Solution?

When I press people who tell me they're determined to see the current form of government in the United States fall, I ask them what format they would replace it with. After all, we've enjoyed a long run as a republic, but I'll concede it's an aging republic and starting to tatter at the edges. This isn't the first time I've pondered this, and I was telling study groups thirty years ago the most likely scenario would initially be a shift away from a republic and toward some form of fascism; I still think that's a likely scenario for both my time and yours.

There are always voices out there agitating for anarchy, socialism, communism, theocracy, and benevolent dictatorships. The handiest thing to do when trying to refute arguments for such political philosophies is give examples of nations which experimented with those systems and how poorly they've fared. With those facts in mind, if you don't have an answer to my initial question, and a pretty solid answer at that, perhaps it's time to pray this republic form of government doesn't collapse yet. This is of course unless you have a better one waiting in the wings or some new and encouraging ideas to share on surviving a societal collapse.

Be very careful not to be taken in by those crafters of words who've positioned themselves to end up in places of wealth or power if your nation is brought to its knees. I've noticed the fellows calling for revolution are also the most reluctant to grab a gun and sally forth to man the breach themselves. Conversely, they do seem to be the fellows calling out for those whose passions their rhetoric has inflamed to take up arms and face certain annihilation at the hands of whatever evil they are railing against this month. I can only surmise they want to survive the carnage because they're somehow more important than the rabble they incite. If you study political leaders who came to power through revolution, you'll notice this trend predominates. They start the wars, someone else fights them, and they survive to rule.

All problems are local problems, and the most effective solutions to local problems begin locally, not hundreds or thousands of miles away in a capital city which has most likely completely lost touch with its own citizens. The rock group, *Buffalo Springfield*, was very popular during the 1960s. It was a decade of extreme civil unrest and a nationwide time of religious and political soul-searching. In one of their songs, in reference to protesters carrying signs, they made it clear the protesters are mostly just saying "hooray for our side". Even at an early age—I was a teen—it made me think about whether people were really seeking solutions or just rallying for their cause *de jour*. It's a thought still worth considering in your time.

Finally, I'd advise you fashion yourself to be a man or woman who is actually seeking workable ideas instead of the repackaging of sad old political and philosophical dogmas being trotted out by political opportunists in order to scratch the itching ears of a new generation of political neophytes. I still believe this or any country can and should be shaped from the bottom up. Now in truth I've heard this same jargon from every politician I've ever known or voted for. So why is it each of them, having expressed these same localist sentiments, then made every human effort to get away from the local level and go to the state or federal capital? If you're going to propose or champion solutions, be certain you'd bet your life and the life of your loved ones on them... because you might have too.

Now That The End Has Not Come

I've been told the end of the world was coming all of my life. I've heard it from preachers, prophets, fortunetellers, astrologers, and seers of all sorts. In its most recent iteration, the end was supposed to come upon us December 21, 2012, as the Mayan calendar was said to have predicted the end of the world by suddenly coming to an end itself. No one wanted to believe any sort of simpler explanations, such as the Mayan stone carver simply ran out of stone or laid down the calendar and forgot where he put it; the end of the world was the only plausible answer. I'm not sure what to make of it all, but I'm thankful, as I cruise social media, to see the spiritual *cognoscenti* are shaking off the dust of their latest embarrassment and moving full steam ahead with explanations for why they missed again.

This reminds me of the admonition I heard often as a boy from my Sunday school teacher at the Houston Avenue Southern Baptist Church. It was something to the effect "Only God knows the day and the hour of the end of this world." After more than four decades of trying to be a Godly person, I can say with certainty the end of this world is coming. However, it could be in the next hour, or it could be in the next millennium. In either case, the other admonition I recall conjoined with the first one was how I should be ready, so regardless of the time it happened, I would be okay. So, as entertaining as you might find all the supernatural drama, the best advice I can offer you kids is be ready. There'll always be people doing their best to get you to climb on their end of the world bandwagon. Each time you'll need to be wise enough, so you don't get fooled again.

While You Still Have It

The earlier in your lives you learn to enjoy the small blessings of friends and family, the richer your lives will be from that point forward. For me and my generation, this didn't seem to set in until we were in our forties and beginning to experience the normal losses which come to aging humans. By this time you'll have also begun to experience some elements of your own physical decline, but the sharper pains will come from the loss of people you always assumed would be there if you needed them. Your grandparents will die, your parents will die, your friends will die, your siblings will die, and people you've counted on for a lifetime for help, guidance, comfort, financial assistance, or basic friendship will all live out their appointed days and die. As harsh as this sounds, you must learn to expect this, learn to accept this, and begin to live your life as though these passings were going to start later today; don't waste a minute more in not appreciating what you have right now.

Every once in a while, I'll get a momentary urge to call an old classmate or friend, or a former coworker, only to remember in the next moment they're dead. The same thing happens to me with regard to speaking to my Momma, my Daddy, my aunts and uncles, my brother, and my son. I'll see something, hear something, or learn something I want to share with them because I know how much they would've enjoyed seeing or hearing about it, and then I realize I can't. The older you get, the more this happens. When I was eighteen years old, I hadn't lost many friends or relatives. Now having passed my sixtieth birthday, I've lost too many to recall in one sitting. These moments of realization are bittersweet and make me see how important each of those people was in my life; I took them for granted. It also makes me want to take the time to savor the friends and family I still have before they too are gone.

I know you're young and the majority of your life is ahead of you. But I challenge you to be wiser than me or many in my generation have been and begin to savor the people who have impacted your life in positive ways while you still have them around you. Now I'll share a secret with you; I still talk to all these people when I can, but unfortunately it's a one-sided conversation… and I'm standing at their grave.

Reality Checks

Humans grow comfortable with their lives very quickly and then fool themselves into believing everything is going to be great every day. As a case in point, I came home last night to a broken cold water line under a sidewalk in my backyard. The irony was I'd been working on some broken water lines at my place of business all day and hadn't arrived home until 7:00 p.m. as a result. I never saw the second broken pipe coming; what were the odds? Unfortunately, this cold water line couldn't be isolated and had to be dug out completely, along with its fellows (natural gas and hot water) so I could make a temporary patch. I'll put in a new pipe later. Did I mention I had to break five feet of the cement sidewalk above it to gain adequate access? At times like this you relearn quickly why plumbers are paid so well; this work would've all been on overtime.

Despite the PhD behind my name, I'm still a licensed plumber here in California (how else do you think I could afford to go back to school in my 40s?) and still have the skill set and tools of the trade, but a much older body. My point in all this rambling is this; a simple broken water line disrupted my whole evening, our nightly routine, and forced me to perform work at a time and in a way I wasn't expecting. I shudder to think what would have happened if it had been a major earthquake, hurricane, ice storm, or tsunami. Every line in the house could have been snapped and not just one old leaking water line. We're spoiled here in America, and sometimes it's a good thing to get a little reality check.

One of the themes I've hammered on both your parents (your daddies have rarely escaped my sage advice), and more recently you, has been of the need to prepare for unforeseen contingencies. Part of this mindset comes from me being an old

Boy Scout and "'Be Prepared" was and is the Boy Scout motto. The other part of it comes from a lifetime spent dealing with crises in businesses and various other organizations. Only a fool thinks everything is going to hum along smoothly forever. We live in a physical world which is constantly in a state of deterioration; things break down from their complex forms to their simpler components all the time. Check on this, but I'm pretty sure there's a natural law to this effect.

Over the years you've probably seen the little kit in the cute red or yellow divided boxes I sent your father. They included spare electrical receptacles, light switches, tape, spare toilet float chains, faucets, and a dozen other items which become so huge when you have a plumbing crisis, an electrical short, or the kitchen oven dies at 10:00 a.m. on Christmas day and all the hardware stores are closed. Those kits cost me very little money compared to the cost of a holiday callout by a professional plumber, electrician, or appliance repairman, but over the years, I believe they've served their purpose to make your lives and those of your parents a little smoother.

In light of the potential benefits of such preparedness, think of all I've just said to you on this subject as a personal reality check. You're now or soon will be out there living on your own and surviving by your wits. The tendency of young people is to think old people like your grandfather are scared, panicky, and alarmist. Even if those things are all true, try to see the value in this advice I'm offering anyway. Give serious thought to being at least a little bit prepared for serious disruptions to life, like earthquakes, hurricanes, wild fires, blizzards, ice storms, floods, volcanic eruptions, tsunamis, and other rarer but not unheard of events which plague the planet earth. I've lived through some of those natural events, and I can tell you it's a whole lot better to be the guy with lights, water, and a functioning refrigerator and toilet than to be the guy begging for them from his neighbor. Get it fixed in your mind bad things will happen in your lifetime; then prepare to live well through them!

Your Small Decisions Matter

I was reflecting recently on how small decisions can make such a huge difference in our lives. Nearly forty-five years ago, when I was in high school, I decided I'd better show up for football practice one afternoon instead of riding to town with one of my classmates on his new motorcycle. No, this isn't headed where you might think; my friend was a very responsible guy (as responsible as any of the rest of us at sixteen) and what transpired on this afternoon was not in any way his fault.

An elderly lady, who was reported to be 'confused' by the investigating officers, ran a red light. My friend, legally passing through the intersection on green, was instantly killed. I chose not to go through any great logical exercise or effort at insight of my own at the time. He was just a young man, only sixteen-years-old. The elderly lady was likely someone who shouldn't have been driving, and today she likely wouldn't be. On that day I was suddenly a sixteen-year-old kid who painfully understood how our lives can turn on small matters.

You're at the place where you're making decisions regarding your life and the future ahead of you. It's impossible for you to make every decision perfectly because you're an imperfect being; accept this now and don't become paralyzed trying to make mundane decisions. Forgive yourself life's minor mistakes. However, you should always keep in the back of your mind how important every decision can potentially be when you reflect upon what happened to my young friend. All your decisions matter, even the small ones.

Saving Your Savings

Money and the need to manage it will be a big part of your adult lives. I know your parents are working on this now while you're young, and I hope you'll have a good financial head about you as you grow into adulthood. There'll be many things you'll need to learn, but one of the most easily overlooked and underestimated is inflation. In economics classes I've heard it said it's too many dollars chasing too few goods. In a pinch it's easiest to remember it means your dollar has less purchasing power right now than it did a day ago. To this end, financial majors learn to calculate what's known as the *Time Value of Money*. It allows financiers to know what money was worth, is worth, and will be worth, accounting for levels of interest and inflation over a span of time.

Inflation is the hidden tax all of us endure. Politicians on both sides of the aisle know this truth, and for the most part will give your concerns about the cost you're asked to bear, lip service, but they won't make any real stab at dealing with it. Even today, with both sides in Washington jockeying for position on who can balance the budget most quickly and painlessly, inflationary forces (read the printing presses at the United States Treasury) continue their wicked ways. The proof some people pay close attention to this issue is revealed in the efforts those same people make or don't make to hedge against inflation. It does little good to for you to be sixty years old with $280,000 in your retirement account if inflation is eroding your purchasing power by 8-9 percent a year. You're going to outlive your money in just a few years.

Here in 2015, people who bought gold, silver, or other precious metals as a hedge against inflation saw their positions decline by as much as 30 percent. Silver, which had flirted with the $30-an-ounce mark, is now down in the $18-an-ounce range and falling. Gold has seen a plunge, though not as steep as silver. This forces some to rethink their whole strategy and look for other ways to secure their futures. While raw land or other real estate are two prime options, an investment in either requires a loss of liquidity and the need for the economy to turn around in the mid-term in order to regain the use of your invested money. Commodities are a tricky game, and even people who've traded them for years periodically come away burned. Let these be cautionary tales to you.

You can take positive steps in your life, such as paying off your house early and paying down/off your credit cards to get rid of double-digit interest rates. Purchasing non-perishable food items is a sure hedge against inflation, but even under the best of circumstances you can only rely on long-term food storage to reach about three years. Purchasing a more fuel-efficient vehicle, especially if you're driving an older gas guzzler, can be an excellent way to spend money now to dampen the effects of inflationary forces later. What I'm pointing up here children, is everyone's individual circumstances will dictate what he or she is able to do to protect themselves against inflation. The one thing each of you can do is to keep full pressure on your elected representatives to regain control of the printing presses. We've failed miserably in my time to do this, and people are suffering for it, though many don't understand why.

Wisdom's Children

I've no doubt all of you kids are going to be smart, each in your own way. But being smart and being wise is not the same thing;

it's the difference between having knowledge and knowing what to do with knowledge. I know many smart people, some extremely smart people, and some outright geniuses. In each of those three special groups I find far more smart people than I do wise people. Consider what I have to say here, and do your best to incorporate a lifetime quest for wisdom as much as any treasure you ever choose to pursue. Some of my colleagues and I were discussing wisdom the other evening before dinner; we speculated at length about where it comes from. Several points of view were expressed, with the school of hard knocks being the group favorite.

I've gone over our dinner conversation in my mind in the days since, and it occurs to me the opportunity to gain wisdom is all around us; it's built into the system. Despite the abundance of opportunity, a lot of folks go through an entire lifetime and gain very little wisdom from the events they experience. Why is that? Well, my position is to gain wisdom in life, you have to be constantly conscious of the world around you, how you fit into it, and how it fits into you. It's those moments of incongruity with the world, or the world with us, which are ripe for learning and developing wisdom. If you're disengaged, incapable of learning, or just don't give a rip, wisdom of the most important sort will never be yours.

If you know who you are and where you're at in any given moment in time, and if you allow yourself to live in the moment, you'll sense whether or not you are experiencing an incongruity. By this I mean you're having a moment which doesn't feel right, be it mental, physical, spiritual, or emotional. If at those moments you can keep your focus and question yourself as to what's wrong with the situation, the moment is ripe for gaining knowledge about yourself. Wisdom will be learning to apply this knowledge to your life and the lives of those around you; for your good and the good of others. Just having an awkward moment doesn't count. There are billions of people sharing the planet with you who have entire awkward days, or entire lives, and never learn a thing from them.

If you can learn from your daily experiences, build on the positives, correct the negatives, and avoid the same pitfalls in the future, it will bode well for you and your progeny. This doesn't require acting like a spiritual weirdo, wearing a robe, growing a beard, or shaving your head. In fact, the wisest people I've ever known didn't make a big display of their acquired wisdom; they simply lived it out in their daily lives, and the positive fruits of their lives bore evidence of the wisdom working within them. An important closing thought here; if you become proud in your wisdom, you'll have failed regardless of how wise others may think you. Someone once said "Pride goeth before a fall" and a million fallen wise men would likely agree.

Mercantile Fatalities

Online shopping is here to stay, and by the time you're grown, I can only imagine how it will have innovated even more! This statement shouldn't surprise anyone among you, since you've known this form of shopping and buying your entire lives now. Most Americans by 2014 have shopped online. I began in earnest more than fifteen years back, and then it was focused mainly on books for grad school. I could buy a volume online for $80 which would have cost me a $120 at the school's bookstore. I wasn't a math major, but I figured out the savings on those deals pretty quickly. When you toss in the convenience, time and gasoline savings, and reduced wear and tear on your nerves from dealing with parking and other shoppers, you can quickly see why the popularity of online shopping is growing by leaps and bounds and will continue to do so for the foreseeable future.

Major retailers, who don't want to simply become local showrooms where people go to window-shop and then head home to buy online, will have to retrench their businesses in order to survive. It's difficult, if not impossible, to name a major retailer (and a bunch of minor retailers) who doesn't have an online presence in my time. From Sears® to Walmart® to Target® and Sam's Club®, they can all be accessed online twenty-four hours a day, three hundred and sixty-five days a year. This is reshaping the way America shops, as well as most other developed nations around the world. One of the features I and apparently millions of others love is how I can shop many stores in a matter of minutes and can often find products and/or services for sale at deeply discounted rates. This ability to rapidly compare pricing and the resultant price competition will only accelerate in your time.

This raises the issue of "Is online shopping killing local businesses?" I think there's a high degree of truth in this question. Just as there was/is a high degree of truth in the statement "Big box stores are killing local mom and pop businesses." This begs the question for me as a businessman and a capitalist as to why exactly it is people shouldn't be able to buy the goods and services they need from the cheapest provider. I've been a small-business person for decades and experienced the price competition from the big-box stores phenomenon more than once. I didn't like it! But I value the way our system makes competing interests wrestle with one another to be more efficient, and therefore favoring the more cost-effective provider. The benefit is to your pocketbook as a consumer, yet you remain free to shop where you want and support who you will.

I encourage you to engage in online shopping as it benefits you. I also encourage you to support all those mom and pops out there who continue to provide value to you with the goods and services they offer. The tough economic times we're in right now force each of us to look for new ways to make economies in our budgets, whether we are businesses, families, or individuals. Tough economic times have been a hurdle in each generation, as they will be in your time. There'll be mercantile fatalities along the way as businesses which can no longer compete are overtaken by new business concepts. This has been the case throughout history and throughout the history of a concept called mercantilism. The Internet has simply provided its latest iteration. No doubt your future will hold other iterations just as tumultuous to the future marketplace.

Study these iterations, embrace them when they benefit you, and make sure if you go into business yourself, you learn to ride on this tiger and not inside it.

We Know What's Best For You

During the cold war of the '40s, '50s, '60s, and '70s, we regularly heard stories from the Soviet Union of how the government watched its citizens. The secret police could show up at any time and demand to enter your home to look for incriminating information. Subversives were hauled off to the gulags. Here we are, forty years later, and I'm hearing an increasing number of such stories right here in the land of the free and the home of the brave. I can't quote it offhand anymore, but we used to teach Christians a government ordained by God is not a terror to good works. This implied to me if the government was or is being a terror to good works, it was or is not a government ordained by God.

In the Soviet Union, these regressive tactics were used to silence critics of the regime and act as a warning to all others who might think about becoming critics of the regime. If you know any history, you may recall the Soviets also had a constitution, and its citizens were also supposed to have rights. I worry similarly regressive tactics are utilized locally for much the same reason and not just by the governments in state or national capitals. In these times we hear and see more and more horror stories where law enforcement has abused the local citizenry, even to the point of death. It now seems obvious to me various branches of our government are borrowing pages from the Soviet playbook as our future doesn't look so rosy and citizens become vocal about it.

If you're to retain any semblance of what my generation has known as Constitutional Rights, you'll have to remain vigilant to the growing horde of folks who feel you shouldn't have rights or it is they who should decide which rights you should enjoy. I see a rising tide to limit and even do away with many long-cherished personal freedoms. Freedom of speech is constantly under attack. The right to keep and bear arms is the whipping boy of the left. Those who wish to limit or altogether remove those freedoms behave this way because of our old friend, self-interest. This crowd will always play clever semantic games to hide the fact what they really want is to have things their way as opposed to you and yours being able to retain rights guaranteed you by our constitution. Don't be fooled; the more noble sounding the name of these organizations, the less noble their motives.

For more than three-hundred years, your ancestors have been on these American shores. My older sisters chose to become Daughters of The American Revolution to honor that heritage. Neeley's and our ancestors have fought in every great war of this nation, including the revolution. I've never joined any of these types of organizations, but I'm wholly supportive of their ideals and feel no less pride in our ancestors than my sisters do. With this pride in your heritage in mind, don't quietly allow these hard-won constitutional rights, and the freedoms which come with them, to be stolen from you by people who think only of themselves. They do this while simultaneously mouthing platitudes about how noble their self-interests are. This same crowd will demean your self-interests and your right to live as free men and women. If you allow this to go without a fight, your ancestors will roll over in their graves.

CHAPTER 4

What's It Worth To Me

In your time you'll have to learn how to establish value. There are many ways to do this, but if you've no method, or make no effort whatsoever, you can be assured other people who understand the importance of value will figure out your naiveté and take what was once your value and place it in their bank account. The only true way I know to reliably determine what something is worth is to see what others are willing to pay for it. I was recently part of the evaluation of a property asset a company wished to sell. In this case they had several million dollars invested and had been trying to get back what they put into it. So far there are no bites because they overvalued their asset.

What you'll need to remember in situations like this is you'll likely only get what value those assets have in the present day's market. It doesn't matter how good the design was originally, how well it's been maintained, or how proud you've been of it over the years. In the case where your asset has become antiquated, you may get less than 10 percent of what you think it's worth. Often, the client will be angry at the report, continue to try and sell the asset at their asking price, or decide to sit on their asset (no pun intended) until the market improves. At some point, perhaps three to five years down the road, they'll decide to give the sale another try. Unfortunately, the antiquated asset will likely be worth even less than it was before.

Each of us tends to place a lot of emotional value on the things we own; I do it regularly. Yet in the clear light of day, you'll have to accept if you want to sell your treasures, they're more likely to be bought by a bargain hunter than a treasure hunter. Since the last economic downturn in these times began in 2007, lots of treasures have sold at trash prices. If you wish to sell, it doesn't matter what it's worth to you. The only thing which will matter is what it's worth to the buyer. This is a harsh reality each of us faces in our lifetime, and you must work through it and accept this inevitability, or you'll need to buy a lot of storage space to set aside all those priceless treasures you acquire.

You're Never Too Young To Die

One of the many peculiarities I've developed with getting older is my tendency to compare my age to those of people I read about in the obituaries. If they're younger than I am, I always see it as a tragedy. If they're older, I hope they enjoyed a good life. If they're the same age, I look at the numbers several times because I'm sure there's a mistake. After all, people my age don't die, right?

I want you kids to take this to heart. Regardless of what you think, or what your peers may tell you, nobody is too young to die. The first time I recall a classmate dying, I was eight years old. Felipe had an asthma attack his parents couldn't get it under control. By the time they got him to an emergency room, it was too late. He never came back to school. Don't deceive yourself into thinking you're too young to die.

The cemeteries around the world are full of people who were sure they had many more years to live. Part of this comes from our well-developed abilities of self-deception. These evolve in each of us so we don't spend every moment in a panic our next breathe might be our last. Conversely, if we get too good at fooling ourselves on this issue, we can become dangerously foolhardy and take risks which almost guarantee our death.

You'll have to learn to strike a delicate balance. On the one hand you don't want to be so concerned about all the dangers 'out there' you become agoraphobic and end up housebound. On the other hand, if you take on the daredevil life, eventually the odds will catch up and death will find you. I want you to go out and live your life, but the two broadest components of living a life involves both the quality and the quantity of the life.

Red-Shouldered Hawks: Enjoy Their Show

If you've made it this far in this book, you know I touch on a lot of different topics from fields which are so far-flung, it stuns people. I'm sure some wonder why I ramble so. As one of my descendants you've known me since you were a baby, so it shouldn't surprise you. I have broad interests and an extremely curious nature (it's gotten me in trouble more than once). It's allowed me to pursue many different fields; I can't imagine having lived my life any other way. I have friends who've done the exact same boring things for the past forty plus years. They now bemoan their choices while I applaud their singlemindedness; I could never have lived such a life.

A case in point is my ornithological interests. Today as I was driving through the major city near my more rural home town, I spied a pair of red-shouldered hawks sitting on a telephone line which passed over one of the city's many irrigation canals. As I went by, one of them dove to the bank, grabbed a rat, and flew to the pole to which the line was attached. The area around the canal was lined on both sides by yards filled with trees and tree litter; a perfect home for the rat and a perfect hunting ground for the hawk. The urban sighting, which had at first so startled me, now made perfectly good sense.

The red-shouldered hawk is cousin to the more common red-tailed hawk which is prolific throughout California's Central Valley. I have to admit red-shoulders are my favorite local raptor. Typically you'll find them as mated pairs, and as far as I know, they mate for life. They're colorful, noisy, and incredibly fun to watch as they hunt, groom, mate, and raise their young. They prefer to live in riparian forests. Even here in the desert, I came to know them from the few year-round rivers and ephemeral streams we have that are lined with a very narrow riparian habitat.

As we've driven critters away from their natural homes, they've done their best to adapt. To a young pair of red-shoulders who have never lived along a true river or stream, an earthen irrigation canal, lined with manicured yards sporting tree canopies to rival the Amazon, will do nicely. Humans attract a lot of wildlife and this wildlife in turn attracts a lot of other wildlife. Did I mention they're noisy? I've sat and listened to pairs of red-shoulders celebrate, fuss, cajole, and challenge for hours. It always energizes me to hear them carry on this way; I'm completely unable to explain why.

I would have ended my comments today with the last paragraph, but it occurs to me even though you're my descendant, you may still be ignorant (not the same things as stupid) of ways you could assist wildlife. If you ever live on or near an earthen canal, trees planted along your fence-line would be a Godsend to red-shoulders. If you're lucky enough to have them or any other raptor nest in one of your trees, keep your distance, buy some binoculars, and when the babies come along, enjoy the show! I pray you too will be energized by their antics and tiny wild voices.

Experiment In Social Engineering

Let me start out by saying, during the middle of my career I worked daily with both the developmentally disabled and the mentally retarded. Today their range of disabilities is more properly termed intellectually disabled. Because of those intellectual disabilities, and my firsthand experience with them, I have a tender place in my heart for these wonderful human beings and the way they face and overcome daily challenges. I do think those of us who are fully abled should go out of our way to be helpful and make allowances for their physical and/or intellectual deficits.

Having said all this, I want to share a word of caution with you. In many homes where there is a person who is intellectually disabled, of necessity their needs come to dominate the entire household. Such families are counseled early and often about the impact this can have on other siblings. If parents aren't very careful, this domination of needs by the intellectually disabled child will begin to affect their siblings, not to mention the toll it can take on parental and sibling relationships.

To my horror, I've seen otherwise normal, healthy children exhibit intelligence deficits or odd behavior traits which seem to be the result of having been raised with a sibling who suffers from an intellectual disability. Competent counselors can and should be warning parents about this and assuring efforts are made in the home to enrich what might otherwise be a less robust intellectual and emotional environment for these normal siblings. There's no reason why other siblings can't have a normal and happy life; it does take steady and concerted effort and often these parents are exhausted already.

I recall an instance when a neighbor agreed to babysit one of my nieces. The woman also babysat her granddaughter, who suffered with severe intellectual disability. In those days she would have been labeled profoundly retarded. Over time, my sister and her husband began to notice new and disturbing behaviors from their previously normal daughter (e.g., acting out, explosive emotional outbursts, hitting, hysterical crying, etc.). It finally dawned on them this might be related to the environment. They changed sitters and in short order their daughter's life resumed as before. Your first obligation in instances like this must be to your child. I make no apology for this view because it's said without any malice. I ask you to take it in the spirit it's offered.

This sad reality points up the constant need of parents to monitor their child's environment. Deficits can be brought on by constant exposure to any negative influence; the intellectually disabled child is one example I witnessed firsthand. It really does matter what your offspring are seeing, hearing, feeling, smelling, and touching while they are growing up. I know there are those who'll tell you mine is an outdated and Draconian approach, speaking of an unenlightened mind. So be it! You only have one opportunity to raise your child, so work to safeguard their development on all levels. If you want to make them part of a living experiment in social engineering, go ahead. If I'm still alive, let me know how it works out for you.

Everybody Doesn't Need A Doctorate

Education is and always will be an important aspect of life in a civilized society. Ancient cultures like the Chinese picked up on this truth thousands of years ago, and those cultures who've come along later figured out the same truth over time. In your time I expect what passes as education, or more accurately the delivery of education, will continue the ongoing metamorphosis we see here in 2015. However, don't mistake education for learning; they're two different things entirely.

Right now we're hearing more and more about a coming revolution in education where people will no longer need to attend a physical school to gain the knowledge required to gain a professional qualification. Pardon me if I'm slightly skeptical of the idea of physicians, psychologists, and physical therapists who just 'sorta kinda' know about their fields based on some reading, a few weekend seminars, and a white paper they wrote once for which they never received a grade or any feedback.

I totally agree the cost of higher education in 2015 has gotten completely out of hand. I know the kind of economic investment it takes to earn a doctorate. You could easily be tied up for six figures. I am amazed today when friends of mine tell me their kids have as much debt for a single bachelor's degree as I amassed on my way to a masters, a doctorate, and four undergraduate degrees. A friend told me recently his son's medical school alone will leave him and his wife in debt for $250,000.

We as a society are trying to find a solution to this problem before it brings us to our knees, or at the very least another financial collapse like we enjoyed when the housing market went to pieces in 2007. I've been all about education all of my life. However, having a fairly significant education in business,

I can tell you kids it makes no sense whatsoever to have degrees in a field where your advanced education will yield a negative return on investment; your goal should be a better than 1:1 return.

Ironically, I'm qualified to teach at the highest levels and I must say some of the wonderful people who've come my way should have stopped long before they sought out a terminal degree. The pressure put on folks by employers (e.g., school boards, manufacturing companies, city councils, widget makers, government agencies, etc.) to earn masters and/or doctorates has reached near hysterical levels. At the end of the day, we often turn out folks with minimal qualifications and maximal debt.

As an alumnus of six different institutions of higher education, I see a lot of alumni chat-strings where people are stunned at the amount of debt they've amassed and how poor their job prospects are. Education doesn't equal employment. In fact, there's well documented prejudice against people with the highest levels of education in most fields other than academia, and even there academic rivalry is often intense. Consequently, if we don't come to our senses regarding higher education in the United States, financial realities will eventually force us to regain those senses in a very harsh manner. Get as much education as you want and can afford, but avoid the debt trap so many have fallen into in my time.

The Final Needle

I commiserated with a business friend today when he shared with me a letter he'd received from the State of California, informing him of a new inspection fee he'll have to pay for his business.

The irony here is the state has been inspecting the device in question and previously charging him a similar fee under another program for years. These inspection fees are nothing more than thinly veiled taxes, and everyone in California who's been hit with one of the many new fees already knows this. You young folks will have to watch your government, or they'll slip in new taxes on you at any opportunity.

As contradictory as it may sound, there truly is a needle which can break a camel's back. It's not due to some magical power of the specific needle in question. It's more closely aligned with the added weight of the needle having finally exceeded the ability of the camel's back to hold the overall weight of the current load, and one more needle. You and any businesses you may own can only be taxed so much before you/they fail. Some sectors of the California economy are rapidly approaching this breaking point here in 2015. As proof, look back at this time's history and consider the number of businesses going under or leaving this state (and other high-tax states) for those with fewer tax needles.

In your time you'll be faced with the question of what state and perhaps even what country you'll chose to live in. The decision will impact the quality of your life and the lives of your offspring for generations to come. I encourage you early on to consider how your current decisions and behavior will affect your children and grandchildren. Your ancestors came here from Scotland, Ireland, and Germany. Our immediate family came to California in the 1930s looking for better quality of life. For several generations this seemed to work out well for us. But somewhere along the way the political and economic ethos here changed, and at this point the 'why' doesn't really matter. What matters is how it informs your decision making and the manner in which you live your life.

You owe your offspring the best quality of life you can provide; if you can't or won't take this duty seriously, then don't reproduce. Use the rhythm method, take the pill, get your tubes tied, get a vasectomy, or become sexually abstinent. I gave my daughters the best life I could; you were taught to pass this along to your children. One of the important ways you can do this is by raising them in a state or country which doesn't keep piling needles on your camel's back. If at some point you feel you have to immigrate to another state or nation… it wouldn't be the first time our family has done it!

Political Terminal Illness

I suspect you'll see days in your time when you are so disappointed with your elected representatives you're nearly in tears. I see those days in my time! I looked at my congressman's voting record recently, and while he campaigns as a political conservative, he lines up with the tax and spend crowd way too often for me. I can only conclude Washington is infected with a virus which almost immediately consumes every man or woman we send there. Even term limits offer little hope of restoring them to political health.

In my opinion it's a rare thing to see a someone go to the halls of power, whether at the local, state, or national levels, and ever return home again the same man or woman, much less a better one. It's for this reason I suggest you begin early to look upon the person you vote for to take elective office as someone you're willing to sacrifice to an egregious terminal illness. In this manner, you'll be forced to tone down your criticisms later when you come to despise them for exactly what you knew from the beginning would come to pass.

A Panel Of Experts

In my time we're inundated with people who pass themselves off as experts. The most recent and troubling examples of this are the folks who bring us the news at ABC, NBC, CBS, FOX, CNN, MSNBC, etc. In addition to the television news I view at home, I have satellite radio in my vehicles, and since my business requires I spend a minimum of ninety minutes each day driving, I hear a little bit from all of those purveyors of truth in the course of a day. As you may have heard, the guest panel is a popular feature on all the networks in this era. In essence, this guest panel is asked a series of provocative questions related to events of the day, week, or month, and they offer their opinions on the matter at hand. This in itself isn't problematic; what is problematic is people listening to them seem to assume these panelists are what academics term Knowledge Area Experts on the topics under discussion.

Despite the fact the panelists are always introduced, but never introduced honestly (i.e., Joe's a washed-up jock who majored in communications at Bagstitch University and tried his hand at standup comedy for three years), I've noticed people I know who've heard them pontificate listen uncritically and take *Expert* Joe's opinion to heart regarding matters of international diplomacy. They do this as though Joe had studied International Law at Georgetown University, followed by ten years at the State Department, and an additional ten years consulting with various governments around the world. Joe is in fact an ex-jock for the most part! Joe may have read a book on the subject at hand, but should you really base your life perspective for how we deal with international matters involving life and death on one of these panels of experts?

We're so demanding we be entertained every moment of the day or night, we no longer want to hear a real expert unless they have Hollywood-level good looks, a designer wardrobe, and enough witty quips to land them the occasional guest spot on late-night television. This attitude is not a minor aberration you can ignore. If we don't somehow regain our collective sense of the gravitas of many current national and international situations, and begin to demand to hear from true experts rather than the flood of pseudo-experts out there, we're in for a bumpy road to perdition. I'm afraid you'll reap the bitter fruit of all this superficiality. Critical thinking and applied logic have helped make the United States the greatest nation in the history of the world. Superficiality, evidenced by the proliferation of glib-speak, can undo all of this in less than a generation.

What can you do? Well, for one thing you can turn off all the experts on TV and radio, and begin to read, think, and discourse with your contemporaries again. If you must listen to others to help you fashion an opinion or adopt a policy, be certain they actually have the kind of expertise you'd demand from any other profession into which you'd place your well-being, lives, or future. Would you really go to a heart surgeon who was actually a washed-up actor who'd only read a book on heart surgery for your coronary care? Would you entrust your life savings to a down-on-his-luck comedian who'd decided to try out financial advising after attending a weekend seminar? Would you let a bricklayer who'd failed Algebra 101 in high school purport to teach you quantum mechanics? If your answer to any of these is no, then why allow unqualified men and women to lecture you on the weightiest matters of your day?

Grounded In Reality

It's okay to be positive and optimistic about your life as long as you are grounded in reality and not delusion. Everyone loves a visionary, but no one loves a mental case once the mania subsides.

Most of us enjoy the company of people who are positive about life and optimistic about future outcomes. Conversely, most of us are turned off by pessimism and those people who seem to live their lives solely anticipating a negative future outcome.

Be careful to assure when you get swept up on the wings of some purveyor of positivity and optimism, he or she is actually living on this planet and not just visiting here when the meds wear off.

Similarly, beware of political speeches and speech makers. On the whole they seem sure of the rightness of their purpose when they're running for office and equally unsure and unwilling to ever again commit to any position so completely once they've been elected.

You've read, as I've written here before, you should trust but also verify. Some of the most remarkable speakers and leaders I ever met were quite mentally ill. Don't buy into anyone else's madness. The Neeley's have enough of their own to deal with.

Class Reunions

In a few years, you'll have been out of high school and/or college long enough you'll begin to hear or think about class reunions. Be gentle with yourself and others as you ponder attending. Life is particularly brutal to everyone the first ten to twenty years after adulthood gets underway; beware of unrealistic expectations.

As I write this, it's December of 2014 and the time of the year when many are starting to hear stirrings about class reunions next year. After the holiday season, the mailings and phone calls will start in earnest. The opportunity to reunite with people you once regarded as lifetime friends, but haven't seen in decades, will be at hand.

The way my old high school and college classmates avoided reunions of any sort over the years leads me to believe either those school days were not as happy for some as for others, or the years since have been so harsh they've beaten the desire to get together completely out of them.

My friends and I are more than forty years out of high school, but I can tell from comments I receive a great number of them still think all the rest of us look just like we did back when we were eighteen years old. Time spares no one and becomes particularly brutal as age sixty looms large ahead and then quickly recedes in the rearview mirror of life.

About ten years ago I decided I would go out of my way to see old high school and college friends; I grew tired of only seeing them at their funerals. In more than one instance I've traveled over a thousand miles out of my way just to drop by for a meal and an evening of conversation about how our lives have gone since graduation day; I've never regretted one such side-trip. They weren't always cheery, but they were always reaffirming.

It takes courage as we grow older to lay aside any facade we may have built about being ageless, or famous, or wealthy. It takes even more courage—I'd call it tough courage—to let your old classmates see how you, like them, have weathered the storms of life and show all the scars the years have inflicted. Attend your class reunions and visit with old friends. You and they have far more invested in one another than you know; enjoy the dividends.

We All Lose

It's funny how a small act can have such a large impact. I've been a lover and defender of wildlife and wild places since I was an eight-year-old Cub Scout. This doesn't mean I'm some sort of environmental elitist who's sure it's the job of mankind to protect every living thing by placing it in a fenced preserve where it can only be enjoyed from a distance. I readily accept many wild plants and animals exist in numbers far too abundant, and they make a pest of themselves by destroying crops, injuring people, or wrecking habitat (e.g., starlings, deer, kudzu, feral hogs, cane toads, feral pythons, walking catfish, zebra mussels, etc.).

I've spent countless hours on volunteer conservation work, and professionally as an environmental engineering contractor. I've donated money annually toward habitat preservation. At the same time, I've hunted, gathered, and fished since I was five years old. So I've been all over this issue and heard all the views more than once. Now let's get back to my opening comment about small acts having large impacts. As I see it, you can wipe out a plant or animal species unintentionally, and you can also wreck the environment by supporting the wrong plant or animal species at the wrong time. These can be small, unintentional, but well-meaning acts; nature doesn't care about your intent. In fact, lawyers would say no specific intent was required to break this particular kind of natural law.

The problem is with the screamers on opposite sides of these endless environmental debates. They're the ones who can never find common ground because they can't hear a word their opponents are saying over the din of their own voices. We've come a long way environmentally since the '60s, and we've got further yet to go in your lifetimes. The vast majority of people in the middle of this bell curve of humanity have to speak up consistently and firmly, but in a reasonable tone. Otherwise, the polarities of these critical issues drive the agenda while the majority of us give up and stick our fingers in our ears. This battle over the environment will grow more intense in your time unless there's a societal collapse. If this occurs mere survival will relegate this debate to the back burner as it becomes every man for himself and/or his family.

In the meantime, please remember your grandfather warned you when all anyone can do is scream at someone on the other side of the issue, every person, habitat, plant, and animal ultimately loses. As a Christian, believe a loving God placed nature here to serve mankind. But I also believe when he admonished our ancestors to take dominion over it, he didn't mean go out and see how quickly you can lay waste to it for a few bucks. The natural world is a gift from a loving God to his ultimate creation, mankind. It strikes me a loving God would expect his creation would act toward the rest of the creation with reciprocity and want to be very careful with such a gift. The concept of stewardship is an old one, but a very reasonable model to be considered here.

Risk And Reality

A friend who'd read some things I'd recently written contacted me. While we were discussing the renewed international interest in electromagnetic pulse (EMP) weapons, he wondered out loud what I'd learned about Black Swan Events during these past couple of years studying low probability events. I offered the EMP weapons as a perfect example. It's never been done before on a broad scale; it seems too farfetched to most non-scientists, and we're sure if there were a true threat, the wise men and women in the District of Columbia would have done something about it by now. But if it does happen, there'll be a great hue and cry from people who are willing to tell you they actually understood the threat, saw it coming, and tried to do something about it.

Kids, think for yourselves! Ignore all the talking heads who assure you they're smarter than you and can make better decisions for you and yours than you can. Plan for you and your family. Who on this planet cares more about you and your family than you do? We can only effectively deal with the information we have. This assumes you and I are always hearing the truth. Be skeptical! It's your life and the lives of your loved ones at stake. If things go bad out there, do you really think you'll be treated like the families of your local, state, and federal bureaucrats and politicians? What I've learned from Black Swan Events is we rarely have enough information to justify going all in, so you might want to hold something in reserve.

Appearances Drive The Frenzy

It may surprise you after reading this how I can be so cynical about education while expressing my love for it. My mindset has more to do with the philosophical concept of the acquisition of knowledge versus the reality of how and why we gain knowledge. I hope a generation from now, when all of you are grown; it will be a more perfect educational world. But if it isn't, suffice it to say these aren't fully settled issues in this time, either. A case in point is based on something I shared with you and some friends earlier.

I hit a nerve with my short essay "Everyone Doesn't Need a Doctorate," when I originally posted it in 2014. It caused a couple of friends to get in touch to ask why I think organizations push their managers to earn masters degrees and/or doctorates. I've been blessed to head up several organizations, I've served as a manager, general manager, executive director, regional manager, vice-president, president, CTO, COO, and CEO at various times. I definitely have opinions on this one, but they may surprise you.

In the way of background, understand the folks at the top, the so-called C-level executives, answer directly to owners (private companies), shareholders (public companies), or stakeholders (governmental or non-profit organizations). At this level, perception is as important as reality. In fact, perception often shapes reality until it becomes reality. Can the boss afford to be seen as not preparing her underlings for greater roles by encouraging them to get advanced degrees, even paying for such degrees with organizational assets?

The gatekeepers in every business are always looking for new hurdles to place on the hiring or promotion trail to thin the huge influx of outside applicants or existing employees jostling for the next rung up the organizational ladder. I believe quite often bachelors, masters, and doctorates are playing these hurdle-roles as much as any other role they serve. I like to remind folks I was a profitable regional manager for a publicly traded entity before I completed my first bachelor's degree in my forties.'

Brains count to me and to a lot of people who are out there every day engaging in the *Talent Wars*. I've met folks with zero degrees who were highly intelligent and brought tremendous value to the organizations which employed them. Conversely, I've known people with bachelors, masters, or doctorates that brought almost no value to the brand they were associated with. As an owner, stockholder, or stakeholder, I definitely want value for organizational assets spent on education.

The Peter Principle comes to mind here, as many are quickly promoted to their highest level of incompetence and are never heard from again. I run into them routinely at conferences, symposia, seminars, and colloquia. No, they're not there presenting a scholarly paper or sitting on a discussion panel. Their boss sent them so they can remain abreast of their field. Meanwhile, back at Black Rock, the wage-only peons are told in hushed, almost reverential tones how the great one is away at an important conference.

A Perfect Plan

> "The greatest enemy of a good plan
> is the dream of a perfect plan."
> -CARL VON CLAUSEWITZ

Build No Nation Before Its Time

Are you wondering yet why it is the United States has spent trillions of dollars and expended more than 100,000 American lives in places like Korea, Vietnam, Iraq, and Afghanistan to create democracy since the end of WWII, only to have those places devolve into chaos once the troops go home and the Yanks aren't there to enforce the peace? Have you watched a child grow angry and lash out at someone trying to force concepts upon her she's too young to understand, much less adopt? After you read the next few paragraphs, you may not like what I've written, but you'll have a better grasp of our nation's past and why I believe we've failed in many of our several attempts at democracy building. You'll also have new information to inform your politics going forward.

When the United States gained its independence from Great Britain it was at a place and time when the creation of a democracy made sense and had an excellent chance of taking root and thriving. You may recall it was a place where immigrants came to seek their fortunes, but also to be able to practice their faiths and pursue their personal philosophies about things like life, liberty, and personal happiness. Many of them were educated, some were very well educated. Some came from societies where there were already elements of self-rule. Most of them shared a common religious heritage, even if they came from different sects of this religion.

Now compare this fertile soil to trying to seed a similar field of democracy in a foreign country under entirely different circumstances. We've taken on what are at times primitive peoples with little or no education, no history of self-rule and celebrating everything from Animism, to Buddhism, to multiple forms of Islam, to multiple flavors of Christianity. Simultaneously we pretended we would easily find a native Washington, Jefferson, or Madison on every street corner. We've pretended we can take primitive and feudal economies and turn them into engines of capitalism in three or four years. Look at China to see how many decades it's taken them to build their present economy and shake off their economic past.

I could go on about this for pages, but this is meant to be short and not a dissertation or scholarly paper. Consider for a moment how nations go through a series of phases as they mature. During each of those phases, certain characteristics can be identified which they hold in common with other societies which are similarly situated. There's a time when the only rule which seems to work is a sword and a strong right hand. There's a time when fledgling self-rule is fought for and won. There's a time when people, through years of arguing and fighting, learn to live with one another or die together. Until a society is ready, you can attempt as much nation-building as you want, all to no avail.

Once you're old enough to consider these words, the next time you see your nation about to embark on an exercise of this nature, run through the checklist I've laid out above. See what the likelihood of success is before you write your congressperson and urge them to invade some country under the pretext we can turn the invaded nation's populace into foreign versions of ourselves. Give heed to whether or not that nation has reached a time supportive of the seed of democracy being dropped upon the local soil. Consider if the people are personally prepared to let it take root within an already fertile philosophical soil. Biologically speaking, if you toss seed on a rock, even if it sprouts, the elements will do it in rapidly.

CHAPTER 5

Rest In Peace John Maynard Keynes

'm writing this to you because I fear by the time you're grown, the writings of this man may have come back into vogue. Here in 2015 we've experienced a seven-year period of misguided effort by the current administration in Washington, DC to apply this economist's ideas on steroids. The result has been an economic disaster which has yet to end and will percuss within the economy of this nation for decades to come. I wrote this piece originally to my friends, and I offer it to you as I did them. Try to put yourself in their place, as so many of them are struggling now to survive in 2015. They agonized over how to pay their bills, feed their families, and keep the wolf away from their doors. Please read the next two paragraphs thoughtfully.

> *Have you been to the market lately? Can you recall what a can or box of anything cost you six years back? Well, if you can answer yes to both of those questions, then you're well aware of the impact inflation is having on your economy. Absolutely nothing around us has been spared the inflationary spiral. If you're buying rice or round steak, the trajectory of pricing has been the same—ever onward and upward. I'd like to once again thank*

both the Democrats and the Republicans for allowing the nation to drift into this economic morass and continue to support the bad policies which have kept us here.

The only good which has come of the folks in DC dumping trillions into the economy, in a failed effort to restart it, is they've once and for all driven a stake through the heart of John Maynard Keynes economic theory. Keynes, as you may know, was an advocate of government trying to stimulate business by pumping money into it. Government doesn't know how to run a business! If it did, would your local, state, or federal government be so inefficient? Get a clue; it was Americans' pursuit of capitalism which made us economically powerful. It wasn't Americans' pursuit of the perfect economic theory which made us the envy of the entire world.

You're young enough you'll live to see our nation get out of this mess, and if you live long enough, you'll see it come back again (it will come back again). Please recognize the futility of this throw money at it approach to fixing a broken economy the next time it comes around. STOP the politicians in your time from buying votes with your money. Inflation works for governments as a means to inflate away debt which governments (politicians) create. They do this to take from those who work and have in order to give those who need or want. The politicians seek the votes of those who want because it's a growing and vocal demographic. Those in true need can't do much for the politicians and may be easily ignored. Ironically, inflation wrecks the lives of *all* the people by inflating away their ability to adequately provide for themselves and their families. It hits the have nots at least as hard as it hits the haves. Unfortunately, you just can't convince politicians and most of the have nots of this truth!

Those Who Can't... Criticize

With the amount of time you spend on different forms of social media where people post their ideas, hobbies, recipes, and so forth, by now you've seen the derogatory items which regularly get posted there. I can only imagine, as our society coarsens, this will steadily grow worse as your years of majority come to full bloom. I've spoken about this to many people before, but if anything, it seems to be getting worse, not better. I hold out some hope for a rebirth of civility, but the chance of this happening grows slimmer all the time.

There's something fundamentally wrong with a person when one human being makes a positive effort to share something which has the power to enrich the lives of many others, and another human being only seems to possess the ability to insult, ridicule, or slander. My hat's off to the people who put themselves out there and risk this kind of unprovoked attack. They remain willing to try and then go on to post dozens, if not hundreds, of new pieces benefitting you and me.

As for these trolling critics, one wonders if they've ever created anything of value in their entire life. I want to challenge you to try to live a life of accomplishment built on a constructive use of your God-given talents and not on attacking the efforts of other people. You gain absolutely nothing by attacking other people's best efforts. It not only hurts their feelings and perhaps their reputation, it also hurts you and your reputation when others find out you have this character flaw. It will definitely make other folks view you in a less flattering light.

Religious Relics

I saw a magazine article recently, claiming some researcher has found a piece of Jesus's cross. I'd jump up and down and make funny noises in support of such a remarkable find were it not for the fact there have been enough purported pieces found of Jesus's cross over the centuries to build a four thousand square foot wood-frame home. Questionable religious relics are housed in hundreds of churches around the world. Even as diligently as Christianity teaches avoiding the worship of idols, we tread dangerously close far too often.

If I sound cynical, I am. As you know by now, I spent the early years of my adulthood in Christian ministry and saw claims like this one rolling in on an annual basis. In time I came to wonder what it would prove if it actually was a piece of Jesus's cross? What would it prove if it wasn't a piece of Jesus's cross? It would prove nothing. Believers will continue to believe. Unbelievers will continue to doubt. Coffee at Starbucks will cost more money next year than it does this year. McDonald's will still be selling hamburgers. There's nothing to see here, move along.

My goal in these writings is to seed critical thinking in you, and if it's already there, then think of all this as feed (please don't refer to it as manure). I want each of you to grow up to love the Christian faith as much as I do. But don't think for a minute I was a dim-witted old fool who didn't realize religion in general and Christianity in particular has long been the domain of every type of sleazy huckster known to mankind. Therefore, take all you see and hear into consideration, but weigh what you've seen and heard carefully. Christianity, and for that matter every other major religion, is full of seemingly sincere con men and women.

It's best to avoid religious disputes in these matters. I suggest this course because I've never met anyone who didn't have opinions about religion in general and the validity of artifacts, bones of saints, and holy water. More than once I've witnessed a truly learned religious scholar confronted by someone whose total religious training could have been summed up in a paragraph or less. Invariably in these encounters, the scholar is disadvantaged by education and discipline, while the would-be sidewalk apologist has the advantage of being loud, angry, illogical, and self-righteous. Avoid these argumentative encounters, don't buy religious relics, and don't venerate dead saints any more than you would live saints.

Be Good To Your Body

At the risk of repeating myself in these essays, one of the truths which comes back to me regularly as I grow older is the old tongue-in-cheek saying, "If I'd known I was gonna live this long, I would've taken better care of myself." When you're young and your body is strong and at its peak, it's easy to overtax it and wrongly assume the cumulative effect of all this abuse won't take a toll. As the years pile on, the damage which was hidden for decades starts to take hold. For me, as I've shared here before, it's rheumatoid and osteoarthritis from early years spent as a heavy equipment mechanic; I used my hands for everything from touching to hammering.

To his credit, my Daddy told me when I was in my twenties and working seventy hours a week as a mechanic foreman, abusing my body would catch up with me one day. He never lived to see the day arrive, but he was correct in his assertions. It was one of the many times I should've taken his words more closely to heart. For some of my friends, it's been the two-packs-a-day cigarette habit which caught up with them, and for others still, it's the six-pack of Bud Light every day. We're cautioned by the great religions to be moderate in all things; there's clearly a reason for this.

Your parents have been relatively health-conscious in raising you, and I feel they've done a good job of giving you a foundation in living and eating well. The temptation, now you're reaching the age of majority will be to test those boundaries, along with all the other boundaries they've given you. Testing them is okay! Making a habit of breaking them will eventually lead to problems you may not yet be mature enough to see coming. Be wiser than I was and heed the warnings of your mother and father. No one in the world will ever love you more than your parents! Keep this thought in mind as you consider the boundaries; they were good for your body before today... they still are!

Rolling In Manure

A friend asked me today if I ever listen to rap music. I don't know if it will still be a musical force in your time, but I mention it here because of its popularity in my day. My friend had spent time with his teenage daughter and her friends recently on a road trip and was stunned by the crudeness and vulgarity of the lyrics. I've had the same reaction, but if you speak up against the content of this music, you're automatically called a racist because you're judging or dismissing the black, white, or brown gangster lifestyle it most often depicts.

I think there's a certain logic here which is so simple it seems to be evading folks. If you roll in manure for hours, day after day, you can't expect to come out of it without manure in your mouth, ears, eyes, nose, hair, and so forth. So, is it any wonder children listening to music dedicated to the thug life, the prison life, or the low life, glorifying assault, rape, murder, drugs, guns, robbery, gambling, and prison, produces young people who are violent, misogynistic, angry, depressed, addicted, gun-toting, and criminal?

I can't speak to all the children of America. They aren't mine to raise or to shape. You're my progeny, and while I don't have primary caregiver status in your life, I nonetheless have a role to play. I want you to grow up to be a responsible and well-mannered member of society. While good behavior, good grooming, and good manners are eschewed by almost every counter-culture which has ever existed, the adult world you're trying to be part of still pays attention to these things and makes decisions about you accordingly.

Great Dividends

I ran into a young man (any man younger than me) yesterday, and it was gratifying to see how well his life has turned out. I got to know him back when I was a pastor. He came to our youth group with some of the other teens and young adults who attended at the time. When I was told earlier in the day the name of the man I was to meet, it didn't click because he was referred to as Jim, and though the surnames were the same, I was used to calling him Jimmy and didn't make the connection. Imagine my surprise on being ushered into his office and introducing myself, he laughed and said, "You don't need to introduce yourself Brother Neeley. I've known you most of my life. It's me, Jimmy."

Twenty-five years after I last saw him, Jimmy is a manager with millions of dollars' worth of equipment under his control and more than a hundred employees. As we went about the task which had brought me to his office, he shared his life and work history. It had been mostly positive, and the trajectory had been ever upward. We reminisced about the old days, people we knew, and the places life had taken us. We spent a total of perhaps twenty minutes together, both agreeing the time was too short but happy for the unexpected encounter. I see many things about our country which disturb me, yet every time I run across someone like Jimmy, it gives me hope.

Despite all the things I say here to you, fight against the sense life is hopeless and good things don't happen anymore. While I don't want you to be childish in thinking life is a bouquet of roses, I also don't want you to go through life thinking it's hopeless. I've made many personal investments in people which have paid off handsomely over my lifetime. There's no doubt in my mind some of the folks I invested in lived failed lives and made life miserable for others around them. Yet by and far, the investments I made in people's lives haven't only broken even, in most cases they've paid great dividends.

Lessons In Business Ownership

People who've never owned or managed a business have no idea how difficult it is, yet often feel by simply peering in from the outside, they've a pretty good idea of the degree of difficulty involved. This is a mistake I fully expect some of you kids to make as you launch in life. My hope is it can be tempered somewhat by what I write here. Huong Thi Tran, my wife and your Ba Kim, had a dream for years after coming to the United States of owning her own business. So, she saved for ten years prior to my coming along and purchased the business where she was working from an owner who wanted out. This should have been her first clue. Despite only knowing her a year, I begged her not to purchase it, but in the end I agreed to be her partner so she could qualify for the lease (I really had to marry her then, didn't I).

At least a hundred times in the past five years, she's lamented the fact she didn't take my advice and forego buying the business. Laws, leases, lawyers, landlords, thieves, tax collectors, licensing agents, insurance agents, government inspectors, and liars have all provided her with an education into what it means to be a business owner or manager in the United States in 2015. Recently she was counting the years until she figures she can retire; I chuckled. Of course, retirement is predicated on whether or not she can find some other dreamer to sell the business to for anywhere near what she's got tied up in it. She's learned some hard lessons, but thankfully she's survived, and her business has as well.

When observed from the outside, being in business looks glamourous. When you're the person mopping the floors, cleaning the toilets, and trying to balance your checkbook long after everyone else has gone home, it doesn't seem nearly so glamourous. There are tremendous advantages to being your own boss. Unfortunately, most of those only kick in if you manage to be financially successful. I tell business clients I consult with at least 80 percent of new businesses fail, and most do it within the first year. Those are worse than house odds in any casino. At least if you burned $100,000 in a casino, you'd have a great story to tell, and they'd likely have 'comped' you some extravagant meals, a great room, and front-row show tickets.

I like business, your mother likes business, and business has been good to our family. But this not to say any of you need to go into business for yourself. Those are very personal decisions you need to make after carefully weighing the costs; you may find it's more than you want to pay. You've seen some of those costs firsthand as the child of a business owner. If you should decide to proceed, you owe it to yourself to get every bit of information you can about business in general and the line of business you want to pursue in particular. It's said "Chance favors the prepared mind." I'm certain a prepared mind is an advantage in entering business of any sort.

The Uncivil Wars

Today I watched a friend of mine work hard to find some middle ground politically amongst a group of our other friends regarding the latest machinations in Washington, DC. I remained silent on the subject because I know how inflamed passions become when people discuss politics. His efforts ended in angry recriminations, and friend speaking spitefully to friend. I have to admit I wasn't surprised. Our nation is more divided right now than it has been in many years. I pray it's better in your time.

This kind of divisiveness places our democratic republic in the gravest of jeopardies. "Can a house divided stand" remains a timeless question we all should seriously ponder. We can look at the breakup of the old Soviet Union and say, "It can't happen here." Yet we've already fought one civil war to preserve the Union. I think it could happen again in your time, and if it does it won't be north against south. I predict it will be four or five different regions fighting to be shed of one another. A war on this many fronts cannot help but be protracted and bloody.

A man who would know about such matters once said, "There never was a good war or a bad peace." I think about how one of the most celebrated generals in all of history could say such a thing. After all, he'd managed to win a war others thought all but lost. He took the position, and rightfully so, war is an all or nothing proposition. His armies burned and pillaged the holdings of their fellow citizens with absolutely no mercy. Thousands were killed on both sides. I think it might be so again. General and later President, Ulysses S. Grant, was this man.

In the end, Grant's armies won the war, and a mentioned he later won the presidency of the United States. In reading about his final years, I'm not sure he was particularly proud of what he'd done, but some would say Ulysses S. Grant and Abraham Lincoln saved the Union. Others would ask, "At what cost?" So, bear in mind, once the talking stops and the fighting begins, nothing will ever be the same again. This is why old timers with a solid view of history argue so hard for keeping even a bad national peace.

I want to add a personal note here for you to think about. My great-grandfather Jeremiah Marr McCormick was born in Charleston, Virginia. When conscription came down from Jefferson Davis, he was 24 years of age. He heeded the call of the Confederacy. He fought, was wounded and captured, and imprisoned in a Union Prison in Illinois. When the surrender came and he was allowed to go home, his mother, brothers, and sisters had all disappeared and their houses had been destroyed and land seized. He lived out the rest of his days in Indian Territory. Unbeknownst to Jeremiah, his sisters and his mother had survived the war and moved west to Oregon territory. Thinking them dead, he grieved their deaths for 58 years; they grieved his. None of them knew the other was alive. Think on your own family and our history when voices are raised in your time, for civil war.

Tax The Daylights Out Of them

I've mentioned this before, but I want to touch on it again to emphasize how important it is. In order to be financially rich (have a surplus), you must either produce more than you can consume, or you must consume less than you produce. Most of us in the United States in this time learned early on how to produce less than we consumed, and we made up for it by living on credit in one form or another. We burned future earnings for today's elevated standard of living. This has resulted in levels of credit debt never before witnessed in recorded history. The truly smart ones among us learned how to spend less than they consumed. The surplus they were able to save and invest was used for goals such as a nicer home, beautiful furniture, a college education for the kids, and a comfortable retirement for themselves.

Saving and investing is certainly not as much fun as a having a way too big house, a new ski boat, or matching his and her Harley Davidsons. You'll see this in your time because these two patterns of behavior are age-old financial approaches taken by all of humankind; they encircle each of us. When the years pass, and those who were frugal in their youth and now well provided for in their old age begin to enjoy the fruits of their life-long labors, you can join those who get every branch of government to tax the daylights out of the frugal to make up for your having practiced the adage "Eat, drink, and be merry, for tomorrow you die." After all, why should you be responsible for your bad decisions when you can force others to pay for them?

Black Swan Events I

This is a section I've written which needs to be read sequentially. As a result, it appears here in five successive parts. Throughout this book I've tried hard not to bore you, but there are times you have to wade into deeper waters to get a fuller understanding. If I didn't think it so important to your overall education in the ways of some of life's critical events, I wouldn't have included it here. So bear with me, and I think you'll find it relevant to your life both now and in the future.

There was a time in Europe when an exceedingly rare event was likened to the probability of seeing a black swan. In those days, there were white swans and black sheep, but there were few, if any, black swans. It wasn't until British explorers found themselves in Australia and New Zealand that reports of multitudes of black swans were being talked about. It wasn't because black swans didn't exist, because genetic anomalies among white swans were known. It wasn't because it should've been assumed they couldn't exist in large numbers. It was because the concept of multitudes of black swans was so far outside the thinking of everyday life, no one had considered there could not only be black swans, there could be thousands of them. Today an exceedingly rare or unexpected event may be referred to as a Black Swan Event. In recent years there's been an effort to address the so-called Black Swan Event; because failures to do so have produced catastrophic results.

A really smart fellow named Nassim Nicholas Taleb has written a book in my time entitled, *The Black Swan: The Impact of the Highly Improbable.* It's caused something of a stir in many circles but especially in government, business, and finance. I want to spend some time in the next few pages sharing this concept with you and why it is we, as rational/logical beings, are often betrayed by linear thinking when oft times in life the appearance of a black swan in a given field can turn the linear thinking world upside-down. I'll assume by the time you've reached adulthood and are reading this, you'll all have seen these Black Swan Events, you'll know the effects of *them,* and you'll have even experienced their ability to destroy the world as you knew it. My reasons for striking this vein are to help you be open to the coming of Black Swan Events throughout your lives and help you be agile enough to survive them, rather than be destroyed by them.

Black Swan Events II
To expand a bit, Taleb's Black Swan Theory posits Black Swan Events (hereafter represented as BSE) are initially 1) a surprise

to the observer(s), 2) has a major effect on the specific field it occurs within, or it may effect the entire world, and 3) is said to be recognizable in hindsight; this is to say with the benefit of hindsight, one feels they can rationalize what has occurred. Taleb claims he developed the theory to help him explain: "1) the disproportionate role of high-profile, hard-to-predict, and rare events that are beyond the realm of normal expectations in history, science, finance, and technology; 2) the non-computability of the probability of the consequential rare events using scientific methods (owing to the very nature of small probabilities); 3) the psychological biases that make people individually and collectively blind to uncertainty and unaware of the massive role of the rare event in historical affairs."

While studying finance, I initially came across this idea in Taleb's work, *Fooled by Randomness*. Over a period of several years, he refined the idea and his most recent book, *The Black Swan: The Impact of the Highly Improbable* develops the concept more completely. What so captured my attention was his assertion while BSE would be regarded as extreme outliers, they're nonetheless extremely influential in their impact on all of us. In fact, I'd say they're disproportionately influential in their impact on human history and all its various facets. They'd include things like major scientific discoveries, unexpected historical events, and unique artistic achievements. My fascination with these powerful random events in history is how often they've entered an otherwise static world and their dynamic power literally turned the world on its ear. Events like discoveries of the laws of physics, the triggering event of World War I, and the ability of artists to create the appearance of three dimensional drawings all register as BSE.

I'd like you to think about your life and times, and consider how many BSE you've already lived through. At first this will seem a difficult task to undertake. But when I mention things from my time, like the development of the atomic bomb, the birth of rock 'n roll, and the advent of the personal computer, you'll start to see where I'm coming from. The fact is your life and mine have been full of these BSE, and there are more such events ahead, many more for you than for me. With this in mind, you have to decide if you plan to order your lives as though life is static and every day from here on out will be the same as every day which came before it, or if you'll realize at any given moment a new dynamic in the form of new ideas, new inventions, or new technologies can burst onto the scene and transform your world for better or worse. Taleb's work initially caught the attention of people like me in business and finance. Suddenly, every other field is watching too.

Black Swan Events III

Let me jump in here in the middle of these pages on BSE and point out the critical nature of this information—even a life and death type of critical nature. Throughout human history we've fooled ourselves into thinking we're able to predict future outcomes based on current knowledge. This regularly happens in business, finance, science, medicine, politics, stocks, bonds, and religion. Beyond those fields, it happens in our everyday lives with far too much regularity to need to exemplify here. The technical terminology would talk about low probability events and most people's eyes would glaze over, and they'd stop caring or reading right there. Yet the reason I find this area both fascinating and important is how often these events happen, and when they do, the amount of creative and destructive chaos they foster.

Admittedly, all chaos is not a bad thing. It sometimes introduces needed change to a stagnant system which may in fact have positive outcomes. But when the chaos introduced is unexpected and adverse to one's circumstances, the importance of BSE begins to come into sharp focus. Let's use the stock market as an example. If you become anything like me, you'll get bombarded with people wanting you to purchase stocks all the time. They'll paint a picture of a rosy path lined with profits and opportunity for ever more profits along the way. Then, seemingly out of the blue, some happenstance will occur which derails the stock you've invested in, and your position is diminished or wiped out entirely. Let's say you bought a stock based on a rare precious metal and within months, a new and almost limitless supply of this previously precious metal becomes available to the world. A BSE has just had a major negative impact on your life.

Remember you went into the metal deal assured your precious metal purchase was rare, incredibly safe, stable, and had been for the entire history of mankind. Then suddenly an entirely new source crops up, seemingly from out of nowhere. This black swan may have just flown away with your life savings. The BSE is no longer a mere philosophical matter. It's now altered your world and the world of your family from this point forward. In my lifetime we've seen this happen to things as diverse as typewriters, Linotype machines, ironing boards, butter, giant steel mills, and family farming. All of these were established products or fields which were blindsided by a low probability event which either diminished their importance or wiped them out entirely. I hope at this point you're beginning to see how this field of understanding isn't just for academics. These BSE have impact on everyone's life.

I'm certainly concerned about the impact of BSE in your everyday lives. But I'm much more concerned with how they relate to matters which affect the entire world. If you're a student of history, you already know how seemingly improbable (low probability) events have repeatedly changed the course of history. Ask yourself how the assassination of an obscure Duke in Europe somehow led to the onset of World War I and the death of millions? If you're a student of science, ask yourself how some mathematical conjecture by a once obscure patent clerk led to the atomic bomb, the cold war, and the world I live in today. If you're a student of religion, ask yourself how the appearances of Buddha, Jesus, and Mohamed changed and continue to change the course of history. Ponder this between now and reading the next passage and consider how BSE could benefit or destroy your existence.

Black Swan Events IV

If you can accept the fact BSE do occur, and they seem to occur without predictable regularity, you must also accept some uncomfortable truths. The fact BSE seem to creep up on us and jump out from behind a moment in history to reveal themselves, should bring you to the realization we're not nearly as clever or as good at predicting critical events as we like to convince ourselves we are. I remember how intelligent I felt when I realized I'd mastered the rudiments of quantitative analysis. I came away from those studies with the sense if I was just given the correct numbers, I could be prescient about how an organization was going to fare in the coming months and years ahead. This is a dangerous form of arrogance which education in general and math education in particular tends to foster. BSE seem to exist almost to slap the arrogant smile from the faces of the various cognoscenti.

Taking this thinking a step further along the road of uncomfortable truths, can we really take the word of bankers, realtors, economists, scientists, politicians, and lawyers as definitive in any matter when so many times in the past, BSE have made them all look foolish? If bankers, realtors, and economists were so prescient, and quantitative analysis so foolproof, explain the Great Depression, routinely unforeseen economic downturns, and the Great Recession to me. If scientists employing the magic of their knowledge were such sages, and assured us they could see the future, explain their historical bewilderment at stoichiometry, black holes, Higgs Boson, powered flight, the personal computer, stopping and restarting a human heart, superconductivity, and relativity, just to name a few. If politicians and lawyers were as on top of our world as they pretend to be, explain to me the legal quagmire, and the economic and monetary mess every country on the planet routinely finds itself in.

Each time the BSE is encountered, it should first and foremost act as a wakeup call for mankind and our arrogance about what we think we know. It should remind you events you cannot easily foresee or quantify are coming down the road of history, and at their given moment will reveal themselves to your stunned dismay. Afterward with the benefit of hindsight, doublespeak, and obfuscation, the aforementioned cognoscenti will assure you they now see the separate links which went into the BSE. In doing this, they hope by convincing you they understand it, you'll also begin to mistakenly think they also foresaw it. In truth, they can't admit they were unable to capture lightening in a bottle, and when it crashed about uncontrollably, they were as surprised as everyone else. Most frightening for you should be the realization they won't foresee the next one coming, either.

Black Swan Events V
By now you've read as much about BSE as you'd ever want to. If you've taken in all I've written here and still don't grasp BSE

theory, I'll take the blame for it. Those of us in business, finance, philosophy, mathematics, or history are aware of the theme and are either presently concerned, or we've already become bored trying to get our heads around the concept. I find myself in the concerned category simply because of the hubris of the leaders in their fields I've met who feel they have all the required facts at hand to make critical decisions for the rest of us. Educated men and women are not the Masters of the Universe, despite how hard we may work to convince ourselves and others we are.

In some circles, BSE theory has caused people to stop and consider how often there might well be circumstances where the information available leaves too much to pure chance and beyond the reach of our ability to analyze. In other circles it's prompted discussion about the fragility or robustness of existing business models and whether or not at times there are unacceptable levels of risk at play we may not be equipped to contemplate. In political circles, where there really should be a long pause for contemplation and discussion about this matter, our elected brain trust listened politely to expert testimony from Taleb and others and then went back to the *status quo ante*.

My interest in this area comes from studying history this past couple of years, in an attempt to see if I can understand what kinds of events trigger economic decline, total financial collapse, or even signal the end of a nation. Yes, this is the kind of light reading I did in my time. What's been most unsettling for me is how 'unpredicted' the events which have brought nations to their knees have been; the sages seem to have been batting zero. When I looked at our historic economic markets, we seem to have seen the end coming, but no one was able to recognize the trigger until well after it was pulled. I'd hoped to be able to see through all the haze and offer some insight for you and your peers. Instead, what I found time after time in my life were BSE I couldn't predict.

BSE theory and the BSE it posits should come as a wakeup call to all of humanity. When I was a boy, I always had this sense of well-being based on the sense all the really smart people out there were making the world go around smoothly. I was sure the finest minds in science, finance, history, politics, and religion were in control of everything, or at least had such a superior understanding of everything a child like me needn't worry. Then I grew to be a man and slowly understood even the finest minds only understand a fraction of the knowledge available within their chosen fields. My conclusions are it might be time for you to take all the wise men around you less seriously, do your own research, and ask your own questions about the future. If you can foresee or create a BSE, the impact would be priceless. It could save your life, the lives of people you love, or make you a billionaire.

Avoiding Other's Negative Emotions

I'm not sure if I'm just noticing it more these days or if in fact there are more angry, agitated, and aggressive drivers out there on the highways. My suspicion is it's the times we live in and the stress people are under. As one of my friends recently noted, there's a sense of anxiety and ill ease in the country which seems to be affecting everyone to greater or lesser degree. I've learned to mostly ignore the angry drivers over the years and allow them to speed past, cut lanes, and in general make themselves a danger to everybody around them. I've seen more than one wreck where I would later hear on the local news was the result of road rage.

Angry people filled with negative emotions are a fact of life you'll have to learn to deal with. The scripture says, "A soft answer turneth away wrath," which is a great way of saying you're smarter if you don't meet angry words with equally angry words. I learned in Psychology 101 negative emotions of all sorts can be ratcheted up by the addition of other negative emotions. Our introductory psych professor also taught us neutral or positive emotion can dial down negative emotions. So whether you prefer a scriptural approach or the psychological one, it's best not to escalate an argument.

I've learned a single angry or agitated person can impact everybody around them in a negative fashion. By your age you've seen it too! In simpler terms, their anger and agitation rubs off on those around them. I think most of us have experienced having an angry or agitated person come around and felt the way it changed the atmosphere and our behavior. In my time we would've called it negative vibes. If for no other reason than self-defense, our mental modality changes when we are confronted with an angry or agitated person, even if it's not directed at us. I know folks who are masters at defusing these types with humor; I'm not one of them. Because you carry some of my genes, you may suffer from the same social deficiency.

In my youth, I would "...get angry along with the angry," which didn't help the situation much and escalated to violence more than once. As the years passed, I learned to give these folks a wider berth when they came around. But even then you're left in a heightened state of anxiety because of the close encounter with their negativity. In those instances, I had to find a way to shift gears mentally. Those of you who've experienced driving a manual transmission know you have to engage the clutch to disengage the engine. In this way the vehicle can be geared down to a lower range. I find a sincere prayer or meditation is my best bet to disengage those negative emotions and shift back into a more normal mental operating range.

These Days Pass Quickly

Many friends my age have a bucket list they're steadily working on. On one hand I'm sorry they put off things they wanted to do for so many years, on the other, I'm glad they've come to the realization it's their life and they should be living it as they want to. I've been blessed to have taken time to pursue most of the offbeat things I wanted to do in my lifetime. I encourage you kids to enjoy your life while you still have the opportunity. Find the things which will make you happy regardless of what others around you may think.

I hiked, ran, swam, hunted, fished, explored, climbed, skied, flew, sailed, dove, snorkeled, and rafted. I've been blessed by the love of good women and have found more than my share of fellows who saw me as their brother. I'd be hard pressed to find anything on a bucket list I still want to accomplish. But if something does occur to me, I'll go after it if I still can. My focus these days is more about being all I can be in the sense of delivering back to the creation whatever few gifts I have to offer. If you have bucket lists, pursue them with passion; the days of your life will pass more quickly than you can imagine and regrets in old age are like an unending toothache

Spending Time Wisely

We speak of the concept of 'spending' time as though it were a currency, and in some ways it is. As I get older I'm ever more conscious of the increasingly rapid passage of time. I've read many theories about time and why it seems time passes more quickly as we age, but all this does is make me feel like I've gained some small understanding. It doesn't in any way slow time down or bring time to a halt. I've learned over the years no matter what mere mortals attempt to do, we can't stop time, and we can't stop the changes it brings into each life.

With those truisms firmly planted in mind, I've made conscious choices to change the way I spend my time as the years fly by and the far horizon comes ever closer into view. I've learned time is exceedingly precious. I've learned there is no assurance of a tomorrow. I've learned the passage of time can be used for good or evil, or it can just be allowed to pass unconsciously as we grind on through the daily routines we've established. I'm not suggesting your time be spent in any particular fashion. I'm suggesting you spend it in ways you don't regret when time runs out.

It's been said no one on their deathbed ever bemoans the fact they didn't spend more time at work. I've sat at the bedsides of dozens of dying men and women. I've listened to their last thoughts and heard their final confessions of faith. What remains with me from these encounters, some which took place forty years ago, is how precious family and friends are and how easily we forget this in the hustle and bustle of this passage of time we call life. Take heed you give due time to family and friends; I've never seen a workplace show up at a deathbed to comfort the dying.

CHAPTER 6

What Lifestyle Can You Sustain

I've witnessed many families climb economically until they reach some sort of economic pinnacle. Occasionally, through some mishap or another (e.g., illness, loss of employment, divorce, death, etc.) they fall from this pinnacle and end up on a much lower economic plateau. Few of us consider this possibility when we're young, but the lesson here for me has been it's not what economic height you can ultimately achieve which matters, so much as what economic height you can sustain. This truth won't change in your time.

Each of you've come from stable families, and while you might not have been wealthy, you were raised in homes owned by your parents, parents who had stable jobs, stable physical health, and stable relationships. As mundane as those items might seem to you now, they're key to achieving and sustaining prosperity. This is not to say there aren't people out there in ill health, with unstable work histories and crazy relationships, which aren't living at an economic pinnacle. On the contrary, they're the exceptions which help validate the general rule I've posited.

My challenge to each of you is not just for you to strive for some early success pinnacle. My challenge to each of you is to always pursue and sustain a lifestyle within which you can live and enjoy your life. By the time you kids reach age thirty, you'll have seen many human shipwrecks who've failed to grasp how important this principle is while they still had the resources at hand to anchor their lives for the inevitable storms we all face. Be gracious to any you encounter who have fallen, but be wise and learn from their failures. If you mishandle your life, you'll be counted among them.

A Fish Rots From The Head Down
Organizations are only as successful as their leadership allows them to be. You can have the best team of workers in your industry, and if those in leadership fail to lead by providing needed resources, creating empowering policies, and then getting out of the way of the team, the enterprise will never be all it could be. This is why those of us in business can see the same players who were at XYZ Corporation (where failure seemed to be a way of life) go to ABC Corporation and almost immediately turn it into a world-class company. I think many CEOs get far too much credit for organizational success and not nearly enough blame for organizational failure.

In your time one or more of you kids will own or helm businesses. Even if you turn out to be a gifted leader, be humble about it. Today's gifted leader is often tomorrow's failed leader and sometimes the only difference is the failed leader's people assets moved on to other venues. Be as generous with those people assets as time and money will allow. The way you treat people comes back to either bless you or curse you. You'll find it's much easier to pull together a great team for a new project when the folks who worked in your last project loved working with you and felt you valued and nurtured them. This is why corporate narcissists frequently have no second act.

As a leader, I've made mistakes many times. I found years ago the only thing which ever makes those mistakes tolerable to live with, is to own them. You need to take as much ownership of your failures as you do your successes. Sometimes the cost to you will be monetary, sometimes it will be to your reputation, and sometimes it will be to both. But you'll survive the cost, and you'll come through it a different person. It won't only make a better man or woman of you in the long run; it will also tell those who consider working with you you're not the leader who's constantly looking for his or her next scapegoat.

No one wants to work with a leader who's always ranting about those who are out to get them. No one wants to work with a leader who takes credit for every good idea from their team and lays blame elsewhere for their own bad ideas. No one wants to work with a boss who receives a huge bonus based on the work of their support team, while simultaneously denying their support team bonuses, benefits, and perquisites. Humble leaders are supported and admired by their teams. Narcissistic leaders are quietly despised and abandoned as quickly as possible.

Lords Of The Manor

We've turned a very troubling corner in my time when politicians are either no longer clever enough to hide their lies, or they just no longer fear the voters knowing they lied. On the one hand, it might indicate subtlety has gone completely out of the game of politics and a coarsening of political society is in the wind. On the other hand, it may just say politicians have figured out we can be made the serfs in this political system and they've become the modern day Lords of the manor.

I have no way of knowing how this will all be, in a decade or more when you read my words to you. But I fear it will only grow worse as tyrants tend to become more tyrannical over time and not less so. There's an old adage which warns of what happens in a society when the electorate fully grasps it can vote itself benefits. I find it amusing this one about the electorate is bandied about often, and yet somehow folks have failed to give much thought to our surrogate electors in congress voting themselves such largess.

For years now they've steadily increased their salaries, benefits, and outright perquisites to the point where most elected officials live like potentates while they're in the capital. Then, once their years in office come to an end, they can't seem to wait to retire there because while they were in office, they voted themselves all these trailing perquisites which are available to them as long as they continue to reside in or near the capital. Take heed while each of them claim to be populists, they're the most elite of all the political elites in the United States, both in my time and yours!

Tactical Trolls

Time and contemplation have caused me to be wary of much social media. This isn't an outgrowth of any antisocial leanings I might otherwise have, so much as it's an effort on my part not to get drawn into questionable debates or causes. Yes, I do believe there are many worthy causes on social media, but I've become concerned about how much personal information people readily give up to the Internet. Call me paranoid if you will, but just who is it behind the organization which wants you to click yes, in order to electronically sign their petition to stop the slaughter of innocent Naugas used in the manufacture of Naugahyde®? Who is behind the group seeking to impeach the president? Who is it asking you to support legislation to ban nuclear power?

The innocent answers to those questions would be people 1) who love Naugas and don't want them to be wiped out, 2) think the president has violated his oath of office and should be impeached and removed, and 3) support banning the use of nuclear power out of concern over its associated dangers. Now take a deep breath! Then ask yourself, "How do I know that?" The correct answers here should be 1) I took a few minutes to do some basic research as to whether or not such a group exists, 2) I determined they're a legitimate group whose stated goals align with my own, and 3) I made sure I wasn't putting myself at risk by being associated with them. Each is a weighty matter and the third one is the weightiest one of all. Your innocent click may have serious repercussions for you, your career, and even your family.

I admit to a fascination with YouTube® and similar social media phenomenon as it exists in 2015. I'd never even looked at a YouTube video until 2013. Since then, the volume of valuable information and total detritus I've seen there is beyond amazing. YouTube® is like we once thought television would be; a terrific medium for improving the lives of people everywhere, which became mired down in the pursuit of advertising dollars. YouTube®, by the mere fact it operates in the wild west of the Internet, can cut a much wider swath than television. I learned quickly everything you see on YouTube® needs to be filtered through a powerful skeptical lens. The pursuit of 'hits' motivates people to produce videos which ruin people financially, injure the foolish, damage relationships, or outright kill the most gullible among us.

This may surprise you, but provided there are sufficient safeguards such as YouTube's policy of having to confirm your age (what twelve-year-old isn't claiming he's twenty-two) to view some of the material, I have strong Libertarian leanings which cause me to support people's right to do stupid or dangerous things so long as they do them to themselves and not some innocent third party. I also understand the role survival of the fittest plays in strengthening the race by eliminating undesirable traits. Having said this, I want to reiterate the search for truth or pure knowledge or whatever Holy Grail it is people are claiming to be in pursuit of when posting to YouTube®, they easily fall prey to the potential revenue streams they derive from those hits. This is why literally hundreds of thousands of people are trying to create questionable videos which might 'go viral'.

I hope by the time you read this, you're of an age to fully grasp the import of what I'm telling you. If you are, by now you know regardless of how high and lofty we human beings claim our motivations to be, trash sells, and it sells very well. It's not just the purveyors of the trash who are to blame; as humans we're all too often complicit with this group in we're titillated by trash. Trash is far more than a single person's guilty pleasure; otherwise the sources of such information would dry up. I can't begin to tell you how to precisely live your life. Your Grandmother and I raised your mother the best we knew how and then had to trust the lessons took. What I can do here is write words of caution based on what I've seen as an aging man; words I write out of an abundance of caution for lives I hold priceless.

I want to come back around to the actual topic of this piece now, 'tactical trolls'. When I began to realize what trolls were, I was disappointed at their efforts to elicit argumentative words from others who were viewing the videos. But over a year of watching both videos and the interchanges of trolls with other viewers, another picture began to emerge. I pay an inordinate amount of attention to the words people use, the cadence of their writing or speaking, and their use of grammar. In my estimation deliberate deceptions were and are in place: 1) a man pretending to be a woman; 2) a woman pretending to be a man; 3) a white man pretending to be a black man; 4) a black man pretending to be a white man; 5) a straight man pretending to be a gay man; and 6) a gay man pretending to be a straight man. The list of deceit and deceivers goes on indefinitely.

Part of the time, trolls are just people who want to mess with the minds of others. Part of the time, trolls have some serious mental health issues. Part of the time, trolls are actually the producer of the video, seeking to drive hits by getting people to return again and again to perform verbal fisticuffs. Yet the scariest trolls of all are those who are part of some organization, cause, or government agency working to find out what you think. We know knowledge is power. I assure you knowledge can be turned against people in ways they never imagined. Let the ether know you have gold and silver hidden in your home, and see how long it takes a clever thief to find you. The sad part is, having your gold and silver stolen may be the least of your problems.

I've been passionate about many causes in my life, and in at least one instance I and my family paid for my passion dearly. So I understand people who are passionate about causes. I get it when people tell me they want to save the baby seals, feed the hungry children in Africa, provide housing for the poor, and stop the draining of wetlands. I tell you this so you'll know these words don't emanate from some bitter old man who doesn't want people to support their favorite cause. It's my opinion many of the trolls and troll sites on the Internet are placed there by people who don't want to save the baby seals, feed the hungry children in Africa, provide housing for the poor, or stop the wetland from being drained. Bear with me and read on. Don't give up on me here as a hopeless old paranoid.

Look around your constantly connected world. Every day you hear about breaches of security related to personal information, cybercrime, identity theft, and the like. By the time you read this, God only knows where we'll be with regard to personal privacy. Of all the freedoms I cherish, the right to be left alone is as important to me as any of them. I like free speech. I like being able to possess guns. I like the right to be secure in my home, along with my personal papers, thoughts, and communications. It doesn't appear possible to enjoy many of the rights granted us in the Bill of Rights if we lose the core right to be left alone. My philosophy in regard to other citizens has long been I don't want to be a bother to them, and I don't want them to be a bother to me. I think these ideals are at the heart of America.

What wasn't at the heart of America for most of my years was the effort by various elites to spy on a person. Governments spying on friendly governments, governments spying on corporations, governments spying on honest citizens, corporations spying on other corporations, and corporations spying on customers have all become accepted if not acceptable practices. A very clever way to do this involves trolling. If I can change your psychological state of passivity by provoking you, I can pull you out of your cave and learn an amazing amount about you from your unguarded outbursts. I'm a perfect example. Despite all the education I have, and all the manners my Momma and others worked so hard to develop in me, get me angry and a really vulgar reptilian portion of this brain kicks in. Then there's no telling what I might say or do. Trolls know these truths about human behavior.

Information about you, your family, your job, your house of worship, your political beliefs, and your sexual preference are valuable to people other than yourself. Knowing what kind of car you drive, the brand of slacks you wear, and if you're in the market for a new house has value to manufacturers, builders, interior decorators, marketers, and sales people, just to name a few. The nature and place of your work are of interest to employers, head hunters, educational organizations, government agencies, planning departments, and suppliers. Knowing what your position is on religion is of great value to those of the same beliefs. Unfortunately it can also be of great value to anyone who hates your particular house of faith or those who have no faith. If I know your political beliefs, I can use this to political advantage.

That last one about political advantage is especially troubling to me since politics over my lifetime has become more and more divisive, confrontational, and socially super-charged. We're to the point where a sort of populist McCarthyism has emerged where we have hundreds of groups out there putting together narrow-band witch hunts. I fear by the time you're grown, it will be even more so than it is here in my sixty-first year. I hope you'll pause and think before you allow yourself to immediately jump on-board the next online petition solicitation, complaint, or recruitment. The problem is not so much the petition, complaint, or recruitment might not be legitimate. The problem is people who would use this information to harm you or your loved ones.

The next time you're tempted to take on a troll, click you 'like' something, share another's post, or add your voice in support of some otherwise worthy cause, please consider what I've said here. Then, if you still feel you must take on the troll, do your due diligence to ascertain the true nature of the windmill before you charge in, young Quixote.

Your Own Worst Enemy

As a general rule, in the course of your lifetime, you'll do yourself far more injury than will ever be visited upon you by all your enemies combined.

Responsible Adult

When I reflect on the entirety of my life, I must admit I've lived through strange and unsettled times. At least once a year, I'll invariably get emails from friends, telling me they're receiving odd emails from me, and they think I've been hacked. Odd here usually means something salacious has arrived under my name. This speaks well for my friends and somewhat for me. It's well their first reaction is "Farrell wouldn't send me something like this." It's well for me after all these years, and all my ups and downs, people still see me as a responsible and trustworthy adult. As such, I try to let people know I've been hacked, and then I go about the laborious task of resetting all my passwords.

My hope is as you pass through this life, you'll be a responsible and trustworthy person. By this I mean a person who takes responsibility for themselves and any of the obligations they've taken on in life. At first this will seem like a simple thing, but as the years go by, you'll find maintaining your reputation for responsibility and trustworthiness requires making a thousand positive decisions and then standing by each one of them. Even a single act of irresponsibility or breach of trust can become a lifelong black mark which is impossible to wipe away. I'm not expecting you to live a perfect life, only Jesus managed such a miracle. I do expect you to strive daily to be the best man or woman you can be; if you do, the rest will take care of itself.

You Raised Them

There are two major schools of thought on the issue of child rearing. There may be a third, consisting of some overlap between the two dominant schools, but here is how I see it in the mean. Some parents raise their children with an eye toward the present; some parents raise their children with an eye toward the future.

Those with an eye on the present are concerned junior is happy, regardless of what Mom or Dad have to do to keep him that way. Junior figures this out early on, and soon Mom and Dad jump at his beck and call. They take him any place he wants to go. They buy him anything his heart desires. They excuse his bad behavior, perhaps even telling others it's actually their fault junior acted out, hit another child, broke a neighbor's window, or burglarized a nearby home. They may also blame you; junior's friends, junior's teachers, or junior's other family members.

Those with an eye toward the future certainly care about junior's present state of welfare, but they also have an eye on junior's life in the decades ahead when Mom and Dad won't be there to protect and guide him. These parents don't jump at junior's call. They mostly take junior places they've chosen. These parents hold junior accountable for bad manners, crude speech, missed chores, and homework. They accept their proper share of responsibility/blame but lay an increasing amount of it, year by year, squarely at junior's door, so when junior reaches the age of majority, he's headed for a career and not rehab, prison, or a cemetery.

There are exceptions to almost any rule, but you know deep in your gut kids with a solid upbringing seem to have a better grasp of being a productive citizen than those who've been raised to see the world as their stage and everybody else as bit players. The constantly indulged child is far more likely to end up in trouble with the law than he or she is likely to make the dean's list. You can listen to all the pop psychology you want, but you and I both know what we've seen firsthand. The easiest way to ruin a child is to give them everything they want. It's for this reason your mom and dad denied your every whim and worked to moderate your sense of self-importance.

I've observed these two types of upbringing at a close distance, with many families, over many decades. I learned early in my years of ministry to recognize which children I'd be most likely to visit in a juvenile detention facility, a county jail, or a state or federal prison. I knew which parents I'd be crying and commiserating with as they agonized over junior's physical abuse of them, his burglaries of their home, the psychological trauma he visited upon the family, or his untimely death in a shootout with the local police. The worst part is often all the children in a household turn out this way, and the parents face a multitude of these kinds of behavior and events; their old age becomes a living hell with golden years nowhere in sight.

Avoiding bad outcomes is always a laudable goal. However, once your children are grown, the die is likely cast. If they're half-grown, you still have half a chance to instill structure and discipline. The most hope I can offer is, if you're reading this in your young adult years, you'll either have no children yet or they'll be small. They're still like young trees and can yet be properly trained. You can put up some props and ropes, and by concerted pressure in the right direction, your little sapling can still become a straight and mighty oak. But if you wait too long to take these corrective measures, social workers, the police, the courts, or the undertaker will take over where you left off.

I'd like to offer some final thoughts on these issues, and perhaps not popular thoughts at all. It's not up to the church, the school, your parents, or the state to raise your child. With rare exceptions (e.g., rape, incest, etc.), it's a job you took upon yourself when you either chose to be part of a conception or do nothing to prevent an unplanned conception. It's not your parent's fault. It's not your neighbor's fault. It's not your congressman's fault. Whose fault is it? It's your fault. I've had parents complain to me about their child and claim their child's wilding is a case being "...a bad seed." When they do this, I respond in a similar metaphoric vein with the comment, "The apple doesn't fall too far from the tree."

I expect you to produce exemplary offspring. This isn't mere arrogance on my part. It's actually more about the way your parents were raised and how I've seen them raising you. Your father has been blessed with 'almost' as good a father as your mother had. Your grandfathers have all been decent, hard-working, God-fearing men who did their best to shoulder their share of the burden for their families and their nation. You have zero ability to point to your family's previous generations and blame them if you falter or completely fail in life. We'll expect no less than those same positive parenting qualities from each of you. Even if you marry someone who exemplifies less than any of the aforementioned standards, your family will expect more of you because of who your ancestors are and were.

Of Diet And Research

As you know, I've spent a portion of my life as a researcher. Sometimes it was purely academic, sometimes it was directed, and yet each time the end goal was to learn something which advanced 'the art' as they like to refer to it in patent documents. I'm old enough to have a fifty-year perspective on a lot of things which go on in our society. As I was finishing dinner this evening it occurred to me I've lived long enough to hear what I was once assured was a great diet, and one I should all aspire to, as now deemed to be a diet which will make me obese, give me heart disease, diabetes, and some horrific form of cancer.

What did I have for dinner tonight? My wife and I enjoyed steamed white rice, roast chicken, and boiled cabbage, all heartily dosed with soy sauce. There was a time when a vegetable, a starch, and a meat would have been regarded as highly healthy. Now I hear the rice contributes to my obesity, the chicken should be stripped of the skin (where all the flavor is), and the cabbage should be eaten plain; boiled cardboard comes to mind here. In my opinion, soy sauce is a gift of God to an impoverished mankind; it makes many otherwise unpalatable dishes delightful to ingest, at pennies per serving. I'm highly amused first-world nations have the arrogance to tell the poorest people in the world how they should eat.

I'm going to share a secret with you as a researcher which researchers don't always share with their public. First, research is inexact and may even be subject to manipulation, depending on who paid for it. Second, researchers are not always as brilliant as you think they are; more than one of them has later been embarrassed when their poor math skills or outright fudging of their numbers were exposed. Finally, I've known researchers who reported on some horrific malady where their research showed a strong correlation to the item or items they were examining, who didn't bother the least to change their lifestyle to match what their research suggested they should be doing.

Your Ba Kim is Vietnamese by birth and lived through a terrible war there where she lost many loved ones. She reminds me often many people in Vietnam struggle daily to get enough nourishment of any sort. To this end, we share what we have with them, and I marvel to hear how little they may have to eat and yet how happy they are with what I've judged as little. I'm embarrassed first-world peoples spend so much time worrying about their overindulgence, while much of the rest of humanity would be thrilled with white rice, roast chicken, and boiled cabbage. So, dear one, take research with a grain of salt, and offer a prayer of sincere gratitude for what you have on the plate before you as well.

Good Or Bad, Eventually Word Gets Around

As trivial as it may seem to some people, I think honesty is essential to good relationships. This goes for both your personal and professional life. My Daddy had quite a range of personal flaws, but to my knowledge I never caught him lying in my entire life. When I'm searching for things to remember positively about him, this is the first one which comes to mind. I hope you'll be able to say the same thing about both your parents when you're my age. As for yourselves, the only way you can develop a reputation for honesty is to work at it every day of your life. I know if you do, there'll be those who ridicule you and tell you how silly and antiquated the idea is. Yet for the people who'll really come to matter in your life, your ability to be honest and trustworthy will become the cement which bonds those relationships. Consider this recent encounter I had and its outcomes.

Twice in recent years, a business associate and I have been misled by people selling services. Regardless of how smart you think you are, or how many initials there are behind your name, you're going to be taken every once in a while. In one instance a salesperson misrepresented the total cost of a construction project by almost half, around $100,000 more than first claimed. This resulted in a project which was already under way, grinding to a halt once the real numbers came to light. In the second instance a rental company failed to disclose their full list of charges (e.g., service, return inspection, and environmental charges, etc.) for a large generator I'd rented. The hidden fees amounted to an additional 20 percent on the total bill. Now before you say pish-tosh, the kind of generators I rent can easily run from five hundred to two thousand a week and I had this one for several weeks.

How did I handle this kind of behavior? In both cases I addressed my grievances to the presidents of these respective companies. In the case of the generator, the money was returned with a letter of apology for not declaring the surcharges initially instead of upon return. In the case of the other project, which had a value of over $100,000 in materials alone, we never heard a word of apology out of the salesman or the company president I spoke to about this bait and switch behavior. This latter silence speaks loudly to me and says, "This is how we regularly do business, and if you don't like it, too bad." I'll do business again with the generator company, and I'll share with my friends how they treated me. I'll also share with my friends how the building contractor treated us. It appears for one company, it was their mistake; for the other it was our mistake to take them at their written word.

Child of mine, if people learn your word is no good, even in the fastest of times, it will have negative repercussions. If enough people learn your word is no good, you'll become known as a habitual liar. Most folks expect the occasional white lie from others; I'm not excusing it, I'm just stating a fact. But even your mother will learn to doubt and distance herself from you if you become a habitual liar who can't be trusted. Your family's good name and your personal reputation are two things you still possess at this age which are fully intact. You should be busy protecting and building on those two valuable assets, or you can begin to take them apart today by being untrustworthy in your words or deeds. Once again, the choice is yours.

Of Presidents And Emperors

A president is a president and an emperor is an emperor. The problems begin when a president begins to see himself as your emperor. Such behavior grows, according to this adage from Lord Acton's quote archive, "Power tends to corrupt and absolute power corrupts absolutely. Great men are almost always bad men, even when they exercise influence and not authority; still more when you superadd the tendency of the certainty of corruption by authority."

Unconsumed By An Earlier Catastrophe

Historically, the value of money was based on the gold or silver reserves a nation held to back up their currency. Throughout history, money was finite and tied directly to tangible assets (e.g., silver, gold, etc.). In this way a country could not spend more than it possessed, and its economy was constrained to growth which could be accomplished within the reserves on hand. I know you've already heard regularly from your parents about living within your means? This lesson is often lost on people, especially politicians.

Years ago someone (e.g., economist, politician, and soothsayer) realized if you could unhinge an economy from tangible assets and instead use intangibles (e.g., full faith, trust, verbal guarantees, smoke, mirrors, etc.); the size of an economy could be virtually limitless. The downside is what my generation has been observing these past few years as the economy tanked. The Federal Reserve printed money backed only by promises, and then used this money to buy bonds from a creditor (The United States of America) who was already technically bankrupt.

The scheme has made billions for banks, financial manipulators in the markets, politicians, and the politician's friends and families. The markets have in fact hit all-time highs during this heated growth period, since the billions of dollars were flushed into the system with no better place for it to go than stocks. Investors love the current bull market, which is driven by this flood of printed money, backed by nothing. Note at the same time all these fortunes are being made, our nation is seeing the worst unemployment since the Great Depression. At this point I've stopped ingesting the government's lies about how rosy things are. I know too many people who've given up looking for work and don't count in the rosy numbers any more. Yes, governments will lie to citizens in order to keep them under control. They'll pull the same sort of flimflam in your time.

The actual value or true worth of all the printing and purchasing is silently being siphoned away from the people of the United States by inflationary gimmicks foisted on us by those we elected to serve us. Hard assets are being purchased with extremely soft money. It's an old game: borrow in today's expensive dollars and pay back in tomorrow's cheaper dollars. Then work hard to cheapen the dollars all you can in the interim. Unfortunately, real people with real lives and bank accounts pay the toll; it's an open secret. All three branches of the government know this is going on. We the people know they know this. They know we know they know this, and we all just go on playing this silly little game which can end so easily in catastrophe for the ones who haven't already been consumed by an earlier financial catastrophe.

At your age I had no idea of the importance of economics or how it would affect my life. I advise you to learn as much about economics as you can and use it to guide you in the way you live out your financial lives. My family was poor, poorly educated, and was suspicious of anybody who understood money. That suspicion arose because more often than not, those people used their superior knowledge to make money at his expense. In the last sixty years this hasn't changed one iota; the financially and economically savvy are still best positioned to profit in all eras. Educate yourself and join them, not so much as a means to exploit others as to prepare yourself to create your own defenses to all forms of economic exploitation.

Get The Facts Before You Make Judgments

I've been frequently reminded of a Physical Anthropology 101 lecture I sat through as an undergrad where the key bit of information imparted to ninety of us slogging through the course was "Any human male and a female pair, could hypothetically produce in excess of 3,300,000 offspring, and no two would be genetically identical." I was never able to independently confirm the professor's assertions, but I often think about this in regard to all the different human configurations I've encounter and muse over why I only see certain combinations as being beautiful or useful. Of course, my line of reasoning assumes there's some reason to life and it isn't just left to chance. If life is all random chance, then it really doesn't matter. Does it?

The perfect truth I attempt to hold is all of the configurations of human beings are beautiful and useful, but you and I are limited in our ability to see this beauty or usefulness. This leads to all sorts of judgmental assumptions from each of us every day. When people deny they ever do this, I smile inside. Once in a while I do experience a moment where the veil is lifted and the autistic child turns out to be a math savant, the horridly overweight man turns out to be a world-class singer, and the crazy woman turns out to be a celebrated schizophrenic artist who's just off her meds. It might be wiser to be gentle in your judgments than to have the facts later prove you to be a fool.

Not everything is as it first appears to be. You and I owe it to ourselves and all the others we share this planet with to give the facts a moment to make themselves known.

Take A Deep Breath

Sometimes there'll be entire weeks or even months when it seems like everything you own decides to break down at once. The phrase, "These are times that try men's souls" comes to my mind frequently as you may notice from its' repetitions in my musings. I'm sure if the research were done, there'd be a logical explanation for why this is, but I wouldn't spend a lot of time musing upon it if I were you. I rarely get really angry anymore. In my youth, as I've shared with you elsewhere in these writings, I learned how counterproductive my anger was after having to deal with the aftermath of letting it get away from me a few times. Someone has to pay for and/or repair all the damage done in your anger, be it physical, mental, spiritual, or emotional.

My being angry is not just bad for those around me. My being angry seems to kill me just a little bit every time it happens. I think it does the same thing to everybody else as well, whether they realize it or not. There's a danger you'll feel so self-righteous in your anger at first, you won't see this negative aspect. However, given time you'll definitely begin to feel it. I work very hard these days to remain on an even temperamental keel; it's not being done solely to benefit those around me. I advise you to work to find this this mental space too. In doing so, we'll both live longer lives, I in my time and you in yours; it will be a better quality of life we each live.

Eulogies

I'm told there's an Australian tune called, "Everyone's a Top Bloke When They're Dead." There's a lot of truth in this title, and as I read obituaries daily, I've never seen one which pointed out all the well-known faults of the deceased. In my twenties and thirties I officiated at dozens of memorial services. There was more than one occasion where I knew the deceased well, as their pastor perhaps too well, and was genuinely stunned at the eulogies which were made. Chronic philanderers were suddenly model husbands. The mean-tempered, wife-beating, child-abusing town drunk became the loving and devoted husband and father. The fellow killed in a shootout with the police after being caught robbing a liquor store was suddenly a paragon of piety, according to the people he'd gone to Sunday school with twenty-five years earlier. I think these flights of fiction generally just embarrass everybody in the room and serve to magnify the failures of the deceased, which they likely all knew too well anyway.

I know nothing I'm saying here will change anything past or future, and while I never extolled on virtues the deceased didn't actually possess, neither did I ever say, "He was a rotten, skirt-chasing, gambling, low-down rounder, and we're all better off that he's gone." I've instructed your Mother I just want her to tell the truth about me when the time comes. You see, God knows all about each of us. He won't be snowed by people at our memorials, embellishing our lives with stories of what a fine human being we were. So people who know me, know me warts and all. Hopefully, the people who know you well, know you similarly and still like or even love you. Also, the next time you're asked to speak at your best friend's funeral, while no one expects you to talk about the time the two of you got tossed out of a strip club drunk, they also won't want to hear you turn him into a saint if he was killed by a rightfully jealous husband.

No Place Like Home

You may recall from your childhood how weekend family outings to the lake, the beach, or the mountains have never been my cup of tea. It seems like such an enormous effort to plan an extended outing, gather all the materials required, coordinate your family and friends, and then journey to your proposed place of fun, sun, and play. Then you find yourself exhausted on all levels long before you get home on Monday evening. The marriage is close to over, the top of your head is sunburned, you crave a real shower, and eating food not prepared over a grill seems like a treat.

I feel the same way about those weekends as I do about business travel. When I was young, I couldn't wait to travel, fly in planes, roll in trains, drive rental cars, sleep in hotels, and order room service. The thrill had pretty much worn off completely by the time I was thirty years of age. Consequently, I admire anybody who can take on a weekend outing or business trip with good humor and some degree of sanity. As for me, I'll make do with my own home, my own bed, my own car, and familiar surroundings as often as I can. I've come to value the comfort of the familiar above all else; in time you may too.

My counsel to you is to accept the fact you'll be expected to good-naturedly go off on a series of extended weekend outings in your life. Grin and bear them. I didn't always do this, and in retrospect I wish I would've. I know your grandmother and your mother would've appreciated it more if I had. On the off-hand chance your weekend outings turn out to be smashing successes in life, you'll look like a cordial genius. Conversely, if they come off as near-disasters, and you've borne them like a trooper, your spouse and family will love you all the more for being so supportive and a good sport under such trying conditions.

Pushing Back

I doubt you know much about my nuclear family, the family of my birth, because your mother only knows the highlights and lowlights and not much of the mundane day-to-day existence of our lives back then. I want to address one such area because it's been on my mind over the past few weeks. It's a flaw in my makeup which was born in my humble but very dysfunctional childhood home. It's a flaw I've had to fight hard over the years to correct. It's the flaw of knowing how to connect with my anger but not knowing how to connect with my assertiveness. The result has been explosive displays of anger which resulted in not knowing how to properly address a personal wrong until it had festered to such a degree both it and I had become volatile.

I came from an alcoholic home. My Daddy drank nearly every day of my life until he was a man of seventy. He ceased drinking completely six or seven years later when cancer was destroying his throat, jaw, and tongue. Some of my older siblings will argue whether or not my Daddy was an alcoholic until they run out of breath, but most of his serious alcoholism came along after they were grown and away from the home. If you're roaring drunk two or three or four nights a week, are sometimes completely drunk twenty-four hours a day for weeks at a time, routinely spend the majority of your income on alcohol for you or your drinking buddies, or if you're jailed for long periods on three different occasions for assaulting your family and police officers while drunk, you're an alcoholic. Having expressed this, let me explain where this ties into my inability to be assertive. My Daddy could be verbally and physically violent when he was drunk; when sober he was as kind as any man I ever knew. Sadly, arguments in my home could easily end in some form of violence.

From these violent events I learned arguing or standing up for yourself, even when I was in the right, could result in an absolutely unwanted display of aggression from my Daddy. I saw my Momma struck more than once. For the most part, this left me crippled in the sense of questioning my rights to stand up for myself; I can't, nor do I pretend, to speak for my siblings. As an adult I saw I could rise up and easily and forcefully defend others and the rights of others; I championed the weak in all their versions. But whenever my rights were violated, I generally remained quiet until the resentment at the mistreatment had festered so long it came out in violent and angry verbal attacks and a willingness to resort to physical violence. People who'd only seen the kindly Farrell were absolutely stunned and frightened at who I became when pushed this far.

I'm not now, nor have I ever been in your home on more than an occasional basis. I've no way of knowing precisely what the dynamics have been as you've grown up, but I've never seen drunkenness or violence as an issue. I wish for each of you a life where you can be assertive without being angry and violent. I wish for you a spouse who behaves the same way. Every human being has certain inalienable rights which I believe are an endowment of a loving Creator. No one human being's rights are more important than the next, but some people seem to feel their rights should supersede those of all others. If you're to survive and not become consumed by your anger at times, as I have, you'll have to learn to recognize your rights, then be able to assert you, your ideas, and your personal rights matter as much as anyone else's do.

CHAPTER 7

Careless, Poorly Educated, Or Illiterate

I know at some point during your childhood you heard from me about my concerns regarding the decline of civilization in the United States. It manifests itself on many and varied fronts. I want to call your attention right now to how important it is you speak and write properly. Each of you came from homes where English was the native tongue, and despite some southern influences which have been part of our family for centuries, you've been taught from an early age to speak properly. I know your first thought will be, "That old man sounds like the worst sort of Dust Bowl Okie when he talks to us." I'll be the first to admit this is the case when we speak at home and among our family and close friends. But you also know I can turn on a dime, and Neeley the public speaker suddenly appears. My point is I don't mind you knowing a less causal form of writing and speaking as long as you know how to do both properly and exactly when they need to be exercised.

I've been part of the faculty of a school of advanced studies at a university for many years. Though I'm currently inactive to have the time to write, the main area for which I was hired was mentoring doctoral candidates who were working their way through the writing of their dissertation. It's the final step in their pursuit of a doctorate. Have no doubt about it, these are smart people, and this work has caused me to be hyper-vigilant about language and how it's improper use brands the user as either careless, poorly educated, or illiterate. I've deliberately chosen not to write as an academic to you children. Your main goal should always be to communicate to the audience in front of you and not one you imagine. In listening to politicians and the folks celebrated in the popular media, I'm increasingly troubled we elect, hire, and promote people who are careless with their public speaking and writing, poorly educated, don't know their audience, or are outright illiterate.

A case in point, and there are many to choose from, concerns listening to the chief correspondent from one of the major media outlets repeatedly talk about the 'vunerable' Democratic members of the House of Representatives as a result of their support of the Affordable Care Act. I'm genuinely not trying to be a Grammar Nazi, but I can't find the word vunerable in the dictionary. I do find the word 'vulnerable' and it seems to fit the sentence in which the non-word vunerable found itself. You may ask rhetorically, "Who are you to correct someone being paid a million dollars a year to keep you and me informed?" These inconsistencies in language beg the question, "Do the people who produce these news segments actually understand English?" I believe a good deal of it comes from sight reading and laziness. Regardless of the source, it paints an unflattering picture of these speakers and writers.

The Human Touch

I like to get to know the people I am doing business with, even if most of my dealings with them are on the Internet. Yesterday I was able to meet two different Internet vendors I purchase from regularly and was delighted with the experience. It's funny how a face-to-face meeting with someone who has previously been only a disembodied series of emails can answer so many questions and either raise or lay to rest so many concerns. I worry we're losing something as a society as we become more and more physically disconnected from people. As much as I love the Internet, it will never replace human interaction... and it shouldn't.

As the years pass, I fear the pace at which humans lose physical contact with each other will escalate. While there are times it's great not to have to deal with a physical presence, there are other times where it's equally important to be able to meet and know people as something other than disembodied beings; voices on the Internet, Skype®, or your iPhone®. Let me encourage you to use the interactive skills your parents taught you and keep them in tune. The man or woman who learns how to meet, greet, and enjoy people has a huge advantage over those like me who would prefer to remain at a distance and struggle to be socially at ease.

Dealing With Mad Men

I read in last week's news the current leader of North Korea, Kim Jong UN, ordered his uncle be executed. This is the same uncle who helped him consolidate power after the death of his father, Kim Jong IL. I'm old enough to have witnessed many other strongmen taking power and then killing off all threats to their power. However, there's a greater danger in this latest would-be North Korean God-man, and it's a danger which may yet be visited upon its neighbors and enemies in an atomic fashion. Pay heed here; he'll be in power in your time.

When the United States and the Soviet Union were heavily engaged in the Cold War during my childhood and young adult years, both appeared to have had a fairly accurate assessment of themselves and each other. Their whole sense of mutually assured destruction (MAD) kept both sides from quickly jumping into a nuclear war or an event which could lead to one. However, when you're a God, and an isolated God at that, you have few equals at hand with which to compare yourself. This self-worship is handy for boosting your own ego; otherwise it's very dangerous.

Setting ego boosting aside for a moment, an isolated God may actually be a very poor judge of how his or her actions will be seen by the richer neighbors and one's better-armed enemies. Consequently, it's much easier to make rash decisions and take rash actions than if the would-be God had more equals to look to for comparison, advice, or emulation. After all, how can you say "No" to a God? It appears in this instance not only can't you say "No," but saying "No" may in fact put you in front of a firing squad.

For any among you who might say the North Koreans will never use their nuclear weapons, I point out they've invested a huge portion of their entire economy for decades in obtaining, improving, and fully weaponizing their nuclear arsenal. Those missile launch platforms and submarines cost the Korean people dearly. Kim Jong UN knows this, and so do his people. Many in North Korea have faced starvation and the loss of family and friends over those same decades to keep this ability intact. If a young God finds his back to the wall and his hungry subjects looking to him for action, you can no longer bet cool heads will prevail.

This young God is at an age where he's likely to still be in power when you raise your families, unless a coup were to dispatch him to the afterlife. I suspect this specter of his continued evil rule will be so because we haven't been able to make any real inroads into bringing North Korea into the modern world, since the end of open hostilities between the two Koreas in July of 1953. At this time it has been sixty-two years since the peace treaty was signed. To date there has been nothing peaceful about the relationship between North and South Korea or North Korea and the United States. Unfortunately you inherit this mess from my generation as I inherited it from my parent's generation.

Like it or not, you and I have to take all mad men seriously. Even in 2030 there'll be no shortage of people with the same world view as this currently youthful Korean leader. You can look to any continent in your time and find at least one. The tendency of people everywhere is to grow fatigued by a constant state of war or near-war; your generation will too. It's at these times you must be more vigilant than ever your nation doesn't make a misstep in its relationships with mad men or child Gods, a misstep which ends up in a nuclear holocaust. He has conventional nuclear weapons and growing ability to project them with missiles. He aspires to have thermonuclear weapons and intercontinental ballistic missiles (ICBM). The conventional nuclear weapons were a nightmare and the hydrogen bomb on an ICBM is a nightmare on steroids.

Altruism Or Competitive Advantage
The next time you see some millionaire/billionaire/trillionaire calling for laws to ban certain practices (the list is endless), consider this truism from the business world. Once I have mine, it's appealing and easy for me to support laws which bar you from getting yours. In fact, this has been one of the credos of the modern age. The minute I've made enough to take care of me

and mine, I begin to demand laws which prevent others from using the same tactics and path to success and prosperity which I enjoyed.

Often such efforts will be assigned some lofty sounding designation; don't be fooled. The heavily hyped designation may in fact be nothing more than an attempt to preserve the competitive advantage the party who has already arrived has been able to acquire for itself, while no such laws existed to prevent it. Simultaneously, the 'arrived' will use clever semantics, emotionalism, appeals to patriotism, and the promotion of even more self-serving laws to prevent later arrivals from competing with them for the new and lofty economic perch they've come to enjoy for themselves and their heirs.

Life Is A Moving Target

Life is a moving target for all of us! Just when you think you have it all dialed in, it moves again. As a child this infuriated me, because in those early years I naively figured if I could just get life dialed in the first time, it would be an easy road afterwards. I couldn't have been more wrong. Life is dynamic and not static; it changes more quickly than I can even write this sentence. While you sit there reading this paragraph, thousands of changes have taken place in your body at the cellular level. Multiply this concept by the seven billion or more people sharing the planet with you, and you get a sense of the magnitude of any single area of change taking place right this moment.

If you consider those seven billion discrete people, and then consider your own cells are only a minor part of the changes going on in all the people in all the world around you, you're going to see the deck in the card-game of life is re-shuffled too many times each day to latch onto some rigid framework for dealing with the pace of change. This is why your parents gave you values, morals, and other high ideals to guide you. Static maps which ignore changing roads will be of little use inside this kaleidoscope we call life. Broad guiding principles which once seemed senseless will become more reliable than you ever imagined, and once seemingly foolish heuristics will become the phrases you live by.

Of Course We Were Young Once

Here in my time, I routinely post pictures from my high school yearbooks regularly on my graduating class's webpage and on Facebook®. Inevitably, I'll get a comment from someone's grandchild or even a great-grandchild who is simply incredulous grandma or grandpa was ever young, athletic, or good-looking. One commenter said recently, "I can't believe my grandma was a hottie." Well, I knew her grandma, and she was a hottie.

I thought the same childish things about my own parents and grandparents. I suppose it's one of those truths every generation has to experience for itself. You too will age and grow old and your children and grandchildren will also marvel you were once as young as you are today. They will also wonder out loud about your existence before you became old, wrinkled, and gray. My Momma said this was, "…the natural order of things; kids have done it forever." The older I grow, the more accurate my Momma's simple phrase becomes.

As I've said to you before in these pages, you should live each phase of your life to its fullest. At every age you're going to encounter experiences which are pleasantly surprising; you're also going to encounter experiences which are unpleasantly surprising. You'll learn to live through them with equanimity, or you'll struggle endlessly to find some way to deal with them. I suggest acceptance of the inevitability of gaining years, but rejection of the growing old mindset which negatively affects so many in each generation, including my own.

What Makes Your Day

I made my monthly trip into the Los Angeles Metroplex today to pick up some items I'd bought from different machinery companies and an auction house. I had a very nice lunch at Panera® with my youngest daughter (Rachel) and my oldest grandchild (Katelynn), both grown women. The highlight of my day was hearing my youngest grandson, Ford; utter his new favorite word, "Ball."

It's funny how what it takes to make your day changes as you pass through this life. Each of you will discover in your time what really matters in life. The things which matter to you in your youth don't seem important at all, even as little as five years later. I challenge you while you're young, to work hard to figure out the people, places, and things which bring you joy. Once you find them, hang onto them at all costs.

In your youth you'll be sorely tempted to believe and then pursue the belief money is at the core of all happiness. Money is necessary to survive through having enough to eat, buy clothes, and provide shelter. What an old man like me misses are the things which no amount of money can buy. They include places and times which no longer exist, friends and family who are no longer alive, and the robust physical and mental health a young person takes for granted.

My Best Laid Plans

Please understand my best laid plans for life and business were just an elaborate and delusional list of things I considered critical to my anticipated undertakings. Once undertaken they never even came close to being critical, or for that matter, actually occurring in the real world. Our imaginations about what will be, seldom match the reality of what is. It's my suspicion it will be much the same in your time, unless you're just a great deal more insightful than I've been. This doesn't mean you shouldn't have plans and do your best to make them good; it just means you'll need to be flexible and learn to work with whatever life sends your way. It does no good to hold on tightly to a plan whose time has passed or whose time will never come.

This act of 'holding on' is akin to folks in my time who were inveterate Luddites and doggedly hung onto typewriters after personal computers entered the scene. They not only looked foolish, they eventually became anachronisms and found it hard to remain employed. In every field of human endeavor there's near-constant change (Black Swan Events). You'll need to adjust to this idea, or go become a hermit someplace where nothing ever changes. The other insight I can offer you here is you have to be ready to let go of things, or you can spend the rest of your life bemoaning lost yesterdays. I fight with this myself, but I've learned an outdated plan, no matter how brilliant or how much you've invested, is still an outdated plan.

One Percent Error

A great deal of my work in the field of organizational development has been devoted to watching and listening to other people's employees and/or volunteers. One of the recurring themes in organizational failure is related to how a simple misunderstanding can lead to eventual decline or outright collapse. This happens when the original misunderstanding is compounded again and again as people new to the organization are oriented and mentored by those who already possess the one percent error.

When people are new to an organization, the last thing they want is for anybody to think they are 1) slow-witted, 2) don't comprehend well, or 3) just can't come up to the required speed of the task. Consequently you'll almost never hear a new hire or new volunteer in their first months with an organization asking too many questions. You'll never hear one asking questions about the same issue over and over again regardless of how poorly they've grasped the concept. And so it is once they understand the concept 50 percent, 75 percent, even 90 percent, they're on their way to becoming another cog in the error-burdened organizational machine.

I visited Philadelphia Gear Company back in 1981. They make cogs, or more accurately they make gears; similar principals. I was there as a buyer, and the company I represented planned to spend $7,000,000 on gearboxes designed to routinely handle a million foot pounds of torque. I toured the entire facility and remain impressed to this day, thirty-four years later, with how important the meshing of the gears is. A minor error in the even the smallest interface can completely destroy the entire gear train and its housing.

I took this path down memory lane with you to make a point related to fit. An employee or volunteer with a 75 percent accurate understanding of your organization may be able to get by for a while. An employee with a 90 percent understanding of your organization may be able to get by for decades. But the day will come when, for all those various misfits (e.g., 50 percent, 75 percent, 90 percent, etc.), there is a point at which the movement of the organization will exceed the misfits ability to mesh, and they (depending on how critical they are to the mission) may in concert function to destroy the organization.

A good example is the acronym F.O.B. It's a term commonly used in logistics for shipping, trucking, air freighting, etc. I like to ask people working in companies where transportation is integral, and throwing this term around with me, if they can tell me what it means. I always tell them that I don't know the term and would appreciate their help. It never fails as many as six out of ten of my would-be mentors actually don't know what it means. This can be devastating and expensive in companies which are quoting freight rates to customers. The term most commonly is taken as meaning freight is Free On Board and indicates who will pay the freight and from what point. If I tell a client the items I've sold them are free on board at my business site they know any freight cost off the business site is at their expense.

Picture people baking your mother's best cookie recipe, and every time the recipe gets shared, they change the amount of, or forget an ingredient. It wouldn't be long before the cookies they're handing out and claiming to be made following your mother's recipe gained your mother an undeserved reputation as a terrible baker. Now, imagine a chemist mixing a critical formula and being unsure of the chemicals, their amounts, and the proper sequence in which they're to be added. If you're lucky there'd only be a bad batch to be discarded; if you're unlucky people, food supplies, or machinery will be impacted; people can die from such errors.

As I've aged I rely more and more on prescription drugs to keep the ravages of the years at bay. What would happen if the people formulating my medicine didn't know if they were supposed to add a microgram, a milligram, a gram, or a kilogram? What if a radiologist treating me for cancer didn't know the difference between a millimeter, a centimeter, and a meter? Now picture those kinds of errors multiplied with each new cadre of trainees as the earlier trainees (now the old hands) pass along their own misinformation or misunderstanding of the facts. You can easily see this is a nightmare; it's a nightmare unfolding in many organizations in the world today.

You can apply this axiom of error to any field. You'll regularly encounter religion, science, and politics in your life. I believe they can each easily fall victim to minor errors if they aren't caught early and dealt with forcefully. In time the unchallenged error leads to a new denomination, a new view in physics, or a new view interpreting old political axioms. Mind you, they're erroneous, but it can take centuries to turn error like this around, if ever. The next time you encounter any of these three fields and sense something is wrong, remember this writing.

There must be a constant battle on all levels within organizations to remain true to the original idea, process, recipe, or formula! If not, the one percent error has triumphed. I'm volunteering for the board of an organization right now which had previous managers who apparently didn't understand basic accounting, much less managerial accounting. What they were able to do was never bounce a check so the accounting would never be called into question. They also never underwent a true audit of their financial records. Unfortunately, it was impossible for this organization to accurately assess its financials and provide the board with answers at financially critical moments. Correcting these errors is expensive, time-consuming, and frustrating for everybody involved.

What did it take to begin to turn this organization around? First it took someone to say, "I don't understand this accounting you've given me," instead of nodding and pretending to understand. Second, after many attempts to explain the accounting, by the staff which was left behind after all the resignations or terminations, it took someone who actually did understand generally accepted accounting principles to say, "Your Emperor has no clothes." In other words, your accounting system isn't an accounting system at all, it's only a disjointed hodgepodge of accounts and numbers which none of you can explain completely. This of course angers people, but frequently pulling off the Band-Aid® is the only way to ever heal this kind of wound.

Once the lack of real accounting was acknowledged and ushered from the room, hope returned to all some solution could be found. Let me be clear, when hope returned, it arrived with some pain brought on by embarrassment for the board of trustees. These trustees suddenly saw it was because they'd really never seen the 100% solution themselves, they now looked somewhat foolish. So here's my lesson for you: if an organization you become part of has been living with the one percent error in any critical area for more than a year, you need to figure out how to take a day of what the military calls 'stand down time' and get everybody on the same page at the same time, while you still have an organization.

Here's a quick and dirty look at the math (with some rounding): Generation (G) 1) $100 \times .99 = 99$, G2) $99 \times .99 = 98.01$, G3) $98.01 \times .99 = 97.03$, G4) $97.03 \times .99 = 96.06$, G5) $96.06 \times .99 = 95.10$, G6) $95.10 \times .99 = 94.15$, G7) $94.15 \times .99 = 93.20$, G8) $93.20 \times .99 = 92.27$, G9) $92.97 \times .99 = 91.35$, G10) $91.35 \times .99 = 90.46$. Over ten generations, a nearly 10 percent error rate has been introduced using a deterioration rate of only 1 percent per generation. What if the deterioration rate in accuracy is 2 percent, 5 percent, 7 percent, etc.? What if there are multiple errors and not just one? This is why world-class organizations are so adamant new employees do it The Company Way, or not at all. This is why you'll need to demand the same unwavering adherence to the official recipe, formula, method, or process in your career.

Lessons Of The Vietnam War

Yesterday I was disheartened to hear on the news the Islamic terror group Al Qaeda is in fact now resurgent in many areas of the Middle East. Simultaneously another more dangerous group called ISIS is also rapidly rising. I was disheartened purely because of the success of the decentralized concepts of leadership emphasized originally by the late Islamic terrorist, Osama bin Laden. Over the years I thought I'd articulated the ideas bin Laden espoused well, but just because I understand them and can speak about them to others doesn't mean others understand them as I do. Apparently many in power haven't understood them at all. Our nation will continue to pay a terrible price for this lack of understanding.

There is this annoying fact present now which hangs around like a late-season fly, and I want to share it with you. The fact is the United States, after investing the blood of its young men and women, and the riches of its people, frequently decides disengagement is the best approach to take once an enemy shows initial signs of defeat. As a case in point, I heard late today Fallujah, Iraq has fallen into the hands of Al Qaeda. This nearly caused me to vomit from the realization of what we've thrown away there in terms of lives and wealth.

My generation has heard the name Fallujah mentioned in connection with dozens of dead United States Marines; many more times than I can recall! One time? Ten Times? A hundred Times? Maybe even a thousand times! This doesn't even take into account the brave young warriors left permanently disabled by their time in Fallujah. So, we took this city and the rest of Iraq, and then we walked away, dumping it in the hands of a weak and corrupt ally. Didn't we learn anything in Vietnam? Look at our nation's history! Look at your nation's history!

Please read this thoughtfully and go look at the history books for yourself with regard to your nation's decisions in Iraq and similar conflicts over the past three quarters of a century. By now you're in some way enslaved in this system as a taxpayer. It's a broken system I might add, where we expend both blood and treasure to win wars to make the world safe for democracy and then give our gains away to regimes unable or unwilling to hold them. No other military power in the history of the world has been this stupid, and it is stupidity, not ignorance. Ignorance would mean we didn't know better and had no previous guidance in the matter.

Your generation needs to do a better job in this area than the ones which have come before it. Your generation needs to be smarter than mine has been. You can't count on politicians to break this cycle of winning wars and then giving away the victory. Only rarely is it the blood of a politician or their child which is spilled in these wars. Politicians are married to the idea of telling you whatever lies they have to in order to be elected and then re-elected. This continues to be so in order they may go to the trough in Washington with the other political hogs, where the tax slaves foot all the bills.

Casualties Of War

A good friend a few years older than me served in the United States Army in Vietnam. Everyone was happy when he came home in one piece, but for all intents and purposes, he died there. It was years later before it caught up with him, but he truly perished in the jungles or rice paddies between Saigon and Pleiku. In Vietnam he experienced violence, mental illness, and hard drugs. When he came home, he pulled himself together and did his best to settle into a normal life. But those of us who knew him well saw a personality which see-sawed between enormous manic highs and violent emotional lows. There were times when he was the same ole boy we'd always known, but then he'd become a devil none of us could reconcile with the man we knew and loved. When the end came, I always suspected an overdose, but since it was weeks before they found his body, I'm not sure they ever determined the exact cause of death. I can tell you for a fact his combat experiences were a major contributing factor.

Fast forward thirty years, three wars, and a handful of police actions later, and I'm now aware of another young man. This one served as a United States Marine in Afghanistan. He completed two tours of duty there before coming home to his wife. I met him when he was a high school senior, and I was acting as a community volunteer for a scholastic competition. He seemed like an absolutely normal kid, was polite, and did his best to bring his A-game to the academic team. Eventually he graduated and went off to the Marine Corp, and I never gave it another thought. Not until his name showed up in the national news after stabbing his young wife to death and then going on a cross-country killing spree. Police officers in Texas finally managed to stop him. There are those who'll tell he died from bullet wounds inflicted by those officers. I can tell you for a fact his combat experiences were a major contributing factor.

As long as our nation, or any other nation, sends young people off to the horrors of war, there'll be casualties long after the battles end. You need to grasp the significance of this early in life and understand just as individuals pay a cost for their personal exposure to war, so does the society which sent them there. Some of your contemporaries will argue you or they lack personal responsibility related to the making of war, the victims among the enemy, and the victims among our own veterans and their families. These same arguments have been raised for as long as humankind has waged war, which is to say since the day Cain slew Abel outside the Garden of Eden. We've all had blood on our hands since then, and you'll have your share as well. Mentally ill, drug addicted, and homeless veterans are just the visible tip of the iceberg.

Always Arguing

Somewhere in these pages I've written about giving the jealous and the angry a wide berth. If you haven't run across it already, I can assure you there'll be plenty of words about them later. Let me add to those first two (e.g., jealous and angry), the argumentative. I'm not talking about the person who will upon occasion debate an issue with you, I'm talking about the person who seems to choose the contrarian approach, no matter what topic is raised.

When you're a child, you'll likely argue more than you will as you age. I think this comes from understanding how ineffective argument often is in trying to get other people to see things your way. Most of us eventually learn the truth of the old adage, "It's easier to catch flies with honey than with vinegar." Accordingly, we sweeten our words and there are now fewer of them when we speak.

In matters of religion there's an adage which says some people "...are always arguing but never able to come to knowledge of the truth." While taking it somewhat out of context here, it still seems like sound advice with regard to those who only want to exchange verbal fisticuffs and aren't interested in what the truth of the matter may be.

If you desire a peaceful life, avoid the chronically argumentative. If you're dating someone or simply working on a friendship, pay serious attention to this matter. People claiming to want to be your friend, who seem to relish their role as one of the constantly argumentative, may have deep-seated mental problems you can't fix. You don't have to and I don't even encourage you to waste your time trying!

When considering a long-term relationship with a potential friend or marital partner, ask yourself if you want to spend this much time going forward in fruitless argument. As the opinionated young person I've already seen you to be, there'll be the tendency to argue as though it's a game. In its proper venue it is in fact a game and one of those venues is law, another is politics, and yet another is religion. Leaving constant argument out of friendship and marriage is wisdom.

Good Intentions

Your great-grandmother always told me, "The road to Hell is paved with good intentions." In other words, good intentions alone aren't enough to keep you out of trouble. Accordingly I've set a personal goal of walking an additional twenty minutes each day this year, and so far so good. However, I'm concerned my new-found habit of killing off some of the last of the holiday candies is not aiding me in developing better heart health.

A lack of self-discipline has cost me greater success in a lot of the areas I had good intentions about. Those chocolates will soon be gone, and I have the discipline in this area to get back on track. I was in my forties before I realized if I worked on a goal even as little as twenty minutes a day, given enough time I could achieve remarkable things. For instance, most of the writing in this book was done in thirty-minute intervals.

Good intentions alone will never be enough. To achieve anything in your life worth achieving, you'll need to put forth a steady disciplined effort. This year my goal is to improve my Spanish. So I bought Rosetta Stone and have set aside twenty minutes each day to work on it as well. Will I become fully proficient? I'm not sure, but I can't help but become more fluent.

You're each gifted in many ways. The greatest danger in this package of giftedness is to think giftedness alone will be enough. In my youth I believed giftedness alone was enough. Consequently, I didn't apply myself to my studies as I should have. Even your giftedness with a large dose of good intentions won't be enough. Only by disciplining yourself and your giftedness toward specific goals, will you ever achieve your fullest potential.

You're The Parent

As I assume you already know, I fathered four children and managed to raise three of them to adulthood. This past Sunday it's been seventeen years since my son, your uncle, took his life at the age of seventeen years and five months. I say all of this not to depress you, but to point out I have a 75 percent success rate in raising responsible adults and good citizens. Your mother, my daughter, is a wonderful, strong woman and is successful in her own right. Those qualities didn't just happen because your grandmother and I decided to allow her to raise herself. It happened because the two of us decided before your mother was born we'd raise her to be well-behaved, well-educated, and God-fearing.

I've said all of that to say this: when I encounter parents out in public with small children who are actually in charge of their parents, I worry for all of us. I encouraged your mother to break this kind of defiance in you. Only time will tell how effective it was. By now know the children I'm referring to. It's the four-year old screaming at the top of her lungs and slapping her mother's face because she isn't getting her way. Or the two year-old who is kicking his mom's shins because she's trying to keep him from running all over the store by holding onto his hand. There are infinite variations of these scenarios, and you'll see them all in your time. The irony is in both of the instances I observed this week; the mother gave me a pleading look as if to say, "S/He is not usually like this."

It's possible this wasn't their normal behavior. What with fatigue and an overdose of sugar, I can see this happening. But with some of these behaviors, it's hard for me to buy into the idea these are model children the rest of the time. I understand we live in a steadily deteriorating society. That's why it's all the more important mothers *and* fathers *and* grandparents are involved in making sure their kids don't end up in the state penitentiary. I hear words coming from the mouths of five year-olds which would have once only come from the mouths of hardened sailors. This didn't happen by accident, and it can't be stopped with good intentions alone. In the matter of your own offspring, you're their parent, you're not their buddy. Act like a parent and discipline your child before it's too late.

If you decide to bring children (my great-grandchildren) into this world, only do so if you're willing to take responsibility for them and their proper upbringing. Otherwise, forego children and buy an expensive dog to pour your affections out on. When you produce children, they have the potential to be either a blessing or a curse to their parents, their family, and the society they live in. You owe it to yourself and the rest of the folks sharing the planet with you and your progeny, to work hard to produce responsible citizens. If you don't, and millions of others don't, the end of the society you live in can't be far ahead. My children, even my dead son, have been the source of extraordinary blessings to me; may yours be the same to you.

Your Work Or Your Life

Here's another view of an important topic I wrote about earlier regarding work/life balance. I've frequently heard it said no man lying on his death bed ever bemoaned the fact he hadn't spent enough time at the office. I suspect this goes for people whose office is a field, a construction site, a mine, a classroom, or an oil field. Everyone who wasn't born into great wealth has to work in order to survive. The mistake I've made, and so have many others like me, is to mistake our work for our life. I admit I saw this error at age fifty and have been doing my best since then to fight against the urge to spend more of my life at work.

I don't know how your generation will view work and workaholism, but I do hope you can find a better work/life balance many years earlier than I did. You only have so many days allotted to you, and when those are gone they can't be called back and there are no do-overs. I believe you've experienced a more stable and balanced childhood than I did, and this can't help but instill a better view of how you should live out your days. Balancing work, family, friendships, faith, civic duty, and personal time are habits developed across a lifetime, so be busy about developing good habits and passing them on to your own children someday.

For most of us, this problem of workaholism was born in our childhoods as a result of experiencing poverty and the fear of being sucked back into that morass. For others, it's the instant gratification which comes from doing your job and doing it well; in knowing you're the expert and this is your domain. For those who helm great organizations or world-changing projects, it's the buzz they get from feeling omnipotent, almost god-like. Regardless of which of these narcotics is chosen, or why, the addiction is the same. In time a workaholic can find themselves happier at work than anywhere else in the world. Trust me on this, all your relationships will suffer for it.

What I saw, and what countless others see, either in a moment of insight or upon their deathbeds, is we have to make the same kind of investment in having a life away from the office as we do at work. This was extremely awkward and difficult for me at first, yet over time it becomes more comfortable and easy. The most embarrassing part is the realization the greatest organization you may ever helm, or the greatest project you may ever head up, or the place where you feel you are the world's leading knowledge area expert, will move right along without your constant attention once you leave, become permanently disabled, or drop dead.

A Thief At Your Side

I was listening to an accountant last night detail some financial security measures he was recommending to the Board of Trustees I serve on for our local cemetery district. Having been a senior manager for more than thirty years, I've encountered my share of embezzlers, and in at least one case helped prosecute two of them and send them to federal prison.

The accountant was sharing with us a money-skimming scam he'd recently encountered which had pulled $30,000 out of one small company in about eighteen months. The details are too long and convoluted to go into here, even if I were willing to share them. I continue to marvel at how clever people are, and how quickly they can spot a flaw to be exploited, when it comes to stealing.

If you are now, or someday should become a business owner or manager, here's a word of advice which comes from my own experience. In every case I've ran across where someone seriously damaged an organization financially by embezzling, it was someone regarded as "…one of the most trusted employees we have." It wasn't some seedy character who had somehow gotten on-board; it was a most-trusted associate.

When you start watching for potential embezzlers, look for a thief at your side before you look very far away.

Relearning The Lessons of War

When enough years have passed where a nation feels it can easily begin to denigrate its former allies from some previous war effort, then this same nation will be forced to relearn the lessons of that war all over again. This happens because the collective national memory of the cost in blood and treasure has faded.

In your time, if you should take part in any type of online historical forum or chat room, you'll be able to see the virulence growing between various peoples (e.g., Brits, Americans, French, Dutch, Canadians, Australians, Vietnamese, Iraqis, Afghanistanis, etc.) who once fought beside one another in some other war.

Pray your generation doesn't fall into this "denigration of former allies" trap, and you or your children aren't forced to pay the price again in blood, which a previous generation has already paid. Be slow to speak ill of a former ally; you never know when you'll need them again.

The Road To Ruin

Your mother will tell you, and it may well come as a surprise to you, despite my hard exterior, I'm as compassionate a person as you're likely to encounter. Yet there are definite limitations to my compassion. This is why I wonder why people who can afford $200 tennis shoes, expensive tattoos, $600 cell phones, and drink $7-a-cup specialty coffee need to be propped up with subsidized food stamps, housing, and medical care. No society in history has gone down the path our nation is currently on, for any appreciable period of time, and ever come back. I'm troubled by the entitled generation mentality of my time.

The wide-spread culture involving the "You owe me a living" mindset can't be sustained indefinitely. There are sad times in my days when I'm not sure you kids will inherit anything like the America I've known. An entitlement mindset is anathema to a capitalist system, and capitalism made this nation great. The biggest obstacle to turning the entitlement mindset around is as more and more people see their entitled neighbors have their basic needs met regularly and also see them pick up some of life's perquisites. The perks were formerly reserved to only the hardest workers. This makes people witnessing this inequity less likely to try and pull themselves out of their financial morass and more likely to adopt an entitlement mindset of their own.

One social scientist I read regularly claims an idea which is taking hold among a larger segment of our society is, "If he ain't workin', and he's gettin' by, why should I go out and bust my hump every day and end up with less than he has." He and I believe it's the underlying reason more and more people are drifting into relying on government aid and why the current economic recovery of 2015 seems to be crippling along. The combined mindsets of a dependence on government and a need for class warfare have never produced a good outcome; they won't produce a good outcome this time either.

As far as I can see at this time, while you're still a child, your parents are doing their best to raise you to be a responsible person and a responsible citizen. You've been raised to take responsibility for yourself and the things you do. In time I expect this mindset to transfer to *you* taking responsibility for your adult life, your marriage, your children, your career, and so forth. I fully accept there can be injuries or illnesses which can destroy one's ability to care for oneself and trigger the need for the public to step in and assist one of its members. But short of this level of illness or injury, I expect each of you to become responsible adults and look at the end of your own arm for the first helping hand.

CHAPTER 8

Define Your Own Success

I find it puzzling so many people I've met feel they have to evaluate the success of their life by comparing it to the lives of others. You should strongly consider whether this is the reason so many people seem to be unhappy with their lives. Individual concepts of what comprises success are as varied and unique as the individual. The metric of my time won't be the metric in yours.

Constantly comparing your life to others is inviting dissatisfaction unless you by chance find a doppelganger that happens to see the world exactly as you do. I believe God made each of us unique. This further implies you'll need to be uniquely satisfied. The dissatisfaction arises when you accept the lie others, no matter how well meaning, should define your success and the resultant happiness which comes with it.

Is Anyone Following You

When I was working my way through graduate school and later post graduate work, the concept of 'Leadership' was all the buzz.

I suppose I've read in depth at least ten or twelve different theories on Leadership. Some I like better than others; some I don't care for at all. The topic is an important one, especially since my favored forms of leadership seem to be in such short supply these days.

I have to credit my Daddy Bill Neeley, who only managed to finish the third grade, with an important view he shared with me many years ago when I was a young pastor. One day while he was visiting me, and I was working alone on some church construction, he said, "Son, you're only the leader if people are following you." He was of course referring to me being there and working alone. As I ponder daddy's insight about leaders, I have to admit his view is at least as weighty as those of many academics who've written extensively on the subject.

Consider well what your ancestor said. People will flock to you for a variety of reasons, and sometimes this will make you believe you're their leader. You'll even believe those who flock to you are actually under your leadership. The reality of people's momentary adulation is not the same as people being willing to engage in a dynamic effort requiring them to step away from the path they were on previously and follow you with their lives. Be careful you don't mistake wealth, looks, dynamism, or having a crowd around for indicators of leadership; it happens a lot.

Bitterness And Bitter People

I'm contemplative at the start of each December, even more so than usual. At that time of the year I know in about thirty days, the year will come to an end and a new one will begin. Perhaps it's a more reflective time for all of us as we look at what we've come through in the past year and consider what lies ahead. In any case, one of the things I see more clearly and painfully in this sixty-first year of my life is how many people are angry or habitually negative; my Momma would've called them bitter. I can't speak to all those who might fall into this category, but I can address what I see or have seen among my own acquaintance.

I've noticed a growing negativism or anger from some over the years, but in the past five to ten years, it's become a steady state of personality for a few people I know. This bitterness is a poison so strong, I've moved away from those people, and in some cases completely cut off relationships. To people who've known me a lifetime, this seems out of character and even excessively harsh. However, it's a simple effort at self-preservation. I find those who've judged themselves as having lived failed lives seem to be the most bitter amongst us. I've certainly not accomplished all I set out to as a teen, but I've accomplished much of it, and I can't blame anyone else for my failures; I can't justify any personal bitterness in those areas.

You'll experience storms, rain, pain, and some exceedingly bitter disappointments during your lifetime. You have the option to pick yourself up and fight on, in an effort to redeem whatever resources you have left, or you can sit down and spew out venom on the parade which passes you by. The habitually bitter people I find most distressing are those who once showed great promise but have now lost the ability to see anything good in even the most beauteous and uplifting moments in their lives, or the lives of others. Beware of those people, as you would beware of a poisonous serpent. While a serpent can wound or kill the body, constant exposure to the habitually bitter man or woman can wound or kill the soul.

There Are No Winners Here

I've learned to take what divorced people say about their ex-spouses with a large grain of salt; you should too. I reached this conclusion after encountering a few of those terrible ex-spouses and being stunned when they turned out to be regular people, leading regular lives, and possessing regular outlooks. Some of them were very nice, and we became friends. Most did not have two heads. Most did not have horns and a pointy tail. Most didn't even breathe fire when they spoke.

All of us know divorced couples; some of us are divorced. For you who've never yet met any, be slow to judge one or both parties when you finally have your first encounter. Inevitably you'll discover in most, but not all cases, both parties are people similar to you and/or your spouse, it's just one day they started to come apart. The rift eventually became impossible to repair, and they both moved on, some more smoothly than others.

There's a great deal of prejudice against divorced parties. Who did what to whom, and who did it first, becomes a matter of constant speculation from friends, families, and onlookers. It's even worse when others feel the need to take sides. This only prolongs everyone's agony and likely loses friendships all around. It's hard to make true friends; it's foolish to lose them over a matter you may not fully comprehend.

Be supportive of both parties. Don't feed the flames of anger—they're strong enough already. Be available but not nosey, and in a year or two or five, life will find its own natural rhythm again and the parade will move on. Make a conscious effort to fairly evaluate divorced people if you must. Rarely are divorces the one-sided affairs some people want to simplify them down to. It took two to tango, it took two to create a marriage, and it also took two to create a divorce; there are no winners there.

Other Career Paths

When I was a kid, authority figures told my generation any American child could grow up to be the president of the United States. In retrospect, and with the benefit of six decades of hindsight, I can tell you this is total hogwash. Look at who becomes president in this country, or any first-world country for that matter. Look at the connections they had. Consider the people with huge resources who championed them, and notice the hyper-elite pathway which unfolded before them throughout their lives. Not only can the average American child *not* grow up to be president, only the most infinitesimal fraction of the most elite of Americans has a shot at it.

If you come from a wealthy family, have well-connected friends, and can afford to go to one of the handful of universities which seem to routinely turn out senators, congressmen, and presidents, there remains hope for your dream of running the country. For all its efforts to appear egalitarian, the United States has its royalty as much as any European Duchy. Occasionally, someone beats the odds and creates a new national royal bloodline (e.g., Roosevelt, Kennedy, Bush, etc.). If you find yourself as part of the other 99.9999 percent of the populace, you might want to think about other career paths.

Handle The Family Business with Care

Businesses can and do crash all the time. Every once in a while, "All the king's horses and all the king's men can't put Humpty

Dumpty together again." When you become part of an organization, my advice is to handle your business with care. Some of you'll become part of family-owned businesses. There are no guarantees just because your family (or your spouse's family) has owned a business for a generation or more, the organization will survive to be passed on to you in your time or your children in theirs. If you have designs on the family business, start working with great care early in your career to assure it survives your tenure, so it can then be passed on to your children's children.

Your War On Poverty

We've been waging the war on poverty in this country since I was a child. To date, we've invested more than $200 trillion dollars on this war. This means for sixty years we've been engaged in an ongoing battle but never gained a victory. I fear you'll be waging the war on poverty in this country when I'm dead and gone. You'll be paying for the war on poverty in your time, just as we did in mine. The irony is we've more impoverished people in America today than when we launched the war all those trillions of dollars ago. Something is wrong with our war on poverty. I hope your generation can do a better job than mine has done in figuring it out, fighting said war, and actually winning this war.

It's very possible our failure to win the war on poverty is related to the fact that instead of firing bullets at the real problems in this war, my generation indiscriminately threw money at them. If the problem intensified, we increased the amount of money we poured on it. Here in 2015 we don't have any new ideas, and we don't have any new source of money to create a surge against poverty as the people funding the war are now themselves likely to become casualties. It seems from this side the best your generation can hope for may be peaceful coexistence with poverty in America.

The only problem I see with this approach is peaceful coexistence with poverty will at some point become impossible because it's economically unsustainable. Programs designed to care for the impoverished continue to accelerate their demand for dollars and threaten to consume the entire budget of the United States if allowed to go unchecked. My generation has lit a fuse on a bomb which will explode on your generation. I worry this will result in economic collapse and chaos or a philosophical class war which eventually boils over into a shooting war. I wish neither scenario on you and hope your generation's efforts surpass the efforts of my own.

Twilight Of Civility

I came across the works of Konrad Lorenz years ago when I first became interested in the behavioral sciences. I don't know exactly how many books he wrote, but I read two of them, *King Solomon's Ring* and *On Aggression*, and I was particularly affected by the latter. I promise to get around to reading his work *Man Meets Dog* soon. Lorenz had earned a medical degree by the time he was twenty-five-years old. I suspect his time in the German army, and his four years as a Russian prisoner of war, provided him with lots of opportunity to observe the best and worst in human behavior. I'm not sure what caused him to drift into behavioral sciences, but while he shared a Nobel Prize in Physiology or Medicine in 1973, he had already begun to apply himself in the emerging field of ethology decades before.

On Aggression deals with Lorenz's observations of animal behavior and how they have evolved a series of actions and reactions (responses and behaviors, I believe he called them) so every encounter between animals didn't have to end in a fight to the death. He would later extrapolate, quite effectively I think, how human beings have evolved manners, aggression-inhibiting behaviors and responses so every negative encounter between humans doesn't have to end in death. In my time I see a fading of both manners and these positive behaviors Lorenz wrote about, which were intended to make it possible for people to co-exist in a civil society. To get a feel for what lies ahead in your time if this trend continues, you must think back to the brutish human behavior of the Dark Ages. This twilight of civility is a regression, regardless of the pretty face we try to paint on it as a society.

Lorenz became a member of the National Socialist Party (Nazis) and held many of their extreme views when he went into the German Army as a physician. After the war and those years as a prisoner of war, Lorenz spoke often of his regret at having joined the Nazi Party and having any role in the horror it unleashed upon the world. I suspect having seen the very worst of human behavior on a firsthand basis couldn't help but impact Lorenz's views about human hostility and our need to keep it under control if we're to survive as a race. I worry at times my own era hasn't produced similar men and women who could speak to present generations about the need for ongoing efforts to stem aggression and retain manners. That we came away from WWII managing not to destroy one another is a tribute to the time and its' people. I hope in your time, people can do the same.

Blessed To Live In America

As I write this, here in the United States it is our national day of Thanksgiving. One of the things I am always thankful for is to have been born and raised in this very prosperous country. You too have been born here and regardless of your present station in life, you'd be much worse off in almost every other country on the planet.

In some instances, you'll encounter folks here in the States who feel they haven't been treated fairly or gotten their share of the American Dream. I suppose this is a natural reaction and everyone's entitled to their feelings. It's not a perfect country, but it's still a place of immense opportunity for each of you.

It's a bitter irony the people in the United States who feel less than thankful today, rarely have the opportunity to see how the rest of the world lives. Few of the world's developed countries compare favorably to ours. Whereas most people on this planet still survive on less than one dollar a day, the average American is forced to get by on a hundred dollars a day or more.

If you can find nothing else today which lifts your spirits when you contemplate your life and condition, consider what I've just written, even if it's not Thanksgiving Day as you read this. It will make it a little easier to accept your many blessings on a regular day and the wonderful gift it is to be alive and living in the United States of America. If this doesn't work, you can always visit the third world for some perspective.

Slower To Judgment

The more I learn and know, the harder it is to make sweeping statements or broad judgments. My hope is this will eventually be the same for you. This is not to say I want you to abandon concepts of right and wrong. It's more accurate to say I understand there are a whole host of factors which go into what's right and wrong, and it frequently takes God-like omniscience to know all the factors and sort them out fairly.

As a young person, you have limited life-experience from which to draw upon. As the years pass, you'll encounter more and more real-life circumstances which will better inform your maturing judgments. This should be true in every area of your life. So it might be fairer to say it won't be so much it's harder for you to judge an issue, so much as it takes longer to arrive at a valid judgment, due to there being more factors you'll then be willing to consider.

Your Holiday Traditions

Yesterday I was blessed to spend the day with two of my daughters and their families. Those families in 2013 included each of you grandchildren. In case you've forgotten that day, or were too young to recall, we enjoyed our annual Christmas fiesta with all sorts of homemade Mexican dishes and party games. I'm certain this combination puzzles outsiders, but each family evolves its own holiday traditions, and I staunchly support engaging in ours annually, regardless of how odd it may seem to onlookers.

As you begin your own family, you'll be able to create your own set of traditions. You may go traditional and you may even add holidays your family never celebrated. It's okay to hang onto to the traditions of the family of your birth, but it's certainly appropriate to incorporate those of your spouse and their family as well. Or you can set out to create a whole new set of traditions which are distinctly your own, and which will be excellent too! The one tradition to never let go of is loving your family. If loving your family fades, the others won't matter.

Wisdom Is Justified Of All Her Children

It occurs to me, as I sit here contemplating my family's migration from Oklahoma to California during the Dust Bowl era, there are far more stories out there than just the one of the mythical Joads of *Grapes of Wrath* fame. Poverty was widespread and not just the purview of a few. In contemplating these same migrants, education and wisdom are not the same things. I know many people, who regard themselves as 'Steinbeck's Okies', who do their best to condense the entire experience down to the events surrounding Steinbeck's one fictional family. Thankfully, many voices have risen over the years and attempted to tell some of the other stories. Never forget your Neeley ancestors have their own story! Never forget there were educated Okies, there were wise Okies, and in a few instances there were educated and wise Okies.

I'm one of those people who revere John Steinbeck for his ability to write in such a way it challenged the status quo ante and forced people who were comfortable into a state of discomfort as they considered the plight of their fellow human beings. Our family came to California short on education but long on wisdom. As a child I wasn't necessarily proud of this; as an old man who devoted more than twenty-five years of his life to the pursuit of education, I see much greater value in received wisdom than I did as a boy. Education has taught us about poverty, class warfare, and social injustice. Wisdom comes only when we know how to use our education to effectively and efficiently address these important issues. Knee-jerk reactions don't fix long-term problems. Knee-jerk reactions are not the products of wisdom.

In fact, knee-jerk reactions, in attempting to deal with issues of social justice, are notorious for creating newer, more, and more-deeply complex problems than the ones initially faced. I've spent a significant chunk of my post-grad and post-doc years addressing the inequities of the social system in

America. What I've seen time and again is education can murder wisdom, and academic solutions have often created more problems than they solved. If you want to fix the problems of the poor, go live among the poor and get to know their problems. If you want to fix the problems of Native Americans, go live among Native Americans and get to know their problems. Gain wisdom to go along with whatever education you have. It won't benefit your soul or your nation for you to be educated if you are not equally wise.

The professional academics, which have planted their feet firmly in the areas of research, statistics, and targeted outcomes, will publish prodigiously and present their papers well, all the while staying in a plush hotel, eating three solid meals a day (not including catered coffee breaks) and happily rubbing elbows with other cognizanti. They'll go on to fill the cherished seats at many of our higher institutions of learning. They'll be called as expert witnesses before committees of local, state, and federal legislatures. They'll be appointed by both Democrat and Republican Presidents to places of honor and authority. This won't change! Yet at the end of the day, you still have to wonder if they'll be able to demonstrate the differences between education and wisdom, which so many of those old Okies understood so well.

Values Can't Be Legislated

The question arises frequently in my time about whether or not the United States is a declining political power. I doubt it can long remain stagnant in this instance and will have moved one way or the other by your majority. However, if the question is asked with regard to the United States military, I'd have to say "No." American warriors remain the best tactical fighting force in the world, and we spend billions to assure them the best in weaponry. From a strategic standpoint, their effectiveness has and always will be tempered by politics. If you doubt this, look at every war they've fought since World War II, beginning with Korea and leading up to the time of this writing in 2015.

If the question about declining power is asked with regard to the citizens of the United States, I'd be a little slower to say "No." Let me state here flatly my generation isn't composed of the same caliber of Americans my Momma and Daddy's generation was. If you look at the educational systems, the religious systems, the governmental systems, and any other key barometers of what makes nations great, we appear to be in steep decline. I believe this decline stems from the fact while a government can tax and arm its military with certainty, it cannot legislate study habits, religious devotion, or involvement in the political life of the nation. Consequently, unless the people themselves once again embrace these ideals, the decline will continue.

In another ten or fifteen years, when you're fully grown, it will either have improved decidedly or the America prior generations of your ancestors enjoyed, will only be a memory. You can't do a great deal about the behavior of your fellow citizens. You can however determine what kind of American you'll be and influence what kind of Americans your offspring will be. If you have poor study habits, lackadaisical religious piety, and are uninvolved in the political life of your country, you can't very well expect things to get better in those areas. The challenge is to discipline you in these small matters. If you do this, the larger matters you confront in life won't be nearly as daunting as they will be for your contemporaries.

The Stupidity Pit

I've quit trying to guess just how stupid people can be. When I think I've finally found the bottom of the stupidity pit, someone comes along and shows me it goes even deeper than I ever believed possible.

Healing Your Own Anger

In my journey with regard to anger, I had to decide I wanted to be free from it; there's an insidious pleasure/power dichotomy at work in our anger. I had to identify old hurts which were the sources of the anger. I had to figure out what acts or efforts it would take to pry these sources of anger from my heart. Finally, I had to practice these acts or efforts every day. With shallow hurts and the resultant shallow anger, they moved on almost immediately. With deep hurts and the resulting deep anger, it took months or even years to finally be free; some I'm still working on. I see ridding oneself of anger as fully worth the effort. The Bible talks about this kind of anger as bitterness and then says, "Bitterness eateth like a canker (cancer)." There are already enough sources of cancer out there without creating and internalizing your own.

Even though you'll have experienced relatively affluent lifestyles as compared to the other seven billion people on the planet, I've no doubt there'll be deep disappointments and even anger which comes up in your time from wrongs, real or imagined. I hope these are relatively minor episodes or losses and they don't come to cripple your life; and cripple your life they will if you ignore them. If they aren't minor episodes, and they are crippling, you must make a greater effort than ever before to rid your life of these deadly parasites. Otherwise, the anger they breed will fester like a dirty wound, and left untreated will smell foul to those around you, all the while slowly poisoning you and the ones you love, and stealing the life you might've had.

You Might Want To Catch Up First

As the years have passed I've learned if you haven't seen someone in a while, it's always good to catch up before you get into any serious conversations. With the passage of time, we all change. Each of us endures different life experiences and makes different choices, which results in very different outcomes, one from another.

I've seen some very bitter and acrimonious exchanges between former old friends who haven't talked in decades; class reunion weekends are notorious for events like this. It stems from our desire for time to have just stood still while we were apart and everything could be just as it was when we last were together. Unfortunately, you're not Peter Pan, and it isn't Neverland you live in. Things can change and they can change dramatically.

The poor boy you knew in your childhood is now a multimillionaire with a trucking line and vacation homes in Colorado and Hawaii. The mousey little girl you worked with in the sewing factory during the summer between your junior and senior year, went on to law school and is now a respected trial lawyer. The athlete you were sure was going to the pros, contracted multiple sclerosis and now struggles to lead as normal a life as possible. The class beauty married well, but caught her husband in bed with the children's nanny. She's now an aging and bitter divorcee.

I hope you get the picture and are mature enough to see the wisdom. We all change over the years. Some change in minor ways, some in major ways, but we all change. I've passed my fortieth class reunion and the fiftieth isn't far off. The mere act of living through this many years will change each of us, no matter how hard we try to remain the same. If you want people to give you the benefit of the doubt regarding your life's outcome, you'll need to be willing to do the same for others.

Take the time to catch up first before you begin to speak your mind.

He's An Original

Despite all you'll hear in your time about self-made men or women, generations are built upon the generations before them. You need to recognize someone springing to prominence or amassing wealth is the product of many small factors which appeared in past generations, and the current beneficiary can only honestly claim to be responsible for a small part of it; he or she did not pre-select the genetic mix or ethnic heritage. I do concede it matters what you do with the genetic mix and ethnic heritage; some use it better than others.

Every once in a while, the random contributions from sixteen great-great-grandparents comes together in a remarkable way, and of course we as the recipients, assure ourselves the outcome is our original creation. It's original, and yet it's not. If you make the mistake of buying into this foolishness, you run the risk of taking on a load of arrogance along with the erroneous notion you're an auto-genetic original. You didn't create yourself from whole cloth, but you can take credit for what you did with it.

Circumspection

I've been building things (e.g., houses, engines, pumps, compressors, refineries, churches, office buildings, gas plants, etc.) since I was a young adult. One of the first things I learned is the damage I can cause in thirty seconds, either deliberately or accidentally, can take thirty hours and thousands of dollars to repair. Consequently, a man of my temperamental persuasion has learned to take greater care than the average person might in how I handle every situation in life. I approach problems more slowly now than I did in my twentieth year. I look at problems from many different angles. I mentally try on multiple solutions to the problem before I raise a hand to begin any type of physical action. I ruminate on the whole issue for another day or two, sometimes even another week.

This has caused some people to wonder if I'm not too bright. It's caused others to speculate I'm hesitant to act because I don't know what I'm doing. I've often been accused of over-thinking a problem. To my credit, I've taken on some extremely sophisticated tasks, completed them in the time promised, and done so profitably. As you grow older, you'll have vast amounts of life experience to draw upon which allows you to consider problems in the abstract, whereas when you're young you might wade in with a sledgehammer and a wrecking bar, and let the chips lay where they fall. It's this hasty, ill-conceived latter approach which has branded in me the wisdom to follow the more circumspect route I now favor in old age. Think quickly, then move slowly, but move deliberately.

I Was Misquoted

I find it infuriating both major political parties and their operatives now seem to find it completely acceptable to lie repeatedly about specific issues or events, and when later confronted with their words, blithely claim they were taken out of context. "I was misquoted" seems to be the standard explanation for a politician making the mistake of speaking their true mind and then crawfishing out of their prior moment of spoken honesty, when later called to task for it.

As you grow up, and it falls to you to take some share of the political reigns of this country, you must listen carefully to what politicians say and place their words firmly in your memory. This will be so because so many of them are tempted to speak off the cuff and then later, when the political winds shift or their evil intent is exposed, they'll look you in the eye (or the television camera) and say it's you who are mistaken or they'll claim their enemies have misquoted them. If you listened and you remember, you won't be easily taken in by this common form of deception.

The difference in my mind between a single lie, or a single misquote and a pattern of lying, or claiming one was misquoted, is the latter brands the person sporting the established pattern of lying, as a chronic liar. It would have once been unacceptable for politicians caught in outright lies to appear and deny their bald-faced lie. Political partisanship is such we're now all too willing to allow this behavior and forgive our guy but condemn the liar from the other party. The lies of a Democrat politician, or the lies of a Republican politician, are still lies and should not be acceptable to any citizen.

Let Sleeping Dogs Lie

The advice I was given by my Momma as a child, "Let sleeping dogs lie," is still sound advice today. Unless you're looking for a foot race or a fight, it's far better to quietly pass by some potentially dangerous people or situations than to draw attention to yourself and have them engage you. You don't have to involve yourself in potentially dangerous life situations.

There are people who are truly vexatious to the human spirit and are best avoided on a regular basis. Some of them are potentially dangerous to your physical well-being. I've mentioned them throughout these pages. Because a significant percentage of your fellow human beings are mentally ill, cognitively damaged, or just downright mean, in your time be careful you don't needlessly become their victim.

As you age you'll gain the wisdom about which dogs to pet and which dogs to avoid. You've a right to self-preservation, to be left alone, and to your own piece of mind. Yet having those rights and exercising them are two different matters. Fight your tendencies toward arrogance and too much involvement in every battle which comes along; you will be rewarded with a more peaceful life.

As you read these words, you're young and full of the sense of your own rightness and invincibility. If you live long enough, those personal magnifications about your abilities and limitations will pass due to real-life experience. I know this sounds confusing, and it is. You're on the cusp of passing from childhood into young adulthood, and your parents and I have shielded you from life's harsher realities, as all good parents do. Time will make these issues less confusing.

Letting sleeping dogs lie is one of the ways you can avoid some of life's certain dustups. If you are of a nature to look forward to skirmishes, don't fret, there'll be plenty of times when you've no choice but to fight. You should rest when you can, eat and drink when you can, and love and laugh when you can. But as far as creating fight or flight scenarios goes, avoid them whenever you can.

Announced Faith Or No Faith

In your time I fully expect the forces for freedom from religion will have a louder voice in American society than those for freedom of religion. I can already vaguely see the outline of coming events in the years ahead, and it doesn't look pretty. I can't imagine the level this will have grown to as you live out these next ten or fifteen years of your young life. Regardless, look around you right now as you read this for the first time and see if people of faith, any faith, are not being pressured regularly by those of no faith to remain silent regarding their beliefs. Freedom of religion is your right as an American; don't let it go without a fight! This is a sleeping dog worth taking on.

You can decide whether to go ahead and bite your tongue regarding your faith and your religious beliefs in an effort to get along and remain politically correct. You can silently tell God how much you love him. Of course it risks God openly rejecting you at the one moment in time when you'll need his recognition and acceptance the most, but only you can make this decision to openly express your faith. The faith you possess can't be my faith, it can't be your parent's faith, and it can't even be your Pastor's faith. Faith and its open expression must be your own or not at all. No one can live it out for you and no one can take your place should you be called upon to die for it.

CHAPTER 9

May Your Future Be Bright

I had lunch recently with a friend who spent many years as a newspaper reporter and editor. We talked at length about how the business has changed and the disturbing shallowness of what now passes for news. We ended the lunch hour talking about feeling old and out of touch with our times. I suspect a good many of our contemporaries feel the same things.

Though he is ten or twelve years my junior, he expressed some of the same frustrations I have with what catches and holds the attention of the masses these days. I suppose as one ages, it's natural to long for times past. I keep praying the future emerging before me is really as bright as the government, the media, and all the advertisers would have me believe.

This desire doesn't spring from my need for a longer better life, so much as it does out of my concern for you and your parents. I came of age in what I think will come to be regarded as America's Golden Era. As a Baby Boomer born after America had perfected its military might, I lived in a world where our nation was politically and economically stable, or at least as stable as any nation in the history of the world has ever been.

I enjoyed the highest average standard of living anywhere in the world at the time. This doesn't mean I was wealthy or from the wealthy class. It does mean even poor Americans lived better than the vast majority of people on this planet. I've no way to see or predict your future; here in 2015 it doesn't look so great for you right now. So my prayer is you'll have brighter days.

For America to return to greatness, you and your generation will have to rise and assert yourselves in ways Americans haven't had to do in many years. The days when you and your peers could coast along on this nation's former industrial and military might have passed. It will require mental and physical toughness; I believe you possess those qualities and hope your peers possess them, as well.

Your Ancestors Are Watching

Your Neeley great-grandparents were farmworkers who rose before daylight to go to the fields. Eventually my Momma took a job as a maid for a hotel. She did so because the work was steady and year round. My Daddy remained a farmworker all his working days. There were six siblings in my family, and we each learned early to be responsible to get ourselves up, make something to eat, and arrive to school or work on time. I remember my Momma being very supportive of us getting an education, but I don't recall her being particularly involved in our homework or learning. I attribute this low degree of direct involvement to her feelings of inferiority over her eighth-grade education. In retrospect my parents were similar to the parents of my peers in our small farming community; to my knowledge none of them were well-educated.

My Daddy had even less education than my Momma, as he was sent to help his dad in the fields after his third year of schooling. Through no fault of his own, he was never able to return to school, and it had a definite negative impact on many areas of his life and the lives of his family. However, all six of us grew up to be responsible citizens and taxpayers, and Daddy taught us to be honest by his example. None of us ended up in prison, and only one of us ever had anything bad said about him on television, in books, or in the newspaper. So when I look at all the privilege and opportunity given to children in the past fifty years, I'm at a loss to explain to you why this nation isn't a much better place today than it was when hardworking and poorly educated people did the best they could to raise a family. I have high expectations of you and your children; your ancestors are watching.

Enemies Of Excellence

I've worked with a lot of machinery over the years, and a large part of this has been high-precision machinery. Whereas a lot of mechanical devices will tolerate sloppiness and still function, precision machinery requires precision fits and limited tolerances; high standards are the norm. It's not uncommon for various standards to be used for exact comparison of lengths, widths, angles, mass, density, and so forth. If in your time, you're to be successful in fields requiring this type of precision, horseshoe close won't work, and sloppy standards will always result in damage over time.

There is an inordinate amount of time spent by a millwright or any other craftsman in checking his fit of the work before him. If the craftsman is diligent, the work in question can enjoy a nearly indeterminate number of years of usefulness. If the craftsman is sloppy, the work he undertakes can be reduced to a pile of rubble in a matter of seconds. Most great accomplishments in life require a similar devotion to high standards. It's not enough to talk about how much you admire standards if you ignore them in your work or your personal development.

If you wish to 'be', you must find the standards for the type of being you aspire to and then pursue them doggedly, devotedly, daily, and with single-minded determination. When others suggest you don't have to be so careful in your efforts to perfectly mimic this sort of being, even if it offends them, you must remain true to the standards. I once read a pound of raw steel was worth a few cents, a pound of nails made from the steel was worth a dollar, but a pound of precision watch springs made from the same pound of steel would be worth thousands of dollars. Your goal, and the precision it takes to reach it, have inherent value. Do you want to produce nails or watch springs?

As you craft your being, you'll have essentially the same material and tools as everyone else. The outcome of your life is sometimes negatively impacted by other people or circumstances, but by and far it really does come down to the standards you adopt, your effort to meet its precise parameters, and your determination not to just get close or accept being sloppy. The world around you is full of those who once had all the material and tools, but chose poor standards, executed the standards haphazardly, or took an on again, off again attitude about their daily pursuit. Those with failed lives will be your worst critics, but only if you choose to excel.

Great Swelling Words

Being experienced in a field is not something lightly dismissed. I find it cavalier when I see politicians running for office and blithely dismissing their lack of experience in business, the military, or for that matter any other real form of non-elected leadership. You should be highly skeptical of politicians making similar claims in your time. Being a great teller of tall tales is an admirable quality in some quarters; I don't find it admirable in politicians.

Your country will need men and women of substance to helm the nation. I fear we've come to the era predicted in the Bible when our leaders can only muster "...great swelling words." I also fear politicians will become so expert at manipulating you; your task of sorting out the cow from the manure will be exceedingly difficult. Even if this becomes so, don't let yourself be captured by mere words when substance is what's required.

Managing Dilemmas

It occurred to me earlier this week, while observing a manager and one of her employees having a discussion about how to best solve a problem, one of the biggest challenges management faces is dealing with people who are mentally ill. Now, this isn't news! Research over the past thirty years has shown routinely that on any given day, somewhere between 17% - 20% of the American workforce is suffering with mental illness. This is a problem in workplaces worldwide. I don't expect its resolution by the time you fully inherit this society.

The problem of mental illness in the workplace becomes truly dangerous when you're no longer dealing with run-of-the-mill depression and other garden variety neuroses, but with employees and/or managers who suffer from full-blown psychoses or personality disorders. Compound this with the increasing use of alcohol and hard drugs and you have a recipe for disaster.

Basic management training generally doesn't spend much time on this topic, and even if it did, the field is far from what we generally train managers for. This leaves the average manager in way over their head and does nothing to address the real problem.

If you should become a business owner or manager, even in a small capacity, you'll encounter workers with mental health issues. You'll run into workers who are addicted to drugs and/or alcohol, and at times you'll come across the full complement we'd call 'dual diagnoses' in one person. I certainly want you to be compassionate and supportive of them, but only if you can do so safely. I don't want you to fool yourself into thinking you're Freud or Jung, and you're going to sort this person out. Mental illnesses and addictions, even mild ones, are serious business and best left in the hands of people who have received specialized training in handling these matters.

In my time there's rarely a week which goes by where I don't hear of some sort of workplace assault or murder. Assaults, batteries, rapes, robberies, and murders by coworkers are a fact of life worldwide; don't be naïve. When times get as tough as they are right now, and as they will be again at some point in your time, these behaviors multiply geometrically. Usually it's some sort of personality conflict, power struggle, termination, or reprimand which sets them off. Regardless of the triggering event, people end up being severely injured or killed by coworkers. I'm confident in well over 90 percent of these attacks, the mental health and/or addictions of the attacker play a key role.

As an undergrad I first wanted to be a psychologist and took sixty semester units in the field before I changed my mind about the personal utility of windmill jousting and other similarly hopeless causes. Years later in graduate school, and as a doctoral student, I took significantly more courses in managing people and dealing with the psychological aspects of mental health and drug-addiction dilemmas in the workplace. Even with all this said, and keeping a loaded handgun in my top desk drawer over the years, I've had some very dangerous moments with drug-addicted, mentally ill, or downright criminal employees who didn't want to cooperate, didn't want to get along with coworkers, and frankly didn't care what I, the law, or the company wanted, either.

Difficult People

I'd venture to say there are few things in life tougher to deal with than difficult people. I understand death and taxes are constants and constantly annoying. Difficult people are like having a pebble in your shoe; they're simultaneously annoying while they're injuring you. I wish I could assure you that you won't have to deal with difficult people, because you will. They come in all shapes, sizes, political persuasions, financial strata, races, and religious beliefs. No one race or ethnicity has this to themselves; difficult people come from every known demographic.

Some will be difficult because they're given to rudeness; others because they're close-minded or their views are different than your own. If you can learn to handle them, you'll be seen as a genius at getting along with people. As I look back over my life and the toll dealing with difficult people has taken on my mental, physical, and spiritual health, I'd advise you to steer clear of them entirely whenever possible. You don't owe anyone the opportunity to destroy your peace of mind for even a minute, and difficult people often seem to delight in being difficult.

Anything But Golden

As you age, be careful you don't spend so much time agonizing over the state of the nation you lose track of the state of your children, grandchildren, and great-grandchildren. Politicians will come and go. Philosophies will wax and wane. Economies will rise and fall. Less about the ongoing ways of the world will change than some people out there would try to convince you they will.

Truthfully, the only things you're likely to have much impact on is your household and progeny. It will do you or your family little good if your favorite president is in office, but little Billy is doing nine to fifteen at Soledad, Attica, or Marion. It won't matter a whit if all the Adams, Roosevelts, Kennedys, Bushes, and Clintons have been president if you have to visit your children or your grandchildren in a prison, an insane asylum or the local cemetery.

Get these priorities straight; if you don't, your golden years will be anything but golden!

Protected To Death

Yesterday I was reading an account of the kind of bravery exemplified by young men who had died during battles in past wars. I'm convinced there was an era where this sort of behavior would've been easily exhibited by most, if not all, young men who entered military service in any major country around the world. However, in my lifetime I've seen progressive nations like the United States work overtime to tamp down the early boisterous behavior of young men which would later have led to exhibitions of moral courage, courageous physical acts, bold leadership, and yes, maybe even injury and death. There remain numerous exceptions, but not nearly as numerous as they once would've been. It's not I see us having turned our sons and grandsons into girlie men, so much as it is in our effort to shield and protect our sons from an increasingly dangerous society; we've instead suffocated the burgeoning roots of the young acorn which would've become a mighty oak.

I offer a single example, though I could think of several others, and given the opportunity so will you. I've watched children being ferried directly from their homes to their schoolyard gate and back again, even though it was only a couple of blocks. Their families have assured them it's far too dangerous to walk to school or ride the bus, since there are so many bullies, rapists, child molesters, kidnappers, terrorists, and general no-accounts in the world. It's also deemed too dangerous to go to the park or play in the street, as previous generations did. This may well be, but in response to all this spare time spent in the house or in afterschool programs, enterprising types found a readymade market for expanded television advertising opportunities and ever more realistic video games. Children became shut-ins and/or couch potatoes, developed obesity, Type 2 diabetes, and killer gaming skills before they were twelve years of age. We now have a primary developmental epidemic which is unobvious and a secondary physical epidemic that is obvious.

Your grandmother and I were married twenty-seven years and raised four children; three daughters and one son. They played in the yard, went to visit friends, had schoolyard fights, suffered scrapes and scratches, caught head lice and childhood illnesses, and in short were pretty much typical kids of the era. They had all the maladies every other kid of their generation had, and three of them came through it pretty well. The fourth, your Uncle Ryan, committed suicide when he was seventeen. Even though his death was tragic and is something I've never gotten over, I wouldn't change the fact he and your mother were expected to be part of the rough and tumble of the everyday life of our small rural community. Any child can be struck down by disease, be it physical or mental. But every child can be socially crippled for a lifetime if his or her parents, or their society, work hard enough at it. It's possible we're now protecting children to death. So, be careful how you raise your children; helicopter parenting can be as deadly as a disease.

The Distant Future Belongs To Graduates

Here are some sobering words from an old academic to his grandkids. As I write this we're at the time of the year when valedictorians, salutatorians, and other commencement speakers everywhere wax philosophical about the future. Youth worldwide are suddenly burdened with the knowledge they're expected to go out immediately and make a difference. I'm not from this school of thought and recognize while there are some very young people who've had remarkable accomplishments, most of the time it comes from people who've finished growing up, completed their education, and stopped believing all those silly things commencement speakers told them. Don't spend the next decade beating yourself up because you aren't a millionaire/billionaire/trillionaire yet.

If you're graduating from high school, you're either headed for the military, a minimum-wage job, or some form of higher education. If you have the right connections, you may be going into the family business or an apprenticeship somewhere. Even though you carry some of my genes, 99.9999 percent of you are not going to be rocking the world anytime soon. This is the good news! Any of us who've lived a life understand within six months you'll be so stunned by the adult world you never knew existed, you'll wish you were back in high school. My advice is to go out, embrace your new scary life, and figure out how to navigate the world. In a few years, you'll have gained your footing and be ready to rock the planet.

If you're graduating from college, the news is not quite as rosy as for those graduating from high school. You've been navigating the semi-adult world now for four or five or even six years. You did it on a combination of scholarships, student loans, part-time jobs, and the charity of friends and family. This charity will soon end in most cases. After all, you're much better educated now than many of your benefactors, and they expect you to go out, get a high-paying job, and behave as a responsible adult. They'll be disappointed with you when neither of those things happens soon enough for their liking. You making a determined effort to succeed will lessen their disappointment.

Here's my parting advice to you on this issue: on high school graduation day, hug every one of your friends tightly, because you'll never see most of them again. If you're graduating from college, look around during the ceremony and drink it all in— the music, noise, color, pageantry, crowd, and speakers. This day is what you've been working for all these years. Don't be in such a hurry to get on with your dragon-slaying you fail to soak in this moment. Be sure to thank your mom, dad, siblings, other relatives, and friends; it's been more of a team effort than you'll fully understand for at least twenty years. Then when you toss your mortar board into the air, realize childhood or your young adulthood is sailing away with it, and the future lies just ahead of you.

Beware The Politician Who Would Save You

I routinely ponder the political class in various nations, but always spend the most time considering political elites here in the States. When I was a child, we respected politicians and saw them as men and women working to make the world a better place for all of us. Fast-forward to 2015, and the American political class seems to be composed almost entirely of people whose sole objective is re-election and the continuation of their life as political royalty. I'm told by some, mine is a very negative view; others tell me it's an accurate one.

I hear more and more of the people I interact with voice their anger at what they're beginning to see as an elitist ruling class, which is solidly in the pocket of big business. They also recognize each political party now engages in this kind of elitist behavior. Yet almost universally those same angry people are at a loss as to how to change the present system. At some point in the near future, a single man or woman will catalyze this latent anger and turn it into a powerful political force. We have to pray the chosen man or woman is more along the lines of Gandhi than of Hitler.

Beware of this undercurrent as you reach maturity and don't be deceived by those who would feign change while actually supporting political royalty's status quo ante. At the same time, you need to be aware of the strong appeal throughout history of fascism when folks become dissatisfied with their political ruling classes. Fascists are simply the other side of the same evil coin, where the rule of a political elite composed of the many is replaced by the rule of a political elite composed of a few. The principles of this republic are sound, and you should strive to embrace and uphold them at every opportunity.

The United States Constitution and the Bill of Rights will remain under fire your entire lifetime. This is so because those political elites of which I speak seek to carve out for themselves, their families, and their political cronies a better deal than the one promised to all of us by these documents. Resist the urge to feel you're better than other Americans; you deserve no more, but you certainly don't deserve any less. Any man, woman, or organization which seeks to diminish or take your Constitutional Rights away is your enemy, not your friend, regardless of how cleverly they may couch the taking! Recognize these deceivers and their deception and treat them as such.

On The Lookout For Stupid

Stupidity is at epidemic proportions in our society in my time. If you observe human behavior for any length of time, I feel you'd arrive at this conclusion sooner or later. I suspect this will be worse in twenty years, not better. I actually don't mind people being stupid as long as it only affects them. I do mind when it begins to affect me, my family, or my friends. Yes, this is a very selfish and self-serving view, but I'm of the mind self-interest has to be given a fairly high priority in life if you're to have and keep your life instead of being disadvantaged or enslaved.

I'm on the road a lot, and as a consequence of all this time spent on our nation's highways and byways, I see a lot of driving. Some of it's stupid driving. A recent and growing trend here in California is increasingly for people to pass other cars on the shoulder. If there are two lanes, I have no problem with this. But when they use the parking lane, the bike lane, or the unpaved shoulder of a road to get past a dozen cars ahead of them, they're stupid. I don't mind them being stupid, but I do mind them risking my life by deciding they're exempt from safe driving habits and have a right to put the rest of us at risk.

We see this passing on the shoulder phenomenon routinely on city streets these days. Yesterday, while I was waiting in a traffic backup of almost thirty miles due to construction on the interstate, I suddenly noticed a young woman driving past us on the shoulder at a high rate of speed. I would understand if it was an emergency, but it wasn't. We were almost at the end of the queue and I saw her a few miles ahead, observing the posted speed limit. Yes, she beat lots of other drivers in her quest to get to the head of the line, but how many people's lives and property did she risk traveling fifty miles per hour on that dirt shoulder?

You'll have examples of your own from your time, but pedestrians have been killed in California by drivers passing on the shoulder when they lost control and went into the bike lane or jumped up on the curb. Pedestrians or bicyclists, a ton and a half of automobile, and someone suffering from terminal stupidity makes a terrible mix. "You can't fix stupid" is a popular comedy line from this time. You can raise your children not to be stupid, you can make a point of not behaving stupidly yourself, and you can encourage everyone you know to behave in a responsible manner. After that it's all about keeping your eyes open and being on the lookout for stupid.

I'm of the opinion stupid people behaving in a stupid manner have killed a lot of innocent people who were guilty of nothing more than believing everyone around them was going to behave responsibly. You need to absolutely put this mindset out of your head. People—even well-meaning people—behave stupidly at times; some folks make a habit of it. The name we give to people who believe this routine practice of stupidity is not true, and also believe everyone is looking out for everyone else's welfare as much as they are looking out for their own, is 'victim'. None of you were raised to be victims, but if you grow less vigilant when it comes to the ways of the stupid, it may literally be your funeral.

Help Or Sympathy

I discovered forty years ago, very early in my years of public ministry, most of the people who ask for help in changing some situation in their lives don't truly want help changing. In my opinion, people who want help changing have come to the place where they either can't or won't go on with their life the way it currently is. Until people reach this point of deep dissatisfaction, they're either searching for an easy way out of a hard situation, or they just want someone to hear them out and sympathize. My daughter raised you and I'm hoping some of my philosophy will have trickled down to you.

People who know me well know I'm willing to hear your story a couple of times and offer counsel before I either tell you to stop bothering me, or I begin to avoid you or refuse to accept calls or requests for my time. I know some people regard this as mean on my part. But I finally realized decades back that I'm not doing anyone any good listening to them go on about a problem for the twentieth time when we identified and agreed on a course of corrective action eighteen hearings ago. Besides this, it grows wearying at some point to cover the same ground again and again and again.

I encourage you to be sympathetic to all people who need and can benefit from your sympathy and the other good things such sympathy will elicit. I'll equally encourage you to end the flow of sympathy immediately if it becomes obvious the people you're being sympathetic to have become addicted to the sweet feeling other people's sympathy bathes them in. At this point it should be obvious they've decided to stay in this place rather than take on the painful work of healing and moving on with their lives. This doesn't mean you have a right to be mean to them if they reject your help, but it also doesn't mean you have to apologize when it's time for you to move on.

Affliction

Edith Schaeffer, the wife of Francis Schaeffer, one of my favorite theologians, wrote a book regarding the issues surrounding affliction many years ago, after her husband's death due to lymphoma. It seems for each of us as we grow older there are afflictions of one sort or another. In some cases they're physical; in others they're mental or spiritual.

Schaeffer posited the ending years of our lives are times which can be great periods of personal growth, specifically because of the presence of affliction and the personal issues it raises in the suffering. I've decided since there doesn't appear to be any way to avoid growing old, other than dying young; I'm going to make the best of this I can. I suggest each of you do the same if you're afflicted in some way.

As I write this, none of you are afflicted with any kind of terminal health issues which I'm aware of. So let me be quick to tell you all the afflictions in life are not just related to your physical health. You'll each encounter multiple challenges of one sort or another which will affect your lives. They'll either become obstacles you grow through and overcome, or they'll be insurmountable obstacles which stymy you in achieving your fullest personal potential.

Only a masochist wishes for affliction. Consequently, I don't expect any mentally healthy person to embrace affliction on any scale or for any purpose. The word 'enduring' comes to mind here, rather than the word 'embracing'. My best counsel to you then is you endure whatever afflictions life may bring your way in the best fashion you can muster, and when you find some way to make these an opportunity for physical, mental, or spiritual growth, you do so to the full extent of your powers.

Giving Less And More

There comes a point in the cycle of aging where most Americans my age own more 'stuff' than they can possibly use. But instead of the mass of this stuff dwindling as we routinely make trip after trip to the Goodwill, Salvation Army, or Saint Vincent De Paul thrift shops, the core of it is refreshed two or three times a year as those we love try to display their love in their birthday, anniversary, and holiday gifting. Consequently, the piles just grow.

Let me propose a couple of alternatives for your gifting. First, if you absolutely feel the need to give a tangible gift to aging parents, grandparents, or friends, do your best to make certain it's really something they need, want, or at least can make use of. Second, consider donating to a worthy charity in their name; I personally like UNICEF's child vaccination programs, Heifer International®, Samaritan's Purse®, ECHO®, Re-surge®, and Smile Train®. I feel equally blessed when they receive a gift in my name. In fact I feel better than when I receive a gift directly and know I don't need it and will have to figure out how to store it.

I don't believe I'm the only aging parent or grandparent in America who still has last year's gift cards in my wallet, wrapped birthday, anniversary, or Christmas packages lying on a bed in the back room, or still need to take the skydiving class which was assumed to be on my personal list of unfulfilled dreams. Special days are certainly about giving, but it doesn't necessarily have to be direct giving to have the intended impact. If you've nothing to offer but your heart, that's certainly more than enough.

In closing, I want you to love your family with all your heart. Yes, I do know if you love your family the natural urge will be to share your love in the form of tangible gifts; it's human nature and unlikely to be entirely avoided. But in your time, understand it's okay to show you love people by doing good works in their names or even in their memory. There comes a time when most of us in the first world have more than we can ever use. It's the memories of gifts given and received, and more importantly the love which birthed those gifts, which lives on in our hearts and memories forever.

Self-reliance

There's a study making the rounds right now which goes into detail about the high percentage of millennials (young people between the ages of 18-34) in the United States who earn in excess of $72,000 USD per year, still relying on their parents to help them pay for basic necessities such as food, clothing, utilities, cellphone bills, etc. I am stunned by this because while I'd consider it normal to assist your offspring in gaining a launch in life, at some point the idea is the offspring will become self-sufficient. Mind you, I'm not talking about parents making little gifts to their kids; I'm referring to parents being expected to continue supporting a child who is earning roughly the equivalent of two hundred and forty times the yearly income of the average human being on this planet. In my opinion, there's something wrong with this picture.

Another survey asserts the average citizen of the United States facing imminent retirement has less than $30,000 USD in their retirement fund. This of course begs the question as to whether or not parents who should've been saving for their golden years have been shoveling money into dependent children, who will themselves, be unable to help those same parents when retirement becomes a physical necessity. In many ways this appears to me to be yet another breakdown of the familial contract between generations. I don't know how it will all play out, but from this angle it looks fairly dire. It also suggests an economic collapse of some sort is out there for both parents and offspring once the parents are no longer earning and the children have built a lifestyle they can no longer sustain.

Your Neeley grandparents raised six children in the best fashion they could. We were poor; factually we were impoverished. Six children were far beyond the economic means of my parents and most other parents of their generation, for that matter. But without reliable contraception, large families were the norm. Besides, if you lived on your own farm, more children meant more field hands when my momma and daddy were born. It's ironic we live in relatively prosperous times, and we've learned to control our reproduction to the degree most folks in the United States today have had an active and reliable means to determine the size of their family for decades, yet some form of poverty may yet be in their futures. I've never favored abortion and still don't. But until you can control your reproduction using the many means other than abortion, which are readily available, it's impossible to control your economic destiny. Reckless spending confounds the old birth control benefit equation, no matter one's position on abortion.

How bizarre this equation has become when people who prospered by controlling the size of their families are now consumed by the pursuit of excess by their own children. An excess

I might add, most parents now similarly situated taught those same children. The expectations they gave their children regarding an entitlement to an ever increasing standard of living may yet destroy them all. The first study I mentioned noted more of this same group of young adults was saving for a vacation than saving for the down-payment on a first home. Clearly the so-called American Dream has been supplanted in these minds by a dream of accelerating luxury and self-indulgence. I want to make this clear to you: Learning to be self-reliant will place you in a position to help yourself, help others, and prepare for your own future. Self-reliance will also make it possible for you to earn enough so you can have not only life's basic necessities, but also an economic surplus which can be used for those nice vacations and other perquisites this confused generation now pursues to its own destruction.

Evil And Evil Men
The path of evil men is sadly all too predictable. This won't change in the years after I pass on, and it will still be so in your time. The outcome here in 2015 of the recent Russian-forced Crimean election should surprise no one since it was a predictable evil. It should especially surprise none of those people my age who are old enough to have lived through the cold war. I'm praying this is a single isolated incident and not just the first shot in a protracted war of annexation by the Russians, a war you would unfortunately inherit.

Awakening The Sleeper
With each new generation entering the workforce, there is great concern they'll not ever measure up to past generations. Expect some of this mindset from people as you reach adulthood.

While I agree certain members of each new generation seem difficult to engage at times, I'm pleasantly surprised to find once engaged they catch on quickly and are excited to learn skills or ideas which don't have anything to do with a video game, a tweet, or an Internet posting. I suspect older generations before mine had some of the same reservations about my generation. I've suggested to clients they don't write off succeeding generations too soon.

Once the younger generation grasps a concept, they can bring tools and ideas to bear on problems, which an old man like me just barely understands. I know older generations are always concerned about those which follow, if for no other reason than concerns about who'll pay for Social Security and Medicare. While I'm not saying unequivocally not to worry at all, I am saying if you'll make the effort to help your kids get their feet under them, they can do just fine. You'll be tempted to these same negative thoughts as you age. Be generous with the young people who follow you; you'll need them just as every generation needs the one which precedes it and the one which follows it.

A Tipping Point

Some of us openly wonder if we've passed the point of no return when it comes to being able to deal with the major social issues which plague the United States of America. A popular book from a few years back was entitled *The Tipping Point* and it went on at length about different phenomenon which quietly built to a tipping point, and something or someone was forever changed by the tipping. I have a sense there are several issues in our society which have been labeled intractable for so long, they have gone from being intractable to being permanent. Some tipping, and the change it brings, is good. But a new status quo ante, made up entirely of problems which we were trying to change has failed. This doesn't bode well for our long-term survival.

I spent part of my career working in a cancer treatment center and later in hospice. I've seen far too many people go from having a treatable condition, with which they were able to live for many years, to being told they've passed some invisible tipping point where the treatments will no longer stop the disease. When this happens, death is a foregone conclusion, and it's only a question of how it will unfold over the coming weeks or months. I don't think anybody knows for sure if the United States has hit such a tipping point yet. For your sake, I certainly hope it hasn't. However, it does appear it's time for some desperate measures to be exercised toward reversing current negative trends in social issues.

The alternatives to stopping the decline include more social decay, rising crime rates, rising illegitimacy rates, ballooning taxes, bankrupt cities, more people on food stamps, and ever greater stratification of the haves and the have-nots in this society. Furthermore, we can expect rising crime rates, further coarsening behavior at every level of society to the point any form of behavior will be accepted, and a general sense people can just do as they please and everything will be fine. Options for dealing with these alternatives include building more jailhouses, more courthouses, and fewer schoolhouses. In fact, those options are so abhorrent to me (I hope to you as well) we should be startled and re-energized in our efforts to turn this tide.

By the time you read this, I may well be gone from this earth. In your time you'll be faced with problems which may seem as desperate as those we now face. The way you live your life has an impact on the world around you. Standing up for what you know to be right will have an impact on the society you live in. I know from personal experience there's a cost to be paid for standing up, but there is an even bigger and far greater cost to sitting by idly while the world you love slowly erodes from evil men or evil times. Many times throughout history, tipping points have been arrived at and avoided, based solely on one individual's willingness to step up or to stand up and be counted.

When Happiness Arrives

The harder I pursued happiness, the further it seemed to slip out of my reach. But I discovered if I ignored the idea of pursuing happiness for happiness's sake and went about making the most of my life, one day I looked around and discovered happiness had arrived.

Older & Wiser

I marvel at how different the aged version of people I've known for years is from the young version of those same people. All the things they said in their youth they'd do when they grew old, they've backed away from sharply. All the things they said in their youth they'd never do when they grew old, they've firmly embraced.

My parents were clearly older and wiser than me in this area, and they simply smiled as I pontificated about how magnificently my own life would play out. As a result of those annoying encounters with my parents, let me smilingly assure you, as you too pontificate, you and all the members of your magnificent generation will eventually grow old, just as every generation before it has. The uninformed and inaccurate comments you make right now about your own aging will eventually become fully informed and 100 percent accurate by the passage of years.

The challenge before you now is to capture life's wisdom as best you can and as early in your years as possible. Once in possession of such wisdom, apply it often and liberally. No human being can ever be expected to pass through life without their arrogance tripping them up at least once or twice or five hundred times. Therefore, your goal now should be to avoid making a habit of shooting crows you're later forced to eat.

CHAPTER 10

Raising Trees And Children

I was admiring my newest tree this morning. This will be its third full summer and it's shaping up nicely. I was struck by the state of my tree and one exactly like it which I gave away at the same time I planted my own. I gave it as a gift, and I gave the owner advice on how to plant and train it. By pure chance I saw his tree this afternoon, and it's about half the size of my own and oddly misshapen. He told me he's moved it twice in the past eighteen months. It's clear from the way the tree is shaping up he ignored my advice about pruning and shaping it. I refused to allow the fellow who prunes my mature trees to undertake the shaping of the young tree. However, the owner of the tree I gifted has not only moved it repeatedly, he's also allowed the same pruner I use on mature trees to get hold of his young tree.

While thinking about these two trees, I began thinking about children. I saw some corollaries, and they've very much been on my mind throughout the day. Trees and children both need to be planted with care in a place where they get the optimum amount of all the elements they require to flourish. Move them too often in their youth, and it sets them back every time. Deprive them of the elements they need, and they'll never achieve their full potential. When it comes to trees and children, I don't mind letting someone else trim off the excess foliage from time to time. But I never let them prune or shape my young trees, and I never allowed anyone else to prune or shape my children. After all, I'm the one who'll have to live with this tree and those kids when they're grown.

Finally, I'm okay with others helping me tend the tree through the week with watering, fertilizing, and other menial tasks which can be explicitly dictated and carried out easily by almost any responsible adult. But when it comes to who'll shape the structure of the tree and how it will appear to the entire world when it's grown, it's up to me and me alone. In the same vein, I'm okay with babysitters, nannies, *au pairs*, mentors, coaches, teachers, and live-in nurses as long as the parents are regularly about the necessary heavy lifting of instilling values, morals, discipline, work ethics, love, and faith. One day soon I'll be through shaping this young tree, and the limbs I saved and trained to create a powerful scaffold won't be endangered in the least when it comes time for wind, rain, heat, cold, or needed prunings.

Be Careful Out There

I read two disturbing articles last weekend which raised all sorts of questions about danger, adventure, and personal responsibility. One was the story of a climber on Mt. Everest a few years back, who became unable to walk, sat down in a cave, and froze over the course of twenty or so hours. The drama there was provided as dozens of climbers hiked past him on their trek to the top that day; most did not even pause. The one who did pause was later blamed for not doing more to save this climber's life. The second article was about the horrific fire of a balloon gondola, where the occupants either fell or were forced to jump from the basket. You may have seen pictures of the latter in your history books or however they record such things in your time. As I recall there are also pictures of the dead climber eternally on Mt. Everest, as well.

Here's where my stories overlap with these other two. For many years I hunted, fished, spelunked, explored, rock and mountain climbed, and most of the time I did it alone. I know altitude sickness, and I know what falling cornice ice the size of railroad boxcars looks like up close and personal. I accepted the fact when I was young and adventurous; under those circumstances you often get no second chance. The two times I nearly froze to death; once while hunting and once while mountain climbing and both times hit by sudden blizzards), my brother-in-law, Randal Moss, my adventuring partner all those years, refused to leave me to die. If I'd been alone I wouldn't be here to write this. The Everest climber was on his third trip up Everest and decided to go it alone his final climb. This was a personal choice, and in hindsight, a bad one. His parents said he'd accepted this possibility, and I respect him for it; each person makes their own decisions and must bear the price of the outcomes.

With regard to the balloon incident, I'm sure the two female passengers (both university-level athletes) had signed consent forms, and the pilot that day had twenty years of experience. Let me digress here for a moment and say I once regularly guided backpacking trips into one of our national forests. You encounter all types of people wanting to experience the outdoors when you do this. There range is from those who are completely competent to those who are completely incompetent. One of the common things they each received was my pre-trip warning about going into the great outdoors. Specifically I warned of heat, cold, rain, snow, sun, wind, two-legged predators, bears, poisonous snakes, mountain lions, poison oak, sprains, strains, bone breaks, heart attacks, and even death. I never had anyone refuse to sign the consent form and turn back after those warnings; some of them should've.

I see people in my time as being almost completely unprepared for the real world because television, movies, and the Internet have given almost everyone a false sense of security about just how difficult it is to injure and/or kill one of us human beings and just how tough the average person is. We die very easily. For my part, I always like to go to wilderness areas specifically because it allows you to test yourself with small hope of rescue; it isn't Disneyworld®. In wilderness areas there'll be no helicopter rescues in the event you're even found in time to benefit from one. Be careful about overestimating your own abilities, as young people often do. Let's get back to those two young ladies, signing those consent forms. They'd probably seen so many neat balloon launches on television this seemed like a great way to see the countryside with zero risk. Tragically, they underestimated the risk and likely consented to their own deaths in writing.

What are the take-aways for you? The Everest climber fully knew he risked death on the mountain because he'd been in the so-called 'death zone' twice previously; he'd no doubt seen some of the nearly two-hundred corpses of climbers on Everest, which cannot be retrieved. He deserves the lion's share of the blame for his own demise, though others, including Sir Edmund Hillary, have attempted to blame climbers who passed him by that day. Conversely, my heart goes out to these young women who were likely out on their first balloon ride and climbed in with no thought of the potential for death on their minds. As a consequence, witnesses will now be haunted for the rest of their lives by memories of their piteous and terrified screams for help as the basket became a fiery inferno. As for the balloon pilot, he was from the same school of thought and experience as the dead climber and me; he fully knew the risks and took them willingly.

Our Debt To Future Generations

Twice today toddlers bundled up in their car seats waved and smiled at me at traffic lights. Both were little girls, and both had enormous smiles. As I drove off I felt my heart lifted by the innocence of the second child, and suddenly the thought hit me, "What does my generation owe these children?" As I write these pages, Ford, my youngest grandchild, is about their age now. So an even more pertinent question would be, "What do I owe my grandchildren?" I think it's a serious topic which deserves serious and continued consideration by every generation. The time for this kind of thinking will eventually be at hand for you as well.

My generation has amassed so much public and private debt even the most optimistic economists I know aren't hopeful about ever getting debt down to livable levels for you children, short of an economic collapse and restart. As a boy coming from a very poor family, I remember distinctly my Momma and Daddy not wanting to be a burden to their children in their old age. When they came to the end of their working years, they didn't want to have unpaid debt which would follow them to the grave. They didn't have much, but they didn't leave their children burdened with unpaid debts. What happened to values like this? I don't know, and I apologize to you now for what my generation has done.

In my time it seems we can't rack up enough debt, public or private, fast enough to satisfy some of the people in this country. I've heard members of my generation speak disparagingly about the future of their progeny and how "They'll just have to make do." As poor as your great-grandparents were, I never once heard an idea like this come from their mouths. Those words of my contemporaries are certainly counter to the age-old idea of laying up wealth to pass along to future generations. However, when it comes to creating debt to pass along to our children and grandchildren, we've got it down pat.

If, by the time you read this, the economy we created has made your life miserable, know I fought against it, and I'm sorry!

No Special Training Required

The move toward specialization in our society has been proceeding steadily throughout my lifetime and shows no signs of abating in my sixtieth year. When I was a boy, generalists were the rule and specialists were the exception in almost every field. However, as knowledge proliferated it became impossible in many fields to stay abreast of the explosion of new information and specializations became the norm. Many of the medical procedures my general practitioner physician performed in his office in the '50s, '60s, '70s, and '80s are today only performed by a specialist, and then they occur at a specialized surgery center, a radiology center, or some other form of specialty medical practice. The same is true of accountants, lawyers, and bankers, as well as plumbers, carpenters, and electricians.

This move toward specializations will only grow more intense in your time because of the vast proliferation of knowledge. This knowledge tidal wave will make it impossible for a mere general grasp of a field to be useful, except on the smallest scale. It's always been tough for young people to figure out what it is they want to do with their lives. It will be even tougher in the decades ahead. Fields of knowledge will likely come along, mature, and go away in less than a generation, whereas in my time we've usually had generations to learn new technologies, master them, and build stable, long-term careers around them. I listened to the CEO of a major corporation recently talking about how this is impacting companies like his. He was of the same mind I am; every organization will have to deal with this rapid pace of change and specialization, not just the major organizations.

I already miss having access to people with a broad knowledge of their field. It appears to me certain forms of specialization have sprung up as much due to what can be charged (more) as for any real need for expertise in a very narrow sub-field of an existing field of knowledge. Yes, I do understand some areas of professional practice are so unique there is and will be a need for specialists. I've availed myself of the services of specialized physicians, lawyers, accountants, engineers, and electricians. Yet more recently I've noticed this trend toward claiming specialization has found its way into other work groups, such as gardeners, pool cleaners, janitorial services, and the like. Do I feel a gardener couldn't specialize? Of course not, but when you tell me you're planning to double your price because you're now a certified lawn-care specialist, I'm slightly skeptical about exactly who certified you and in what.

There was a move a few years back for physicians to attend plastic surgery training for as little as thirty-two hours on a couple of weekends. Then to come back to their practice claiming they were 'board-certified'. Yes, they were board-certified, but who certified them? Were they certified by The American Society of Hotel Banquet Room Trained Plastic Surgeons? What I'm getting at here is you have to be very careful when you pay extra for someone who claims they're a specialist. Make sure they actually have trustworthy credentials and/or experience which supports their claim and the accompanying inflated billings. The next time you get a bill from your gardener and his explanation for the price increase is he took a weekend course at the community college, congratulate him and assure him you're not going to ask for money back for all the years he practiced on your yard on his way up the gardening ladder.

In a similar vein, be wary of everybody with a string of initials behind their name. I can say that without even the slightest sense of being jealous because I'm entitled to use several sets of initials I don't even bother to list anymore. If this were Europe, I'd be expected to list at least nine different sets of them at a minimum. Few people here or there would know what they meant, and even fewer would care. I point this out because years ago I saw a proliferation of national certifying organizations which seemed to spring up from nowhere. What it amounted to was two or three people banning together after a conference at a bar or office water cooler to form societies, associations, or fellowships which constituted little more than one sending in their name, resumé or vitae, and a check (the most important element) in return for certification, registration, or 'Fellow' status. There was the appearance of specialization without any of the difficult hurdles normally associated with becoming a certified specialist in any field (e.g., education, hands-on training, examination, etc.). They were then entitled to add initials behind their name; you might not know what they meant, but you didn't argue so much when the bill came.

Realistically, almost all specialized schools and societies sprang up in similar fashion, and many of them have gone on to perform a valuable service in creating and promoting professional standards within their fields. The shaky ones were those who told me my having six college or university-level degrees in the field, state-recognized professional registration and certification, and four state licenses in other specialized fields wouldn't be adequate for inclusion. Ironically, they said if I'd buy their training course for $300 and then complete an open-book exam for another $125, I too could be certified, registered, or a Fellow in their society. Annual dues were $100 a year for the rest of my life. I've passed on these 'Fellowships' just as I passed on diploma mills here in California and elsewhere offering a PhD for $5,000 and the submission of a ten page essay in one's field of specialization. I can assure you a PhD from a regionally accredited university costs about 20 times this amount these days. They also require classes, residencies, and hundreds, if not thousands, of written pages before you're through.

Don't be taken advantage of by these questionable associations and societies. Don't be hoodwinked if you're being referred to a specialist. Be sure to do your homework in advance, ask lots of questions, check out the proffered credentials, and don't become a source of enhanced income for a specialist if no specialization is required!

Competition Of Religious Ideas

During my childhood my Momma was the person most responsible for my religious upbringing. She dutifully took my little sister and me to church when we were children and sent us there later, when financial necessity required she work Sundays. My Daddy was an infrequent attendee at best but was never shy to argue about the Bible at great length. My opinion then and today is he was earnest but ignorant. I love him, but earnest and ignorant didn't impress me then, and it doesn't impress me now. I say this because it's been my observation most people who argue for a religion, and not just those who espouse Christianity, tend to fall into this earnest but ignorant category. Daddy seemed to be of the mind whoever argued longest and loudest was correct in a matter; religious matters were no exception. I fear most people arguing causes they're passionate about tend to fall into this school of practice.

Allow me to get back to my Momma now and what was different about her approach. Don't get the impression she couldn't get loud or passionate about something, because she could. But for the most part she did her best to offer reasons for her religious beliefs based on what she'd read in the Bible, heard in Bible Study, and gleaned from listening to various Christian expositors over the decades. Even when I was her Pastor in her seventies, she continued to be a diligent student of the Bible and was not in the least shy about arguing with me if she felt I was becoming theologically incorrect or nebulous. There were issues she changed my mind on; there were also issues I changed her mind on. Yet the most important thing she left me with was a respect for the competition of religious ideas. We have a right to believe, but we also have a duty to understand our faith well enough to defend it intelligently and without resorting to being loud, angry, or violent.

The church of my childhood was Southern Baptist. It had typical Southern Baptist theology, views, and arrogance about its position as the one true denomination of the Christian faith. It was never verbalized from the pulpit to large degree, but we were taught in every other fashion we'd gotten the Bible completely figured out and anybody who wasn't a Southern Baptist was in grave error. I was assured at one time or another Catholics,

Pentecostals, Presbyterians, Methodists, Nazarenes, the Church of Christ, and just about any other Christian group were operating in error, and if not already Hell-bound, at the very least had one foot in the flames and the other on a banana peel. During those years my Momma would tell me and my little sister what she truly believed only once we got home and away from the Sunday school teachers and preachers.

Momma was much more tolerant of other people's Christian beliefs and said we should treat everybody well, and when we all got to heaven, Jesus would sort all the details out to his satisfaction. In major and minor ways, this view has colored my attitude toward other groups unless they were such obvious lunatics or heretics; their craziness couldn't be ignored or tolerated. When I first became aware there were other religions besides Christianity, and I questioned Momma about them, she took much the same tone as she had with other denominations. She favored evangelizing non-Christians, but she also told us we had no right to treat people with other beliefs badly, and one of the beauties of America is we're all privileged to believe as we wish. Every time I encountered a new religious group, I took Momma's words to heart. Even today, I believe in evangelizing, but I also take a live and let live approach in these matters and won't force my beliefs on those outside my faith.

This brings me to the actual point of this writing. I want you to respect other people's sincerely held religious beliefs. What I don't want you to do is begin to tolerate extremist views, whether they are Christian, Muslim, Hindu, or any of the world's other religious cadres. No one has the right to abuse, imprison, murder, rape, rob, torture, or kill people who are part of other religious groups. We've had enough religious warfare on this planet to last us a few more millennia; untold millions have been killed in the name of this god or that prophet. We seem to have come to another religious flashpoint with militant believers in this time. We again have varying numbers of militant Christians and Muslims. When this occurs, Momma's teaching of a competition of religious ideas goes out the window as fanatical people on both sides resort to violence to drive their theological views home.

In your time you could well see this extremism explode as one group or another competes through violence to impose their religious will on the rest of the planet. I can tell you as a student of history, it will likely turn extremely bloody at some point, and with the proliferation of nuclear weapons, millions could be dead in a matter of minutes. I don't want you to become paralyzed with fear at the thought of this. After all, our faith remains in Jesus Christ, and at the end of the day I ask you to trust him. You can also reach out to other men and women of different faiths you encounter who want to be able to live in peace and worship as they see fit. Yet the danger remains to all a small fanatical group can force the larger populace to choose sides with deadly consequences. In this I'd say, there'll be no neutral parties one the line is crossed.

Lifetime Implications

Please seriously consider what an important matter meeting members of the opposite sex, dating, and selecting a marital partner is. In my time as many marriages end in divorce as survive for the term. This is not how it always was. On the contrary, when I was a boy it was expected people would marry and the vast majority would marry for a lifetime. I married initially believing it would last forever. As you know, in the case of your grandmother and me, our marriage ended after twenty-seven years. The reason I'm raising this issue is the seeds of the destruction of our marriage came along many years prior to its end, and if both she and I had been wiser and taken steps to save our marriage many years earlier, we too might have made it to term. My point is not to lay blame, but simply to say there was serious work needed early on, which neither of us recognized at the time.

Let's consider you meeting members of the opposite sex, and yes I'm old-fashioned and actually expect you'll want a marriage with a member of the opposite sex. This doesn't mean I'll hate or disown you if you don't go down this road, it just means your twentieth-century grandfather really does believe there is a God, and this God ordained marriage between a man and woman. To go any further on the thought is another book for another time and considerably more ink. At the moment I'm focused on your need to get out and meet members of the opposite sex as a prelude to finding a spouse. This doesn't mean I expect you to be making the cattle calls at the local bars or spring break spots. It means I expect you to be looking in places where men or women of substance, with values similar to those you've been raised with, come together. This could be a school, a church, a university, a club, or some similar social venue.

Where you initially find people will be a good indicator of where you'll find them the rest of their lives. The things people value highly in their youth have a strong impact on the course those lives take and the road they head down. If they're gamblers, sports fans, hunters, fishers, or basket weavers, you can expect this to continue to one degree or another in the years ahead. My old pastor, John Sciford, used to tell people if they found their future spouse in a bar, they might be going back to a bar to bring the spouse home the rest of their life. I think there's a lot of truth to his words. Even if you find them initially in a place you like and approve of, do you really want to make such a place the focus of your future and the future of your children? If you don't, this doesn't mean he or she is a bad person, but it may well indicate they're not a good fit for you.

When you do find someone you think could be a good fit, then and only then should you consider dating them. I know this concept seems quaint to you, but why would you date someone you are not at least considering as a candidate to spend the rest of your life with? I married many couples who went on a date or two, and passion being what passion is, took hold and they found themselves 'with child'. You should never need a meal, an outing, or a period of companionship so badly you'd waste time dating a person you see as a non-starter for a marriage partner. Dating is serious business, or at least it should be, as it's intended to give you and the other person time to get to know one another and each other's family. Let me say this right now: if they start acknowledging their family is composed of perverts, jerks, or weirdoes of any sort, but assure you the relationship is "Just between the two of us," run, don't walk away from this one. You really do marry their whole family!

During an engagement young people should be talking over the serious matters of life (e.g., personal values, handling money, sexual attitudes, parental relationships, children and child rearing, and religious values in the home, etc.). Instead the engagement period has become a period devoted almost solely to planning a huge wedding extravaganza and how to beg, borrow, or steal enough money to pull it off. There should be pre-marital counseling; the more of it, the better. I married over a hundred couples, and at least half of them are divorced today. I always insisted on counseling, and I always wanted to do more of it than the couple wanted. After all, they argued they were in love, and love was all that mattered. It was all that mattered... until the divorce! My greatest accomplishment in this area was talking young people out of getting married. They always came back years later and thanked me. The ones I did marry sometimes came back and were angry with me for not having argued more forcefully against their nuptials.

Keep in mind marriage is what happens in the days, weeks, and years after the extravagant wedding. Wise young people would hang onto the $50,000 or more they pump into a wedding and put it into having a better financed marriage. Marriage can be the most blessed state two people of the opposite sex can exist in. Ignoring for a moment all the spiritualizing which is done about the union between a man and a woman, and how it is a type of the relationship between Christ and the church, understand a relationship where two people are in love and supportive of each other, offers them the best chance they'll ever have to become fully self-actualizing human beings in the very best sense of the concept. Husbands and wives who love one another are not jealous of one another. They're not running around holding a grudge against one another. They're not back-biting one another to family or friends. They're their spouse's dearest friend, closest confidant, and staunchest supporter!

This being the case, you can scarcely afford to be without a good spouse once you're grown. Yes, I know the Apostle Paul says some people are given singleness as a gift, and I can see how this too could be a blessed life, but most people don't fall into this category. With this in mind I advise you on the one hand to keep your eyes open for the man or woman God has for you, while on the other hand recognizing there could be many possible good spousal fits out there. I know both men and women who've spent years searching for their perfect soul mate. While

I love the romantic notion, I spent enough years in pre-marital and post-marital pastoral counseling to have seen many who believed they'd married their long sought after soul mate, only to end up divorced. Conversely there were others who were initially trepidatious about the less than perfect person they'd married; only to learn in time he or she really was their soul mate.

Please take these matters with the utmost seriousness, because they have lifetime implications.

Ethical Slippery Slopes

In my time we're starting to worry here in America about the militarization of our police forces and government agencies. Americans from my generation who were raised during the cold war haven't forgotten what the old Soviet Union and other totalitarian states looked like or how significant a role militarized police forces and government agencies played in the enslavement of once free peoples. Fascism always starts out as a beneficent effort to "...protect and serve" the people. Eventually it convinces the people the only way left to protect them is to totally control them. Constitutions are ignored or suspended and *de facto* marshal law is suddenly and irreversibly in place.

When I see stories in the national news stating various government entities all across the country are likely to start pressuring their police forces to write more violations and citations in an effort to boost government revenues, I'm very concerned. These efforts are actually designed to offset the continuing recession we're currently living through, and its resultant drag on the public coffers; they're not about making anyone safer. This revenue-driven approach to law enforcement creates a growing mistrust in a government which goes out of its way to make citizens outlaws. This doesn't sound at all like the meaning we expected out of the protect and serve mantra we keep hearing about.

This kind of manipulation of what's legal and what's illegal in order to boost revenues should give every person committed to the United States Constitution and The Bill of Rights serious pause for concern. Couple this with increasing militarization and one must wonder what happens if the revenue-boosting effort fails? How far will we take this venture into moving societal guide lines to boost tax revenue? Do we encourage law enforcement to plant evidence so they can confiscate property or haul people before the magistrates for fines based on falsified evidence? These are serious issues, and they'll still be serious in your time. Once a society crosses the first line, where does it stop? Civil arguments carry little weight against police forces and tactical teams mounted in armored and armed vehicles which amount to nothing less than light tanks.

There are already enough Americans who see law enforcement as a growth-industry; government doesn't need to add to this perception with these kinds of bad decisions. Yet it does so by making it appear ongoing, predictable, and increasing revenue generation is more important than the public trust. Allowing police departments to become armies of occupation is not the American way. In considering these matters, I suspect citizens encounter law enforcement more than any other arm of government. This carries with it the opportunity for law enforcement to be goodwill ambassadors for good government or the poster children for what's wrong with government today. Looking like an occupying army does a disservice to the citizenry and those who really do want to protect and serve their fellow man.

Living With Yourself

When I was ten years old, I envisioned myself passing through the life I expected to live in the years ahead and never making any serious missteps. By the time I was fifteen, I had pretty much been disabused of this notion and settled on a course where I hoped to make as few mistakes as possible in how I conducted myself. When I reached the ripe old age of twenty, I was pretty much a wreck with regard to living out a flawless life and just hoped to be able to get through it without making it totally impossible for me to exist at all. One of the things life will do to you as you grow up is throw a large dose of reality into your pot of every day dreams. This doesn't mean you can't dream, it just means if you get too hard on yourself, you'll end up a bitter old recluse, sitting in a cave on a hilltop someplace, watching everybody else live out what appear to be flawless lives.

Every son of Adam and daughter of Eve have long been destined to be less than perfect. You know me well enough to know I'm far less than perfect. We humans are at various times, and for nearly indecipherable reasons, ignorant, willful, angry, conceited, jealous, and stubborn. This doesn't help us understand ourselves any better on the days when we are kind, generous, loving, selfless, self-effacing, and otherwise brilliant. Those few verbs don't sum up mankind, but they would give a visitor coming here for the first time from another planet a sense of what a confusing little creature we can be, which brings me to the point of this whole ramble. The thoughts which seeded these pages are about my personal integrity, or lack thereof. Let me see if I can make any sense out of this for you and connect the two in a way which would be instructive and helpful to you as you go about your life.

As far as I've ever been able to determine, and no I didn't do a serious amount of scholarly research to arrive at this conclusion, the only two people who know what's in your heart are you and God. Your mother and daddy never truly know; your spouse and friends never truly know; and your children, who'll think they know all there is to be known about you, will most certainly have only the faintest clue. Who are you? It's very simple; you're the man or woman who shows up everywhere you go when absolutely no one else is around. You're the man or woman nobody else has ever met. We can do an outstanding job of appearing to be kind without actually being kind; we can do an outstanding job of appearing to be intelligent without actually being intelligent; and we can do an outstanding job of appearing to have faith in God without actually having any faith in God. We can mimic the key human behaviors our lives require, and no one else suspects the brilliant disguise.

My advice to you, my flesh and blood, is to work as hard as you know how to develop the positive attributes which don't require either guise or guile in dealing with others. Do your best to inculcate God's Ten Commandments in your heart; God knows it will be hard enough to live by them even if you do this. If you don't go to the trouble making them part of your personal makeup, you don't stand a chance of winging it successfully as you try to navigate the moral morass you'll be expected to survive in. Do your best to embrace Jesus's advice you love the Lord your God with all your heart, and you love your neighbor as you love yourself. I've travelled far and wide, and these were always solid advice on every continent or country I ever touched down in.

You're going to be tempted to do things which are dishonest, say things which are false and openly or covertly desire to take the possessions of others. If you fail to resist temptation, even if you get away with it, you'll know what you've done and how wrong it is. Your respect for yourself will be eroded each time this happens. Eventually the erosion can become so massive the man or woman you once were is no longer recognizable to you or those who once trusted and loved you. In Western civilization most of us spend some period of time each day looking into a mirror as we wash our faces and otherwise get ready for the coming day. I usually have questions for myself at this time. I ask if I'm angry with anyone, if I've knowingly wronged anyone, if I'm satisfied with myself. Narcissistic... I think not. I see it as the mandatory daily reality check which allows me to continue living with myself.

Where Will You Live

One of the matters you should give attention too is where you'll live. In the case of much of my generation, we ended up in the same town we were raised in, or in the place where we attended college, or perhaps the first city we were able to find gainful employment in. I suspect it will be the same with your generation, since mobility in the workforce has been on the increase for the past forty years and shows no signs of abating. You, or you and your spouse, will make these decisions, or life will make them for you. If you're not proactive on this matter, you'll look around one day and realize you're sixty years old and aren't necessarily in love with the place where you live, but it's your home.

Let me, with the benefit of twenty-twenty hindsight, suggest an alternative approach. While you're young, definitely before you're twenty-five, you should begin to think about where it is you want to live. Is it a big town or a small one? Is it in the desert or at the seashore? Is it high on a mountain top or down in the deepest valley? If you don't have enough travel under your belt to be certain, make a point of visiting different locales and spending a few days. If you find one you particularly like, plan to visit in all four seasons before you relocate. Your great-grandmother's old saying about "...jumping out of the frying pan and into the fire" comes to mind here. Be certain it's where you really want to be before you commit your life and resources to be there.

What then? I'd suggest you, or you and your spouse, then do some serious talking regarding moving. Where will you work in this new place you wish to live? Where will you recreate, send your offspring to school, and worship, and how far is it to a grocery store? Our lives are made up of dozens of mundane issues we often don't stop and think about adequately. We deceive ourselves by saying lightly "It will all work out." Yet sometimes relocation becomes both a financial and mental ordeal. Chance favors the prepared mind, so do your homework and your legwork before you call the movers. It's harder to return to your old home-town than you might think.

I've addressed this issue with you because quality of life is about a whole lot more than waking each day and discovering you're still breathing. Your surroundings, the weather, the air and water quality, and other aspects of local ambiance have an impact on your life and health and loved ones. I've lived most of my life in a desert transformed into an oasis by irrigation. Unfortunately, it's a hot, dusty life, and the air quality here has been deemed one of the worst in America. I never gave it any thought when I was your age, and I should have. Many friends left here after high school or within a few years and never returned. They moved to the plains, the mountains, other deserts, and the seashores; I envy many of them their choices.

Fear of the unknown and unfamiliar have held back more would-be migrants than all the border fences ever erected and all armies which were ever raised. You'll be right to have some fear, but it must not paralyze you. Rather it should be the kind of fear intended to protect us from foolish choices or actions which will injure us. By now you've developed schemata for conducting your life, and examining and learning about potentially dangerous people, places, or things. If you follow the same course of easing into new situations while figuring out the literal and figurative lay of the land, you'll do fine. Yes, there'll be moments and even days of anxiety as you enter your new world, new job, new friendships, and your new life. Don't be dissuaded from a great life in a great place by fear of the unknown.

Child Of The Universe

When people choose to violate ethics, cheat other people in their business or personal dealings, or outright break the law, and you refuse to agree with their behavior, I find it odd they'll tell you you're the one who's wrong and then try to recruit others to join them in their negative opinion of you. The older I get, the less slack I'm willing to give people who feel they're somehow entitled to treat everybody else as though their opinion, values, and rights don't matter.

My opinion, my values, and my rights carry at least as much weight as the opinion, values, and rights of any other human being. Yours do, as well. They don't necessarily carry any more weight, just not any less. So if you want to part company with your old granddad, begin to behave as if you are more important than everyone else on the planet. We're all sharing this very small planet. Technology makes it smaller all the time. We're all special in some way.

The idea one person is more special than everyone else is at the core of every theft, murder, rape, robbery, adultery, and war which ever took place. The people who have somehow inculcated a sense of superiority to every other human being represent a danger we too often ignore. This danger brought gas to the trenches in WWI. This danger built Buchenwald. This danger says I should eat, and you should starve. This danger has been around since the Garden of Eden and it will be mankind's nemesis until the final trumpet.

Here's my counsel to you on this matter: carefully consider your fellows who have been arrogant and dismissive of you throughout your relationship. Don't expect this attitude to change as the years go by. What must change is your willingness to put up with them and to get along with such people. The fact the rest of us behave too often like sheep is why others are routinely emboldened to behave like wolves. You and I are children of the universe. We're no less than these who would hold themselves out as our superiors, leaders, or masters.

Based on my understanding of scripture from the Bible, I used to teach congregations it was clear many people would be happy with a king they could turn their lives over to and he'd run their lives for them. The end of the Jewish theocracy and the anointing of Saul as the first King of the Jewish people come to mind; it didn't turn out like they hoped. I've never been this kind of sheep, and I hope you're not either! If you are, you betray hundreds of years of ancestors who resisted the flow and refused to knuckle under to the self-important and self-centered among us.

CHAPTER 11

Pleasure Versus Happiness

The older I've grown, the more I've noticed people busy pursuing pleasure because they equate pleasure with happiness. In looking for definitions of pleasure and happiness, I see, among other things, pleasure can be 1) a state of gratification, 2) sensual gratification, 3) frivolous amusement, or 4) a source of delight or joy. While happiness used to be defined as good fortune or prosperity, Webster's now says this definition is outdated, and I tend to agree. The commonly accepted definition in the modern era has been 1) a state of well-being and contentment, 2) personal joy, or 3) a pleasurable or satisfying experience. I want to talk with you for a minute about how important happiness is and the danger in equating pleasure with happiness.

It's been said my generation exists in a pleasure-mad era. It actually started at the end of World War II, as best I can tell, when in the heady days after the war ended, the victors came back to their home countries with all the experience they ever needed in war and the elements of war. They'd had their fill of anger, hatred, violence, death, and destruction. The men and women who fought, whether on the battlefields or in their nations' various war efforts at home, wanted to take a deep breath and replace their fears and wartime deprivations with eating, drinking, and being merry. And there was nothing wrong with this. In time, as the worst days of the war faded in memory, the simple pleasures no longer satisfied, and new and larger pleasures were created to take their place.

Here in America we saw an industrial boom begin which gave people more disposable income, which led to bigger houses, cars, hair, clothes, families, and vacations. Recreation of all sorts became one of the key sources of pleasure. We swam, boated, golfed, skied, raced, flew, danced, and sailed. And there was nothing wrong with this. However, if you fast forward to the '70s, '80s, '90s, and the first fifteen years of this new century, you'll notice we now have to take any of those things to an extreme level in order for it to bring about the same level of pleasure its simpler versions once elicited. As people began to pursue pleasure to the exclusion of many of the other elements of what we term living, the lines between what made us feel content or happy blurred. More and more people could no longer tell the difference.

Pleasure activity is not in itself a powerful drug. But I think research would show pleasure has an incredibly strong ability to set off receptors in the human brain which release some of the most powerful drugs on the planet. I'd go further and suggest additional research exists which supports the idea people can become addicted to the drugs in their own brains and the delivery system which provides them—all in the pursuit of our old friend, pleasure. Happiness has always implied a sense of well-being to me. Having experienced my share of both licit and illicit drugs, I can tell you some have the ability to bring about a sense of well-being. But unlike a sense of well-being which flows from a sustainable source, derived from an overall balanced existence, drugs require a near-continuous effort on your part to find, purchase, and ingest them; you can think addiction here.

Like most people, I've spent a lifetime pursuing happiness. In my younger years, I made the same mistakes most members of my generation did and sought to be happy by being continuously pleasured. This took all the commonest forms of my day, including drugs, alcohol, sex, music, sports, travel, and eating. Many of those I did too excess, and there came a time when they began to lose their ability to bring me pleasure, much less happiness. The same thing will happen to you if you pursue a path bent on pleasure rather than looking for actual happiness. For me happiness began to grow in my life when I had a personal encounter with the savior, Jesus Christ. It didn't immediately make me a happy or perfect person. It did set my feet on the path to real happiness for the first time.

Today, happiness is about being at peace with God, being at peace with my neighbor, being in love with my wife and my family, being satisfied with what I have and what I've accomplished, and my personal efforts to make the world a better place for others and not just for myself or my clan. At your age you see life as a great mystery you're going to go out and unravel. This is the arrogance of youth, and every man or woman who ever lived suffered with the same delusion. Every generation has deluded itself into thinking they alone understand the mysteries of life and each new thing they encounter is their personal discovery and no one else's. I'm amused at this thought in these years, just as I'm sure your great-grandparents were amused by me when I made so many earth-shaking discoveries about life.

Happiness is 1) a state of well-being and contentment, 2) personal joy, or 3) a pleasurable or satisfying experience. Happiness isn't about great wealth. Happiness isn't about great education. Happiness isn't about great accomplishments. Happiness isn't about great fame. There are happy people all over the world who lack one or more of those things. There's a scripture which says something to the effect "Godliness with contentment is great gain." Happiness is about well-being and contentment with the life you have and the things you possess. Happiness is about personal joy, and this kind of joy can only come from inside you. Happiness is indeed a pleasurable or satisfying experience, but don't settle in your life for mere pleasure when happiness is what you and every other human being truly needs.

Friends And Friendships

Friendships have been on my mind a great deal lately. Much of this reflection is born of puzzling over what happens to friends as the years go by. Some of the people you regard as your friends may still be around forty years from now. Conversely, some of them won't be your friends forty days from now if the circumstances warrant it. People change, grow, and move on with their lives. At times people leave other lives in their wake. There isn't necessarily anything underhanded or nefarious in this; it's just the way life is.

You'll have friends you feel as close to or closer to than a sibling, only to fall out with them over some matter or another and never speak again. I've had friends like this I still miss, but I'll no longer keep company with them because of their attitudes, behaviors, politics, or religious persuasion. Neither you nor I are obligated to hang on to or be hung on to by people who've made choices we can no longer abide. It's back to the old theme

I harp on about of you having the right to be self-determining. When you realize you need to go in one direction and your friend needs to go in another, insofar as it's possible, wish them well and be on your way.

In my opinion, friendships need an elastic quality if they're to last. There are people I've been friends with for five decades. In the parlance of this time, "We aren't all up in one another's business all the time." This implies people can be friends, even close friends, and not have to know everything about each other, be involved in every aspect of their lives, and/or hang out with them every moment of the day or night. One of the things which make friendships so valuable is friends are not identical copies of one another; they're real people with real lives and real differences. Learn to see this diversity as a benefit, not a problem.

An important consideration is friends stifling friends. If you have friendships where those involved try to speak for you, think for you, or just in general control you, this is not friendship. It's a psychically unhealthy relationship. Friends like this are more likely to be mentally or emotionally ill than just overly friendly and may even represent a physical danger to you over time. If a friend is starting to feel more like a stalker than a welcome guest in your life, start putting some distance between you and them until you can completely extricate yourself from the relationship. When you realize a friendship is impoverishing your life rather than enriching it, the friendship has actually ended and some other dynamic is at work.

Being a friend is about more than hanging out together or sharing common interests. As the years go by, your friends represent an important line of support for the inevitable vicissitudes of life; you'll need them, and they'll need you. At various times it will be for advice, a loan, or words of comfort or correction. True friends should be able to do all these things; in my opinion this is where proof of friendship really lies. My Daddy always believed he had many friends until he was old and dying with cancer. He was crushed to learn what he'd had were drinking buddies, hunting buddies, and even working buddies; in the end a true friend was not to be found among them.

I still recall the sadness in his voice when he shared this realization with me. He said, "I thought they would at least come see me when I was dying."

Mayberry Is Gone Forever

When people speak wistfully to you about the town of their childhood, in cases where they've moved away and you've remained, they'll often say they wish they could come back home. I know, because I've heard it repeatedly by having mostly remained in the small town where I was born and raised. On the surface they really believe if they could just get back to their old hometown, things would be as they were, and their place in the universe would be as it was. What they're really wishing for is not just the place, but the people and the time as well.

It's easy enough in these modern times to be anywhere in the world within a day or two. But bringing back a period of time, the people who populated it, and the cultural values of the time, would require the hand of God. For my generation there was a mythical small town known as Mayberry that was featured in a television series from the '60s starring Andy Griffith, Don Knotts, and a then-young man named Ron Howard. I'm not sure what Mayberry will be in your generation, but there'll likely be some equivalents. Let me take on the sad task of informing you your Mayberry is already gone forever by the time you're reading this.

I encourage you to think wistfully of your childhood and your hometown; it was a major factor in shaping you into the man or woman you're becoming. What I don't encourage you to do is to spend so much time looking back on your Mayberry you fail to see the vista of life unfolding before you. Here's something positive to contemplate, the very place you may be uncomfortable living in today because it's not your Mayberry, could very well be the place your children think of someday as their Mayberry.

Making Allowances For Imperfection

You should accept early in any relationship people won't be perfect and flaws will definitely exist. Unfortunately, this moment of acceptance doesn't happen because in relationships which appear bound to be long-term, we'll pass through a phase early on where we seem to lose our ability to see flaws. It won't matter if it's the courtship of a boyfriend or a girlfriend or simply making a new friend at work or in the community. As my Momma used to tell me, "At first you'll want to eat 'em up... then you'll want to spit 'em out." I've reflected at length on Momma's words, and like so many things she said, they've proven to be uncannily accurate and great wisdom to live by.

You'll meet people who are destined to become life-long friends. You'll also have friends who over time will become strangers again. This is the normal way of things, and we can probably attribute it to lack of common interests, growing apart, or serious disagreements over serious issues. I'm not so focused here on those people who come and go in your life as much as

I am those who are there for a lifetime. Once you've passed through your chase, courtship, and pseudo-marriage phases with friends, the grind of life will expose their flaws. Conversely, it will also expose the flaws in your life to your friends. You'll both have decisions or adjustments to make if the relationship is to flourish. If you make the wrong ones, it's very painful.

Marriage between a man and woman is a serious matter and as it's said, it "…shouldn't be entered into lightly or ill advisedly." All this aside, if the marriage is to last, you'll also pass through the phases I mentioned earlier (e.g., chase, courtship, marriage); shouldn't a marriage first grow from friendship? You'd hope so, but often it's just as much about proximity and passion as any other factors. It's in the day-to-day of the marital grind we come to know the people we've chosen as our life-mate. We also come to know their flaws. If the marriage is to survive, we learn to acknowledge these flaws and accept them. If you're unable or unwilling to do this, your marriage will be troubled, perhaps to an irreparable degree.

Most of us find in time we can easily live with and entirely forget our friends' and family's flaws. In fact we may not think about them at all unless someone else raises the issue of a friend or spouse's imperfection(s). I find in-laws to be exceptionally well qualified in this area, often to the destruction of their children's marriages. You can't escape in-laws, so you'll have to learn some way to deal with them if this spirit is part of their makeup. However, you should escape friends who make a habit of tearing down your spouse or other people. They will poison your relationship. You'll have to decide which relationship means more to you. By the way, I found it interesting how people who've previously criticized spouses try to pick up on them after the divorce.

The points I want to reiterate here are you're flawed, your spouse is flawed, your friends are flawed, your family is flawed, and the folks who appear or claim to be without flaw are likely the most flawed people you know.

Anger Will Be Your Only Companion

"Be not quick in your spirit to become angry, for anger lodges in the bosom of fools." Ecclesiastes 7:9

Do you currently have friends, family members, or coworkers who always seem to be angry? Now I'm not going to pretend for the sake of publication anger hasn't been an issue in our family history. I'm referring here to the type of friend or family who show up for a visit angry, get up in the morning angry, or come to work every day angry. I've encountered a few of them over the years and long disabused myself of any notion I could help them get over their anger. I feel sorry for them, and I'm certain their anger is bad for them. I'm equally certain it's destructive to everyone around them.

I had an unwanted interaction recently with one of these types. It happened despite all my best efforts to avoid this person. It happened despite being completely unable to convince him there wasn't some plot against him to shut him out of an event. It didn't matter the event had been held routinely for years; it didn't matter it was open to anyone who bought a ticket; it didn't matter there was publicity in both regular and social media; and it didn't matter his own friends and family knew about the event and participated regularly. What mattered apparently was a giant chip being carried on his shoulder, just waiting for someone to knock it off. He took the lack of a personal invitation from people he hadn't seen in forty years as a source for anger.

Quite often people who are continually angry have some deeper issue (e.g., jealousy, childhood abuse, addictions, mental illness, personal failures, etc.) which is eating at them, and their anger and its associated lashing out are just symptoms of the hidden issue. My guess is the only way to ever turn this problem around in people would be to discover what the core issue is and deal with it. In addressing my own anger issues, this is all that ever truly helped. In the meantime, these angry folks can wreck a family, clubs, churches, businesses, and friendships. My advice continues to be to give the angry man or angry woman a wide berth.

I was recently sharing with someone about a coworker I had more than thirty years ago now. He was the longest-serving employee the company had, but because of his lack of customer skills and an inability to get along with people, he was constantly passed over for promotion. One Friday afternoon he and I had a particularly volatile conversation, where he railed at me for not being able to read his mind. I say this facetiously because he was supposed to be training me at the time, and whenever I couldn't give him answers for product line information which he hadn't shared, he'd explode, scream at me, and tell me what an idiot he thought I was.

I was in my early thirties at the time, in excellent physical condition, completely fed up with his treatment of me, and had determined if it started up again on Monday, I was going to deck him and go home. I never doubted for a minute he'd fold, because at his core he was a bully. I knew I had superior education, training, and technical skills to his, and I was tired of the constant verbal abuse. When I arrived Monday morning, the owner came to me and told me I'd have to step up and run the shop because my coworker had suffered a heart attack Friday night and died. He'd gone out on a late service call after I left, gotten into one of his usual arguments with the customer, and in the middle of a screaming rage, he fell over dead of what was later determined to be a massive heart attack.

This very angry man left a wife and kids. I had to wonder if they were as relieved as I was he wasn't there anymore. I later learned he'd been just as angry and abusive with his wife and family as he was with coworkers and customers. The ending here can't be called positive because the children lost a father and the wife lost a husband. My own interpretation of this all these years later is his constant state of anger had to have put him in perfect condition for a heart attack. What was the core issue? I learned later he'd actually been put out of the family business years earlier for always being so hard to get along with. This had only served to fuel his sense of being the victim of a family injustice.

I've no idea how long this had festered by the time I met him. But I'm sure the anger it bred is what eventually killed him. You likely have friends who were great students or athletes, beautiful cheerleaders or talented musicians, or possessed some similar early exceptional skill or trait which never quite blossomed into the professional life everyone told them it would. Most of them took it in stride and went on to forge a productive life. However, I'm going to wager some of you know the angry ex-whiz kid, ex-athlete, ex-cheerleader, ex-musician, or any of the other exes you recall whose star burned out early. You're not to blame for this, and you shouldn't be expected to subject yourselves to any of their vitriol.

Having failed to fully achieve one's potential is not an excuse to then go out and rain on every parade. Having failed to fully achieve one's potential is not a license to verbally, emotionally, or physically assault people. I taught your mother, your aunts, and your uncle "Life is not fair," dreams don't always come true, and every day we try to make the best of the lives we still have by pressing hard to get as close to those dreams as we possibly can. We all suffer heartbreak. We all experience loss. We all come to know failure on a first-name basis. Cry, pray, meditate, medicate, or seek out a counselor. Do whatever it takes to keep this kind of anger from becoming your constant companion... because if you don't, soon anger will be your only companion.

There Are Words
I'm not sure if I've already addressed this topic with you or not, but even if I have, I want to reiterate the point because it's so important; there are words, which once spoken, can never be taken back. Yes, sometimes you can apologize and move on, but this doesn't erase what's been said. The memory may linger for the rest of one's lifetime.

Be very careful when issuing final words; those being the words spoken before the death of one or both parties makes it impossible to ever make peace over the issue. My advice to you is to seriously think before ever speaking or writing to other people in anger. It won't matter how sorry you are later. The damage will be irreparably done. Since none of us knows the future, it might be wise to be careful with all our words.

Give The Jealous A Wide Berth
Jealousy is a terrible and mystifying thing to behold, but it's even worse to be the focus of. You've seen it throughout your life, first with the jealousies you had with your sibling(s). You saw it again in the schoolyard, where someone was always a better athlete, speller,

mathematician, or reader than someone else. Ultimately you've encountered it in the workplace, but it usually appears there in all its refined and more disguised forms. The passive-aggressive, the saboteur, the bully, and even the office character-assassin/gossip have learned how to get a pass on their jealous behaviors.

Wherever you encounter jealousy, you're best off to give it distance and at all costs avoid feeding into it if you possibly can. Jealousies have the strangest habit of boiling over in the family, the schoolyard, and the workplace. In recent years the manifestations of a rage brought on by jealousy have become increasingly violent. Post Garden of Eden, Cain is said to have killed his brother Abel in a fit of jealous rage. The same levels of family jealousy found in the Garden now provide routine headlines in the media, where whole families are wiped out by a jealous member.

There are people who, because of an innumerable list of mental and emotional problems, operate almost completely under the control of malignant jealousy. They become expert at plots, manipulations, innuendos, half-truths, and outright lies. They engage in these behaviors for reasons most of us cannot grasp, because they never enter our minds. This often puts the victim of the malignantly jealous at a disadvantage because they don't think the same way. For the rest of your life you need to be ever vigilant of the potential danger created by both generic human jealousy and the malignant jealousy so common in my time. The jealous spouse, family member, or coworker can all become a danger to you. It's a brave new world out there; don't become a victim.

A Shared Resource

I attempted to explain to a business group recently how the idea of a global commons, or any widely shared resource, actually works. In a nutshell it means if you have a group of one hundred people who share something equally in common, let's say a pasture (commons), and one hundred new people come along who want to share the same pasture, each of the now two hundred people will only be able to receive one-half the use or benefit the original one hundred people enjoyed.

We see this all the time in cases where the resource is finite (e.g., air, water, etc.). It's also a problem in situations where a resource is not severely limited (e.g., food, farm land, energy, etc.) but simply hasn't been developed yet to the degree necessary to handle the growth of people wanting to use the resource. This is why we're routinely expanding roads and highways, water and sewer systems, and parks and cemeteries: To keep up with the burgeoning number of users.

Where the problem begins is when new people come along and want to use the resource. The people who originally developed the resource see their share diminished unless the new arrivals are required to ante up for the cost to expand the resource to keep the shares at the same size they were previously. As you can imagine, the 'user pay' approach is a popular concept with the early users and an unpopular concept to the later arrivals.

The shared resource concept is the driving force behind so many of the regulations in our country today which add costs to the development of housing. We now often demand developer impact fees of those wishing to expand the housing pool, because of the increased demands it will place on roads, bridges, water systems, sewer systems, schools, parks, cemeteries, police forces, and fire departments. There can be no free riders, or the system will collapse under the constantly expanding demand.

I'm a fiscal conservative. I'm fairly tolerant of people's social behaviors as long as they don't attempt to force them onto me or ask me to pay for them. Consequently, I encourage you to think in terms of paying your fair share in life. By now you've had friends who wanted the rest of the group to foot the bill for food and fun; how did this work out for you? Not too well I imagine, so keep this life lesson in mind each time either you or other people think they can have something for nothing.

Burning Bridges

By this time you'll have experienced one of those painful occasions where a friend, family member, coworker, or even a co-parishioner has sent you a 'hot' email or text while they were drinking, drugged, angry, or all of the above. In fact, because of the accelerated pace of communications now and in your era, it probably already happened to you years ago. Later, when the 'sender' was sober, saner, or calmer, they thought better of their words and reached out to you in an effort to explain to you what 'truly' caused the written outburst.

The truth is with this kind of an outburst, most people likely will forgive it unless it's a habit. But the troubling and corrosive part is those words likely remain in the receiver's mind forever; they then return to their active memory at very inopportune moments for the sender. Many of us believe the "The words of a drunken man are merely the verbalized thoughts of a sober man." So don't deceive yourself into thinking others will be fooled by a later claim it all came about because of your being buzzed.

Please think carefully before you speak, write, text, email, or upload into whatever medium it is you're using to communicate.

When I was young, I learned the painful truth behind the axiom, "Act in haste and repent at leisure." I have no doubt you will learn this as well. If you must police yourself, tape a sign up at your desk which says, "Don't post, text, email, or upload while drinking, on drugs, whether legal or illegal, or just having a bad day." Some bridges, once burned, can never be made whole again. In this age of instant communications, it's easier than ever to strike that match.

Speaking Truth To Power

One of the most disturbing trends in the United States in my time is people seeing themselves as powerless to make any kind of important change in government. I certainly have a limited view of what can be done, but as I've pointed out in my speaking and writing before, I try to make a difference at the local level. There's no reason why you can't do the same.

Please don't ever think I'd want you to simply give up trying to make macro change in your state and national governments. Even if you can't have the big impact, don't give up on making small changes. Micro-level change has a powerful, cumulative effect over time. Keep on speaking truth to power in the best way you know how and with all the legal means at your disposal.

Our family has a history of speaking up to government and demanding to be heard on important issues. Your Irish, Scottish, and German ancestors came to this country in no small part owing to the fact they rose up against the current state of affairs in one capacity or another in their homeland and living on meant going someplace where the current government couldn't take their lives or livelihoods.

I see the fire already burning in you, even as young as you are. I trust your mom and dad to help you temper and channel this fire into positive outlets. But never get it in your mind you can just go along with whatever those in power want you to accept as "The way things ought to be," those are the thoughts of a slave.

History has taught our family evil men and women can come to positions of power, and if they're left to their own devices, they'll violate everyone's civil rights repeatedly. The only thing which ever stops this sort of behavior is to rise, speak up, and resist them with all you have. To do so is dangerous and costly to you and your family; not to do so is even more dangerous and more costly!

Not Conducive

I'm soberly and seriously contemplating a statement from the field of international development which was posed to me by a former student. It's an unfortunate reality a child can easily be conceived, born, and partially raised in a location on this planet which is not conducive to supporting human life, much less the fragile life of a child. I say partially raised because so many children around the world die before the age of nine.

As a consequence of this terrible truth about the unfitness of some geographic locales for birthing and rearing children, in my time we regularly see young children die by the thousands each year in places which are ravaged by drought, famine, disease, pestilence, or endless civil wars. As cynical as this may sound to you youngsters, and despite the money and personal effort I've poured into trying to change these realties, they've not changed appreciably in my lifetime, nor do I think they'll change much in yours.

I hope I'm wrong! But if I'm not, I'll surprise you by saying you shouldn't stop trying to improve the world; only a heartless man or woman can ignore those levels of human suffering and do nothing. However, unless you want to suffer routine depression over these issues, you'll need to accept early on while you can often effect micro-change in the world, macro-change is a more difficult matter altogether; it's not impossible, but it's much more difficult.

Macro-change requires people unite in large numbers, for a large purpose, with large dollars, and an equally large amount of sustained impetus in order to assure certain changes occur. Human history does have a number of success stories where peoples and nations united in some great effort to carry out a transformative work. As sad as the third world appears today, it would be even more of a shambles, and there would be even more dead babies, without the micro-change efforts the heart-driven have made.

Brain Injured

I'm constantly mindful of the number of people in our society who have suffered a traumatic head injury; you should be too. When I've witnessed this, it was primarily caused by car wrecks. However, the wars in Iraq and Afghanistan have swelled the supply of brain injuries; there are plenty to go around! I recently sat on a panel, interviewing job applicants, where one of the candidates clearly had something going on which wasn't making sense in the context of all his other positive attributes; I suspected a head injury. A major cause of epilepsy in our society is automobile accidents. Improvised explosive devices are steadily gaining on capturing a spot in the top five. The fact head injuries are so prevalent, and yet so often mistaken for other mental health issues, is a problem for both employers and employees.

Health care privacy laws make it difficult, if not impossible, to get to the core of these issues. Having worked for two years with clients who were intellectually disabled, I tend to be compassionate and understand. Despite their limitations, people with these sorts of disabilities can be an exceptional employee. The wars we fought in Iraq and Afghanistan assure us a burgeoning cohort of both men and women with brain injuries, who'll work their way through our society for the sixty years. This health problem will continue in your time. If you should come to own or manage a corporation, your organization needs to take a leadership view on this, sit down with your lawyers and human resources experts, and work to find a way to avoid allowing a diamond to be cast into the coal pile.

Taken With A Giant Grain Of Salt

YouTube® is one of the most fascinating and dangerous places on the entire Internet. As you kids know, long before I was Dr. Neeley, I was a craftsman who made a living with my hands. Routinely on YouTube®, I'll see some purported expert expounding at length on areas I've spent thirty or more years working in. The details at times are so erroneous, I fear for the people who take these so-called experts' advice.

A friend sent me a link to an electrical lecture on YouTube® which was obviously given by someone who didn't have a clue what they were talking about. This kind of information is incredibly dangerous. I've been a licensed electrician in the Golden State since I was thirty-five years old. I don't have a problem with his bad advice; I know how to perform the task he erroneously describes, both correctly and safely.

On the other hand, if a layperson were to undertake the repair using this alleged expert's advice, it may well leave them dead. All I can do is comment there, vote thumbs down, and ignore his channel. I sense most of these folks on the media making these videos are trying to sell their services; I understand the need for advertising. What I don't understand is someone who is clearly incompetent purporting to teach on a dangerous topic he's not equipped by education or experience to teach.

We've been admonished by great thinkers for two millennia to beware of allowing the blind to lead the blind. Please remind yourself of this after I'm gone, whenever you're watching some of these purported experts on YouTube® or anywhere else. Some of the folks out there are not just good teachers, they're great teachers. On the other hand, some are self-important dolts trying to make a few bucks. As always, take everything you see, hear, or read with a gigantic grain of salt. Your papa doesn't know everything, but I do know a few things well!

Technological Trojan Horses

One of the most amazing things for a man my age to see is how rapidly technology is advancing from month to month, week to week, and even day to day. Having said this, please don't interpret it to mean I think all of it's positive. The changes in your time won't all be positive either. On the contrary, many of the current advances are unidentified Trojan horses' we've released upon ourselves and only the passage of time will reveal their true cost in terms of their potential for good or bad. Some of those costs will only come to light in your adulthood, and then you and your fellows will be charged with trying to correct the shortsightedness of my generation. I apologize in advance, but the truth is every generation seems to do this to its offspring, to one degree or another. Sorry!

Assuming The Worst

I saw an article in the local press here last year about a family dog which gave birth to a large number of puppies; it almost tied the world record for puppies born to the breed. When I began to read the comments after someone posted it to Facebook®, the majority were decidedly negative or actually attacking the owners. I've never supported puppy mills, but this was obviously a champion breeder of quality animals and a caring owner.

Apparently the disparagers hadn't even bothered to read the newspaper article which talked at length of how prized and valuable these purebred pups would be, before they launched their attack. Instead, the comments castigated the owners and assured all who read their words these pups would end up in a dog pound and be exterminated. The commentators were self-professed experts.

If you should ever become tempted to be one of the haters in the world, get a life! Read every post or article fully before you comment! Listen to people before attacking half a statement. To my knowledge, during the last sixty years, no one has been appointed emperor and given the right to criticize everything they see posted or said on the Internet or in any other medium.

Despite any temptation you might feel to aggrandize yourself by tearing down others, no one appears truly intelligent to the truly intelligent, solely because they've a penchant for criticizing others; they appear in most cases as simply an uninformed critic. Again, my advice is trolls add nothing to the human experience. Don't become a troll.

What Goes Around Comes Around

I encourage you to be careful how you treat folks. Mistreatment of any sort can come back to bite you. As a case in point, in late 2013 I came back in contact with a licensed professional I first encountered in 1987. I was just beginning my career in the construction contracting business, he was already well-established. I sought to hire him to provide his services on an early project I was undertaking. To my surprise, in our first and only meeting, he was rude and dismissive, telling me he didn't need to work with someone inexperienced like me; he told me to be on my way. I was shocked, I was hurt, and I was angry. Ironically, his rejection brought me in contact with another member of his profession who was to have a powerful influence on me by acting as a sounding board, friend, and mentor for more than a quarter century.

Fast forward twenty-six years, and this same dismissive professional is now at the end of his career. His practice has suffered because he apparently treated several youngsters as he did me. Consequently, as his older clientele retired or died off, he found himself with less and less work. I ran across him occasionally through the years and he seemed to have gone out of his way to make enemies. At one point it was rumored his last big project became so rancorous his attorney and the client's attorney had to both be physically present in the room for progress meetings; other communications had to be by letter. In retrospect, it's clear his treatment of me was not personal; he mistreated everybody.

Brilliance, and when he was young, he had a reputation for brilliance, will only take you so far in life. I've seen others in the trades, the professions, and later in academia who fancy themselves so superior to their fellows they eventually find themselves working entirely alone. I still get involved in occasional projects where a professional with this man's skill is required. I was told by a common acquaintance he was excited to hear about one of those projects when they were first out for proposals, but when he learned I was associated with them, he told the acquaintance he wasn't even going to the bidders meeting to hear the details.

I found his reaction ironic; based on what the acquaintance said, he seems to have judged himself in this matter without even being willing to try. I'm a fairly forgiving person, and both I and the organization involved would've given him the same opportunity anyone else was given. As it stands now, it's clear his professional practice is winding down; he's seventy years of age. Whereas others in his profession work well into their seventies, eighties, and even nineties, he seems destined to be sidelined years earlier. The beauty of intellectual labors is as long as your mind is sound, you can have a career. The ugly side of sowing and reaping is the unkind or downright evil things we do through life may actually be lying in wait for us up ahead, when we're older, wearier, and less able to meet and overcome them.

CHAPTER 12

These Are The Times

I'm not ever really certain whether or not these are "The times that try men's souls," but they're certainly the times which give our consciences a good workout. I'm sure there'll come days in your life when you can identify with my opening sentence. Understand, as a man or woman of conscience and principle, you'll experience personal anguish in living out your conscience and your principles. You'll struggle with your conscience many times. Accept this fact and take it in stride. It's not now nor has it ever been easy to do or say the right thing every time. What it has been, what it is now, and what it will be in your time is the key to whether or not your world remains a fit place to exist. A world without conscience or a world without principle is a world which has cast off civilization and returned to the law of the jungle; where the claw and the fang alone determine right or wrong.

Your Electronic Tethers

One of the ongoing acts of self-defense which has been adopted by businesses in this time is to make it more difficult to contact them; I fear this will only grow worse in your time. I understand this action when the business's intent is to keep away constant solicitations or auto-dialer programs from every person wanting to make a sale or every group out there with a cause. It's self-defeating though when it keeps your customers away from you. In your time you'll need to find a balance between too little contact and too much contact.

For years I've made a point of having caller ID on my business lines for exactly the reasons I mention above. But I have no desire to block contact from customers, and therein lays the problem; how do I keep away the pests without keeping away the people who pay the bills. More recently I purchased a system which allows me to block all calls which come in as unknown, anonymous, or are otherwise blocked with regard to identity. While it may unfortunately repulse the occasional well-intentioned caller; it certainly deals well with the ill-intentioned ones.

I live in a time where being able to have an extra moment or two to myself is a real luxury. This is entirely due to the invasive nature of new technology. This constant time consumption places my generation in the position of having to weigh the benefits of our electronic tethers. Striking the perfect balance is a work in progress for most of us and with the rapid changes in technology, a never ending battle.

I worry your generation's idea of face-to-face contact will grow more difficult even if you desire such contact. There's a danger in having all your time eaten up by constantly being connected, but I concede there's an even greater danger in cutting off actual human contact and conversation. You need to work to create an acceptable life-balance in this area; moderation in all things is still good advice. Guard your time and your privacy; just don't guard it so well it becomes self-defeating.

Real Problems... Faux Problems

Early in my career, I was a pastor and later a health care administrator. In health care I worked with Home Health, In-Home Health Care, programs for the at-risk elderly, hospice and palliative care, and federally-qualified health centers. Consequently, I've decidedly different views from most people about what constitutes a real problem. Hearing your child is dying, learning you have amyotrophic lateral sclerosis, or discovering you're going blind are real problems. Real problems in life have horrific consequences and lasting negative impacts on people's lives.

Not being able to go to Aruba on your winter vacation, not being able to buy a new ninety inch flat screen television, or missing your favorite singer in his third farewell concert tour, are faux problems. I challenge you to be men or woman of character and rightly weigh the real problems in life versus the imagined problems. Faux problems are like anything else designated faux; they simply deceive people into thinking they're dealing with the real item. A final caution, don't let other people draw you into their faux problems.

Evil With No Consequences

When they begin to compile the list of names of those who died in the Syrian and Iraqi slaughters going on in my time, your generation will someday desperately need to take a moment to consider how the indecisiveness of our president and congress added to the death toll. It occurred because he/they made it appear America was so weak and unsure of itself, the butchers who gleefully entered the power vacuum this impression created could do as they pleased, with no consequences.

Take a lesson from this and understand evil people in the world are constantly testing the resolve of good people in the world. This will be as true in your day-to-day life as it is in international politics. You must know your values. You must live them at all times and not just when it's convenient. You must be decisive in your actions in this area. I've paid a price in my life for opposing evil; I would gladly pay it again in the light of eternity.

If you and your generation should choose to stand weak and idle while evil men and evil nations carry out their treachery, then rest assured their brand of evil will grow until it covers the earth. The same will be true in your cities. As much as you might like to go to home each night and take your leisure, if you ignore the works of darkness around you, soon there'll be no place which is safe for you and your loved ones. Be vigilant against such weakness, and champion vigilance in your time.

The Proof's In The Pudding

My Momma had another wise saying which was, "The proof's in the pudding." I think most people already know this implies whether or not the pudding has the proper ingredients and preparation will all come out the minute the pudding is put to the taste test. It works this way in every area of life. The way you know whether or not something is genuine, accurate, and professionally executed will only come about when you have to taste the fruits of the effort. This is true in business, religion, sports, medicine, philosophy, politics, and all life's other endeavors.

If you've cooked and tasted the pudding, and the pudding is bad, something is off with the one who claimed to be a cook. You can't blame the suppliers, the manufacturer of the stove, or the maker of the saucepan. The cook selected the ingredients and executed the recipe. Before the cooking began, the cook could have made any change required. The cook must now shoulder the blame for the failure of the pudding and the truth those highly touted cooking skills were not all they were hyped to be.

The Slough Of Despond

The concept of American exceptionalism has been under heavy attack for at least half a decade now as I write these words in 2015. I strongly disagree with the proposition there's nothing exceptional about America. Having said this, let me say right here I also think each country is exceptional in its own way. As I ponder this I have to wonder why there are some folks working so hard to convince Americans there's nothing exceptional about Americans or their country.

Last night I was thinking about Irish, Scots, German, and even Scandinavian ancestors of ours who began coming to America as early as 1713. I have no doubt each of those ancestors came from peoples who believed they were exceptional in some way or another. It's only in this modern era the unique character of the people and nations of this world have come under such relentless attack. We're all being told there's a need for homogeneity if mankind is to survive, and no one is any more exceptional than anybody else.

Here's how I see this issue: each nation, and ethnic groups within those nations, has an inherent, even God-given right to be proud of itself and proud of its people, so long as they are not using this pride as an excuse to abuse other peoples. Adolph Hitler and the Nazis made an art form out of the "We're superior to you so we have a right to abuse you" mindset. Until Americans routinely embrace the idea there are things about this country which are unique, our nation and our economy will wallow in the self-doubt and apathy akin to the 'Slough of Despond' in Bunyan's *Pilgrim's Progress*.

In your future, there'll be periods of national self-doubt, perhaps even extremes of it. A little national self-doubt can be a good thing if not allowed to go to extremes which produce faulty decision making or political paralysis. A little self-doubt can cause self-reflection and a re-examination of the national status quo ante to make certain a nation is still on track with its stated principles and values. Conversely, any nation allowing itself to be told there's nothing good or exceptional about it long enough where the self-doubt becomes chronic, is doomed to fall to rival nations which are sure of themselves and their brand of exceptionalism.

Dangerous Deceivers

I make a point of listening to what is actually being said when people argue or debate. I hope you will as well. If you do, you'll often come away from these moments with a completely different view of the event than those who just got caught up in the rhetoric or the emotion. I notice especially when the topics are religion or politics, how quickly people revert to what we call in Logic the fallacies approach in order to get their point across. It's an important skill to be able to see these drifts into fallacy, because they'll assist you in determining truth from fiction and fresh hay from horse manure.

These fallacious approaches to argument usually proceed along the line of one party saying they're a member of a certain religion or political group. This is followed by the second party immediately producing a straw man caricature, representative in his or her mind of this group. He or she then attacks his or her own biased creation. What makes this dishonest is the straw man only slightly resembles reality. This tells me the father or mother of the straw man cares not a whit for truth and just wants to win the argument at all costs. For your own sake, stop talking and start listening!

In my time we're increasingly surrounded by angry and deceptive voices. In many cases they do everything from bend the truth a little to completely tossing it out the door and downright lying to get their point across. We've recently had politicians admit they lied about important issues in order to gain votes because the voters were stupid enough to believe them. I've made a point as I've aged to part company with people and parties of this sort. Any man or woman who'll resort to fallacies or outright lies to be the winner has something pathologically wrong with them. Their need to be right all the time, even when they know they're wrong, makes them dangerous deceivers.

Are You Qualified

I was reading an obituary yesterday and thinking about the bad advice people sometimes give. Most of the time advice is offered with the best of intentions and is meant to be genuinely helpful. Truthfully I think people may be way too liberal in offering advice in areas where they have nothing to give but their opinion. Unprofessional opinions can cause others great hardship, illness, injury, financial loss, perhaps even death.

Allow me to insert a word of caution at this point; our family does have a tendency to offer a lot of advice. If you should encounter people with serious mental, emotional, or physical challenges, you may want to tread lightly in the advice department. In my time, I've seen well-intentioned people offer direction in situations when they weren't qualified to comment at all, and the outcome was disastrous. The death by suicide of your Uncle Ryan is an excellent example.

Ryan was under the care of both a psychiatrist and a psychologist. The turnaround in his mental health in the year prior to his death was remarkable. Ryan had put on weight, he was laughing, he was smiling, and he was enjoying life again. Enter a well-meaning but totally unqualified youth minister offering him advice. This advice was if he would discontinue his medications, God would heal him of his OCD, depression, and schizophrenic problems. As you know, this didn't work out too well.

This doesn't mean people may not have a wealth of common sense and life experience to draw upon. But if common sense and life experiences were enough, there'd be no need for physicians, lawyers, psychiatrists, psychologists, accountants, and other professional advisers. It's okay to be a friend, and it's okay to care deeply about people. In fact, if you care this deeply you'll want people to receive the best in care and counsel.

Finally, it's not okay to ignorantly offer advice, no matter how well-intentioned. On the one hand, you could be sued by the party or parties involved if they can demonstrate you owed them some sort of special duty based on your relationship. On the other hand, someone could be financially damaged, severely injured, or die from bad advice. The best approach you can usually follow is to direct your friend to seek professional help in the matter.

Intellectual Dissemblers
The more I look at what passes in the online world as philosophical debate, the more I realize people really don't want to come to any kind of philosophical synthesis. They just want to win an argument. This approach is so intellectually dishonest and hollow; it doesn't deserve to be met with anything approaching intelligent dialogue. Let these dissemblers agitate among themselves. Anytime you allow yourself to be drawn into one of these efforts, you cannot win and will come away feeling slimy. Once again, don't feed the trolls.

Talking The Talk
I find it odd and simultaneously laughable so many of the folks out protesting against this or that cause in my time, seem almost universally unable to articulate a clear plan of what they propose to put in place when they collapse the system they rail against. I'm not talking about some pie in the sky approach. I'm talking about a real nuts and bolts, down to brass tacks detailed plan of what we should do from moment one, once we help them destroy this present world order. Many talk the talk, but they lack any kind of walk to back it up.

Who'll plan it? Who'll implement it? Who'll pay for it? How will they pay for it? Decrying what's wrong with the system is a simple thing; it takes no great intellect, no great education, and no real leadership ability. So, go ahead and rail and rant and tell me what a monstrosity the present course of action is. But until you can be part of the solution, and not just one of the naysayers, you're deluding yourself into believing by your words and symbolic actions alone, you're changing the world.

If this describes you, all you're doing is providing a moment's backdrop to the parade of history. It's a parade the talkers eventually have to watch go by, and yet they never quite seem to manage to find their permanent place in the retinue. Our family has worked hard for centuries to be relevant to our world; I expect no less of you. I fully expect an idealistic era in your life, as there's been one in all our lives. But at some point I expect you to pull your head out of those books and begin to do more than read and talk. Start to create and cease to tear down.

On The Lookout For True Need

We have a cadre of men and women who've been holding 'Hungry and Homeless' signs at heavily trafficked intersections and freeway on-ramps in our community for years. I've seen every one of them so often; I recognize them on sight and know if they're out of position on any given day. This morning I noticed one fellow at a nearby intersection who's usually working a location on the freeway off-ramp five miles east of today's outpost.

The odds are, if you live as an adult in a city of any appreciable size, you'll have your own cadre of the professionally homeless as well. I reflect on these folks a lot because I've worked with the homeless over the years, and you develop a sense about who's really homeless and who's only at risk of not picking up enough loose cash to get drugs or alcohol. My next book even delves into this in greater detail. Some say I'm cynical, I say I'm wary.

The chronically homeless are a heart-wrenching and pathetic lot, generally consisting of people who would be or have previously been labeled with dual diagnoses. Professionals who tried to help them realized they were suffering from mental illness and addiction to drugs or alcohol. The latter is usually their effort to self-medicate the mental demons they fight daily. Far from begging for cash, many of the chronically homeless fear being approached at all and avoid human contact.

If you truly want to help the hungry and homeless, you have to stop dropping a buck off with the man or woman with the sad sack look on their face and the ubiquitous Hungry and Homeless sign in their hands. Most cities have churches, synagogues, or other forms of religious outreach and other helping organizations operating genuine outreach to the hungry and homeless. You have to fight your urge to give them a dollar in order to instantly relieve those sad feelings these people deliberately work to induce in you. You need to give your dollar to a program or ministry working to break the hungry/homeless cycle.

Another sign to look for if you're looking for the genuinely down and out is many of these folks are ill-clothed, ill-fed, and often physically filthy; mental illness is a constant companion and personal nutrition and hygiene are not high on their list of items of most importance. They'll usually need a bath, a meal, and a change of gear almost every time you run across them. The man or woman begging in two hundred dollar tennis shoes and obviously clean but tactically worn-out clothes is a professional panhandler or a scam artist who wants cash for drugs or alcohol; he or she is deserving of neither your pity nor your money.

The chronic homeless man or woman is likely to be a schizophrenic ex-music teacher, a bi-polar ex-corporate manager, a brain-injured veteran, or a former homecoming queen with a combination of problems which requires a cocktail of expensive medications for control. In the case of the former homecoming queen, she can no longer afford the drugs which would help her, but she wouldn't take them if she had them because her paranoia won't allow it. She was once a child, a sister, a wife, or a mother. Now she wanders aimlessly in five layers of filthy clothes while pushing a shopping cart full of equally filthy possessions. Do you get the picture?

You can't fix all the problems in the world; God knows I've taken a shot or two at it. However, you can take a responsible approach to the encounters where you actually could make a difference. Be on the lookout for true need. True need isn't showy, it isn't always in your face, and true need isn't running around better dressed than the working-class folks who are being asked for their dollars. True need is all around you; tuning in to true need takes effort and involvement; both are more expensive than your causally dropped dollar.

No More To Take

When I was young, your great-grandmother taught me I must share what I had with others. The concept was laid down early in our home among all siblings. As we grew older, we were taught to share with folks outside the home. Then a funny thing happened. I began to notice I knew people who never shared anything but always wanted to share in what was mine or others. When I asked my Momma about this, she simply said, "Some people are selfish." I've seen a lot of the world, and Momma's words are a truth in every country I've ever been to.

Over the years I learned to avoid people who were selfish because I always seemed to be about giving, and those folks always seemed to be about taking. I'm concerned with many people; taking from others has become their way of life. Unfortunately, taking from others has become institutionalized and even codified into law in my time. The danger in codifying something into law lies in the truth that as more and more people realize they can simply demand what they want, soon there's no desire to give because the giver has less and less of his own to share.

Eventually the givers are either forced to look to the government to satisfy basic survival needs or forced to revolt against those institutions now dedicated to taking those things they possess. There's a delicate tipping point here, where some either reject the status quo ante or accept their lot as perpetual givers. Revolutions are born out of the rejection of a taking society. Additionally, there are many economically stagnant nations where the perpetual takers have become dominant to such degree there's no more left to take. Guard against these evils in your time.

Are You Buying This

I once joined a non-profit group which purported to be diligently seeking to improve the lot in life of a large class of people I identified with. I admired the group's stated goals because I cared deeply about who they claimed to want to help; I felt by joining my efforts to theirs, I could be more effective. In time I came to understand there was a hidden elitist attitude within the group. The truth finally came out the people in charge were only interested in improving the lot in life of a small subset of people within the larger class I identified with, a subset they judged to be intellectually superior. It was a shockingly tiny fraction of those I wanted to help, so I moved along.

You'll need to be very careful not to be taken in by people who claim one agenda when their actual agenda is hidden from you. This example I offer is a good one of the concept of 'false light,' which I've raised elsewhere in my writings. Please understand hidden agendas can and will at times be carried out by politicians, preachers, prostitutes, and every other person or organization which has something they want to sell. I'm often reminded of how the Bible warns us not to allow others to make us mere purchasers of whatever flimflam is currently being sold. The saddest part is these purveyors of false light often appear the most sincere and devout in their efforts.

Nature Isn't Perfect

There is a tendency I see in people in my time to believe if something is part of the natural order, whatever is being referenced must somehow be perfect. Perhaps this is due to the mistaken belief nature and any evolutionary processes involved always result in perfect outcomes. I can easily see and accept examples of micro-evolution in the world around me; I do have trouble however with macro-evolutionary theory. Regardless of whether you embrace one approach, both approaches, or neither, there is a danger all parties may begin to worship natural processes as though they were God. This God-likeness would imply a built-in perfection; this is a dangerous mindset. In these past six decades, I've found nature and the natural processes to be anything but perfect or God-like.

On the first Earth Day, the tendency of scientists was to see all of nature as perfect, and even when viewing higher life forms, the consensus seemed to be to behave as though mankind was the one bad apple in the barrel. But as I grew to manhood, and many of these same scientists took off their blinders, they started to report behaviors similar to infanticide, rape, war, and outright murder among many of both the greater and lesser life forms. I wasn't particularly shocked by any of this since I'd spent a large block of time in my life out in nature hiking, climbing, exploring, hunting, and fishing, and had already seen animals would kill not only prey, they would kill their own kind, and some seemed to kill for sport. I was later to supplement this empirical knowledge with college work in physical anthropology, biology, botany, environmental science, chemistry, ornithology, entomology, and geology.

The understanding I came away with, through a combination of being in the field and sitting through hundreds of hours of classes and thousands of pages of reading, was "Nature seems to make mistakes." You might wonder what I regard as a mistake. The simple example I'd offer would be the times when an evolutionary track fails and natural selection come into play. Albinism in wild animals represents one such failed track, or more accurately, represents natural selection at work, eliminating one such genetic variation. Animals born with natural colorings which blend into their surroundings survive at an astronomically higher rate than those born as albinos. Now, through special efforts made by humans on their behalf, animals born with albinism can survive. Is an albino animal then a perfect work of nature? If it's not, who or what's to blame?

I'm not writing a treatise here on evolution. What I'm trying to do is introduce into your thinking the reality nature is in many ways imperfect and attempts to correct for this with sheer numbers in hope of one of the number being 'correct'. This information implies simply citing something as natural doesn't necessarily mean it's how life forms will best function or even how they'll best survive. This grows even murkier when people try to make claims related to social evolution and our need to accept everything crops up in the human species as natural and therefore perfect. I've encountered people who wanted me to be sympathetic to habitually violent and dangerous people, such as serial rapists and murderers, because "They were born that way" which is to say in the minds of their supporters, their behavior is natural and therefore perfect for them. Unless you embrace and can fully support the need for serial murderers and rapists among us, the argument fails.

Allow me to close this out since I don't want to write so long on a topic you become tired of the idea and abandon considering it as a consequence of mere mental fatigue. Beware the activist, politician, environmentalist, scientist, or religious leader who launches an argument for the acceptance of some theory, concept, theology, or behavior simply because he or she believes "If it's cropped up in the natural world, it's natural and therefore perfect." The logic breaks down in there somewhere, and I leave it to you to sort those claims out as they come your way. What I hoped to do here is to awaken you to another fallacy which has seemingly crept into all areas of human dialog and drifts back and forth between the natural and the social sciences. If in your time you encounter this fallacy, and there is a gut check, even if you can't place it exactly, may it cause you to pause and really think about the argument being made to you and whether or not it's valid?

Commercial Affection

The term 'commercial affection' has been around for as long as I can recall, and in my youth was a part of a country song title: "*It Was Only Commercial Affection.*" The reference was to 'love for money', or more accurately 'sexual favors for money'. You're old enough by now to understand how this works in our society and that it works on many levels; the most basic level being pure prostitution, where money is exchanged for sexual services. It has much subtler forms and nuanced variations from there. You'll encounter the variations throughout your life. Having said all this, sexual prostitution is not what I'm writing about in these paragraphs.

The seed for this particular writing was planted the other day, when I was reminded of an industrial equipment salesman I once did a great deal of business with. I'm guessing there was a time when I spent as much as a quarter million dollars a year with his firm, and he drew the commissions from those sales. Bear in mind, thirty years ago a quarter of a million dollars was a goodly sum of money. The commission on the sales would have been equally handsome. But as fate would have it, the industry I was in slowed down, and we quit buying so much of the material he sold. This salesman quit calling, and we went our separate ways. Since I no longer had any contact from him, and absolutely none of the previous commercial affection he'd shown me in the form of attention, catalogs, Christmas cards, and year-end calendars, when it came time to buy once again, I looked to other vendors who'd kept calling in his absence of two years.

The salesman I'd formerly purchased from heard about this and sought me out; he wondered why I hadn't given him a chance to bid the project. I can be quite blunt at times, as each of you has learned from your encounters with me; I was blunt with him. I reminded him it was as if he'd fallen off the earth for two years, and then he'd suddenly shown up thinking our relationship was still intact. He could have changed companies, moved from the area, or even died, so complete had been his silence for two full years. Our parting was terse, and though I saw him from time to time through the years leading up to his retirement, we never conducted business together again. It was clear the interest he'd so devotedly displayed was just cleverly feigned commercial affection.

Here's where my words of advice to you come in. In the course of your lifetime, you're going to encounter commercial affection, and it won't always be as obvious as a sexual prostitute offering his or her services. More often than not, it will be people who pretend to be your friends for business, financial, political, and yes, even religious purposes. Think about this for a moment: you only hear from sales people when they have something to sell and they see you as a potential customer. The bank or the finance company only calls when it thinks it has a way to make money off you. Your president, senator, congressman, governor, state representative, county supervisor, mayor, selectman and so forth only make contact with you when they want a political donation or your vote. Sadly, you might even only hear from your house of faith, television pastor, or favorite para-church ministry under similarly commercialized circumstances.

Worse than this are those people who will hold themselves out to you as dear friends. It's been said by many we can choose our friends, but we can't choose our families. I'd add my voice to this chorus with an important proviso. Be certain the people who claim a desire to be your friends, and this must include those who may try to move from friendship to love, are in the relationship because of an altruistic view of you and them and not just what they can gain out of the relationship. True friendships and loves should be based on a rough balance of give and take between the parties involved. If the balance becomes uneven, something has gone wrong and you may have simply been receiving a parasitic form of commercial affection which your would-be friend could just as easily term "What have you done for me lately."

Looking back over the past six decades, I can count dozens of such friendships and even still encounter these old friends from time to time. For most of them, there seems to be a distinct case of being ill at ease in my presence since I'm rarely silent when the end of this subterfuge finally comes. For the very cleverest in the bunch, they've long ago mastered the ability to keep selling the idea to people like me we're as close as we ever were, and it's simply life hasn't allowed them to see me or spend the time with me they once did. You owe it to yourself to protect your heart and your mind from people who only want to use you when it benefits them. Their goals can be lofty or they can be the basest of base, but you're merely their stepping stone.

For the sexual prostitute, the goal may simply be getting enough money to keep their pimp happy and buy the next hit of crack. In matters of love and friendship, losing a bit of money would be a small price to pay if you can get away mostly unscathed. But you must take great care you don't lose your self-respect, optimism, joy of life, mental and physical health, willingness to love and be loved, or your personal happiness. These aficionados of commercial affection are much more expensive a proposition in the long run than any prostitute you might encounter. I know the human temptation is to reach out to others because we're social creatures. You must temper this desire or it will become a liability and not the asset God intended. Keep your eyes open and guard your heart from those who would use you for their own purposes.

The True Face Of Evil
I've reflected a good deal over the years about evil and its manifestations. My perception today is much different than it was when I was forty years younger and nearer your own age. When I was a boy, evil was easy to identify, and the good guys were always easy to distinguish from the bad guys. Hitler, Nazis, communists, and other such black-hatted villains were easy to

spot and if there was ever any doubt, there were always societal guides there to make it clear. Novels, movies, and television always made it seem so easy to identify the bad guys.

As the years have passed I've began to realize evil is present in all of us and in the entire world, and the degree to which we're able to repress our own evil plays a large role in others overall perception of us as being either good or bad. I don't have any real problem with this very real and human struggle with right and wrong, it's just somewhere along about the same time, I also realized some people, who were exceedingly evil, were expert at concealing it while routinely pointing up the mundane day-to-day evil present in the rest of us. In one of my other works, I address the concept of thieves being found routinely among the poor, neglected, dispossessed, infirm, and dying. For me it epitomizes the cleverly concealed nature of evil.

I was to discover, much to my youthful horror, some men and women who I'd once taken to be wonderful human beings since they were educational, religious, social, community, and political leaders, were in fact not nearly as loving, altruistic, and kind as the persona they'd carefully groomed for public presentation. The fact is most people learn they live in a world filled with 'studied deceivers'; they use other people's naiveté and childlike desire for a good and kind world against them. One of their worst crimes in my opinion is destroying those childlike qualities in those they encounter. By now, as you've approached your own age of majority, you too have seen the truth behind the old adage, "All that glitters is not gold." It wouldn't hurt to add here that attractive and charming narcissists and sociopaths are at work in all areas of society; top, bottom, and all levels in between.

In this lifetime you'll no doubt see the face of evil at close range and be entirely unable to recognize it. The first reason for this is evil is, by its very nature, all about the ability to deceive in some fashion or another. The second reason is evil can be most effective in achieving its own nefarious goals when its real intent is hidden. So don't be surprised when a religious leader turns out to have been a serial adulterer; don't be surprised when a political leader turns out to have been taking payoffs; and don't be surprised when a supposedly selfless community leader turns out to have been secretly working to feather his or her own nest through kickbacks or other gratuities. I'm reminded at this moment of the old fairy tales, where the monster was in fact someone who concealed themselves in a guise such as that of a beloved grandmother, a kindly old man, or a beautiful child.

As long as you're alive, you cannot escape a world with evil in it. I've watched every sort of do-gooder throughout my life put forth Herculean effort to rid the world of its various forms of evil. I've seen great nations expend billions of dollars in their efforts to eradicate every form of evil. I've heard religious leaders from every major world religion preach and teach passionately in an attempt to wipe evil out. Guess what? In my estimation evil is worse now than it's ever has been; it's likely to grow worse still as more and more people begin to view themselves as a God. As a Christian I regard this as a direct result of mankind's original sin of rebellion against God's law and his revealed will for how men and women are to relate to one another, to God's creation, and to other members of society. This state of steady moral decline, and the resultant proliferation of evil, promises to only grow worse until God declares a final judgment.

I could leave it at this, and this would be both bleak, somber, and without hope. I think any ability to make macro-scale change to evil is an illusion. Certainly you can contain some forms of evil by waging wars, arresting and incarcerating evildoers, and you can even execute people in an effort to rid the planet of their personal manifestation of evil. None of those things has ever accomplished any more than further suppressing the face of evil and forcing it to become more adept at achieving its ends without being recognized. However, I'll admit executions render the individual bad actor void. There's hope, and what you can do is to work on yourself, your children, and your grandchildren. Then perhaps you can work on your friends to encourage them to live lives of good. I can say with certainty if I've had any lasting impact in the war against evil, it will most likely be found in you, your children, and your children's children.

That Final "I Love You"

Today is April 29, 2015 and your Uncle Ryan is thirty-five years old today. If he hadn't taken his own life, he'd be here on Earth to celebrate with his family and friends. As it is, each of us does the best we can yearly to remember his life and honor him in positive ways. In recent years, that's been a high school scholarship or fundraiser to support music and the other performing arts in grammar, middle, and junior high schools. I'd estimate we've helped to raise or directly donated over $100,000 in his name throughout the past 17 years. This brings a small measure of comfort to those of us who loved him and miss him every day.

Ryan loved your grandmother and me, he loved your mother, his friends, his grandparents, his uncles and aunts, his cousins, and he loved his only niece, Katelynn. He was remarkably talented, even gifted, when it came to music. All of us expected him to go on and make a life in music; he played seven instruments I know of. Not only was he an accomplished musician, he also had an incredible talent for repairing and/or restoring old musical instruments. Each of us had dreams for your Uncle Ryan, but due to mental illness, Ryan ceased to have dreams of his own.

Mental illness should've been listed as the cause of his death, though the coroner ruled it suicide. In the four years Ryan was ill, our family came to understand depression, obsessive compulsive disorder, and borderline schizophrenia all too well. He suffered with these maladies to varying degrees every day those final four years. Like most of us, he could put on a happy face and go about his life. But at one low point, he tearfully asked me, "Daddy, what'll happen to me when you die? Who'll take care of me?" I assured him his sisters loved him, he was going to get better, and homelessness would never be an issue. In time he did get better. Some of the modern medicines provided us tools which are miraculous; at least they were for Ryan.

The one flaw in this medicinal approach is when mentally ill people begin to feel better; they frequently want to stop taking their medication. Ryan complained the medicine re-zeroed him. That's a radio term he shared with me related to putting a radio back onto its precise channel/signal. His genius was being off-signal from the rest of us, and he knew it. Not liking the medication was an issue with your Uncle Ryan. This is where the confluence of more than one bad idea can be deadly. As I've mentioned previously, there was a young minister in his church who suggested he could stop taking the drugs because God either "…had healed him or would heal him." So Ryan, wanting to be faithful to his beliefs, pretended to take his medicine in my presence (cheeking the pill) and then later threw them away. All the ground we'd gained in the previous year was soon lost, and then some.

Regardless of how his life came to an end, in celebration of him and the joy he brought me while he lived, tonight I'll have a piece of birthday cake and eat at Taco Bell (his favorite fine dining). He was a wonderful son and as true a friend to me as I ever had. The loss to your grandmother and your mother is certainly different, but no less painful, than my own. Perhaps the greatest pity is today he'd have two more brothers-in-law and four nephews he never knew. They would love him and be loved by him, in addition to Katelynn he already knew and adored. His family and friends cherished him more than he ever realized. When you have children of your own, hug them close and tell them you love them at every chance you get. You truly never know when you've spoken the words, "I love you" for the final time.

Author's Afterward

As I mentioned at the outset, when I began to consider writing this book three years ago, I knew I wanted to talk about the wisdom I've seen, heard, and experienced during the course of my life. In many ways this writing has simply been an offhand recounting of my passage through the school of hard knocks. As I said in the preface, my goal was to leave it primarily to my grandchildren and, to a lesser degree, to my children. It never occurred to me it might have any broader audience than this until I began to share its pre-publication drafts on my blog and with friends and colleagues. To my surprise several, though certainly not all, said they wanted to buy a copy or copies when it was published to pass along to their own children and grandchildren. If this should happen, I'd be honored they'd feel these words have application beyond my own family.

Farrell F. Neeley, PhD
May 31, 2015

www.ingramcontent.com/pod-product-compliance
Lightning Source LLC
Chambersburg PA
CBHW022353040426
42450CB00005B/165